ET   33092

THE HISTORY OF
THE REFORM BILL OF 1832

THE
HISTORY
OF THE
REFORM BILL
OF
1832

BY

W. N. MOLESWORTH

[1865]

AUGUSTUS M. KELLEY • PUBLISHERS
CLIFTON 1972

First Edition 1865

(*London*: Chapman & Hall; *Manchester*: Ireland &
Company, 1865)

Reprinted 1972 by
Augustus M. Kelley Publishers
REPRINTS OF ECONOMIC CLASSICS
Clifton New Jersey 07012

I S B N 0 678 00893 0
L C N 68-30533

PRINTED IN THE UNITED STATES OF AMERICA
by SENTRY PRESS, NEW YORK, N. Y. 10013

THE HISTORY

OF THE

REFORM BILL OF 1832

BY THE

REV. W. N. MOLESWORTH, M.A.,

Incumbent of St. Clement's, Rochdale,

AUTHOR OF THE PRIZE ESSAY ON THE "FRENCH ALLIANCE,"
&c., &c.

LONDON: CHAPMAN AND HALL
MANCHESTER: IRELAND AND CO.

1865.

PREFACE.

THE Author is fully aware that, in the present state of public opinion, the appearance of a work of this nature from the pen of a clergyman will provoke some censure. He is therefore happy to be able to justify himself in words borrowed from a recent article in one of the ablest of our weekly newspapers. Speaking of the recommendation of a London coroner's jury, the writer of the article in question says:—

"They were simply expressing the feeling becoming engrained in the popular mind that a pastor should be ignorant of all but theology, that art and science are irreligious, that a minister should confine himself to preaching and visiting, with good books for his sole reading and gossip for his only recreation. There are parishes in England where the clergyman must study chemistry on the sly, and geology in silence, and there is scarcely one in which the sight of an easel in the vicar's sitting room would not give deep offence. By an odd but explicable whim, the study of astronomy—of all sciences the most absorbing—is exempted from censure; but it is the only one which would provoke from a party in the parish no kind of hostile comment. Such narrowness is, we are bound to say, almost confined to laymen, but it is lay opinion which in England creates the external law of the church, and the opinion expressed so clearly by the city jury has two permanent and most pernicious effects. It forces on the clergy a kind of hypocrisy—an appearance of ignorance they do not feel—and it lowers throughout the country the clerical ideal. The true pastor, to our minds, is the man who, learned in all human learning, familiar with all human practice, physician and teacher, *savan* and divine, farmer and orator, uses those rich stores of capacity to higher ends than gain, who, touching life at all points, comprehends it in all, and derives from his comprehension the power of healing the physician obtains from the study which the St. Botolph's jury have taken on themselves to condemn."—*Spectator, November 19th,* 1864.

This eloquent paragraph expresses the convictions on which the Author of this work has acted for many years. Indeed he has found it absolutely necessary to the maintenance of his mental and bodily health, and to the effective discharge of his pastoral duties to have always in hand some study or occupation which would serve as a mental diversion from his ordinary pursuits, which he could follow without interference with them, which he could take up and lay aside at pleasure, and the materials for which were within his reach. All these conditions he has found in the work now presented to the public, in which he has endeavoured to trace the progress of one of the most important struggles that has ever taken place in this country If, on the one hand, he labours under some special disadvantages in the preparation of such a work, arising from the distance at which he resides from the metropolis, he hopes that he may lay claim on the other hand to some special qualification for its due performance. Old enough to have received an indelible impression of the passions which that struggle evoked, he is young enough to be able to regard it with the impartiality which belongs to posterity. His profession and habits of life, while serving to keep him aloof from the strife of parties, have directed his thoughts to what may be termed the philosophy of politics, and while they have prevented him from being an active participator in the great events which have occurred during his life, they have caused him to be a thoughtful and interested spectator of those events. There are no doubt others who are in many respects better qualified than he is to write this history, but they have not done it. The time when it ought to be undertaken has arrived. The generation that witnessed the struggle is passing away; the generation that is succeeding them can hardly realize the opposition it encountered, the enthusiasm it awakened, or the extent and importance of the changes it has produced.

The point to which the Author has especially directed his attention, and to which he desires to draw the attention of the reader is, the influence exercised by the people on the character and success of the measure whose history he has undertaken to write. He believes that in its main features the Reform Bill was virtually their work, and he has endeavoured to discover and point out the true causes of the interest they manifested in it. But as parliament, and particularly the House of Commons, was the arena in which the battle was fought, the debates of the two houses, and especially of the lower house, must necessarily occupy a prominent place in any history of the Reform Bill. And yet it would be impossible to give an account of all the numberless and often tedious and unprofitable discussions which arose on it. The Author has therefore adopted two principles of selection. In the first place, he has chosen those debates which occurred before the subject was exhausted; and in the next place, he has preserved the speeches of men who might be regarded as expressing the opinions and wishes of large bodies of their countrymen. Of these speeches, he has only given, in a very condensed form, those portions which serve to illustrate or carry forward the history of the period in which they were delivered. If any one should complain that the passages he has thus given are too many and too long, he can only plead that he has laboured most diligently by all the compression consistent with the fair exhibition of the style, individuality, and arguments of the speakers, and by the careful elimination of personal allusions, parliamentary conventionalities, and those repetitions which are almost unavoidable, and sometimes even desirable in public speaking, to reduce them within the narrowest limits consistent with his plan and objects.

While diligently examining all materials of every kind that have come within his reach, and which could by any possibility throw light on his subject, the Author has not been very solicitous to pry into the secret history of court or other intrigues, whether employed for the promotion or the defeat of the measure, and which, in his opinion, had very little real influence on its fortunes. As it has been his chief aim to trace and exhibit the working of the popular mind, he has sought chiefly those materials which seemed best adapted to answer these purposes, and he trusts that he has not been unsuccessful. Mr. Roebuck's "History of the Whig Ministry" is a work which embraces the period of which he has undertaken to treat. Of course he has consulted it. But he purposely abstained from looking into it until the outline of his own history was completed and nearly filled up. After having carefully weighed Mr. Roebuck's statements, he has not thought it necessary to alter any of the conclusions which he had previously and independently reached. The Author feels bound to acknowledge his great obligations to the daily and weekly press of the period, especially the *Times* and the *Examiner*. The former of these newspapers has furnished him with a very large amount of materials for his history, of a very useful and reliable character, and they are all the more valuable and important, because, while its pages faithfully reflected the variations of the public opinion of the period, they exercised a guiding and controlling influence such as no other journal ever wielded.

The Author cannot conclude this preface without expressing his grateful thanks to Earl Russell and Lord Brougham, for the kind readiness with which they have afforded him information. At the same time he thinks it right to add that for every statement and every opinion advanced in the work he alone is responsible.

W. N. M.

Spotland, Rochdale,
Nov. 28, 1864.

CONTENTS.

CHAPTER I.

033092

CHAPTER III.

CHAPTER IV.

HISTORY OF THE REFORM BILL.

CHAPTER I.

WHATEVER differences of opinion may have formerly prevailed respecting the great struggle which I have undertaken
to record, it may now be regarded by every Englishman with
feelings of unmixed pride and satisfaction. If it yields in
stormy grandeur and world-wide results to the first French
revolution and in dramatic interest to that of 1830, it is
inferior to neither of them in the benefits which have resulted
from it to the country which was the scene of it, and it
presents a spectacle without parallel in the history of the
world,—that of a mighty change, invading the most powerful
interests and meeting the most pertinacious resistance, accom-
plished without a crime, nay without a violation even of the
forms of the constitution of the country in which it was
effected.

In tracing the course of this struggle I shall have to point
out to the reader the circumstances which had given to the
landed proprietors of this country a legislative monopoly
which once, perhaps, properly belonged to them, but which
the growth of other interests had rendered it right that they
should no longer retain. I shall show how this exclusive
power was abused, as all such power is sure to be, by its
possessors ; how the abuse gave rise to discontents and
violences ; how those who possessed it entrenched themselves
behind the forms of a constitution whose spirit they violated;

how for a long time they resisted and defied the just demands of the people; and how at last the nation, profiting by a favourable combination of circumstances, triumphed after a desperate struggle over the most powerful aristocracy in the world, and tore from them the rights which they had not the wisdom to concede.

In narrating this struggle I shall not confine myself to that part of it which was carried on within the walls of parliament. I shall rather seek to trace and exhibit the great social and popular forces which originated and over-ruled the legislative conflict. For we shall not rightly appreciate its nature if we regard the Reform Bill merely as the work of certain statesmen and legislators who took a leading part in the preparation and discussion of its various provisions. They indeed gave it its outward form, but the substance and the leading principles were the outgrowth of a long chain of causes by which they were themselves controlled. No doubt they exercised a very important discretionary power in framing and modifying the details of the measure, but they never would have triumphed over the obstacles they encountered if the bill had not responded to the wishes of the people and the requirements of the times. The abuses which they succeeded in removing were the silent growth of a period during which the landed interest was dominant, and the commercial, manufacturing, and trading interests almost unrepresented in the councils of the nation. Throughout the whole of the eighteenth, and still more during the preceding part of the nineteenth century, these interests had been advancing with rapid strides, and for a long time their growth was favoured by the dominant interest, because it evidently tended to raise the value of land and increase the demand for agricultural produce. But no sooner did they begin to demand that share in the legislation of the country which their rising importance fairly entitled them to claim, and which the increasing magnitude and complexity of their ill-understood operations rendered more and more necessary to them, than the jealousy and apprehensions of the ruling class were roused and manifested. The consequences of this exclusion from political influence were felt not only by the leaders of the national industry but by the great bulk of the working classes, who are always the chief sufferers in periods of national distress, whether proceeding from mistaken legislation or from other causes, because while in such circumstances those above them find their superfluities diminished, they are deprived of the comforts or even the necessaries of life. And this is the true explanation of a circumstance which was often triumphantly referred to by the opponents of Reform. "It is only," said they, "in times of great distress that we hear much about Reform. In periods of prosperity and abundance scarcely a meeting is held or a petition presented on the subject." The fact is that the clamour for reform sprang not so much from a sense of the theoretical imperfections of the then existing state of things, not from any strong moral disapprobation of the bribery, corruption, and other flagrant abuses that flourished under it, but from the actual and severe distress which ignorant and selfish legislation combined with other causes to produce. The people cried out because they were suffering, they ceased to cry when they ceased to suffer, and they called for Parliamentary Reform because they justly believed that it would bring with it an alleviation of their sufferings. No doubt they greatly exaggerated the effects which that measure would produce, and overlooked many causes of distress which it would not remove, but still they were right in their belief, that it would tend to a great amelioration of their condition, as the event has abundantly proved. The carrying of the bill was, above all, their work—the work of men on whom it conferred no privileges, and who might be supposed by superficial observers to be rather losers than gainers by it. Their very exaggerations were fortunate, because they tended to keep alive that popular enthusiasm for the measure, without which it would certainly have been rejected.

The mining, manufacturing, and commercial interests were not the only ones that were affected by the monopoly of power which the landed proprietary enjoyed. None suffered more severely from this cause than the farmers and agricultural labourers, because the course of legislation was naturally favourable to the landlord and unfavourable to the tenant. Under a normal and equitable state of things, those important classes, connected by ties of strong sympathy and common interest with the great landlords, commonly voted with them from conviction rather than coercion ; but on this occasion an unerring instinct taught them that their interests and the claims of the territorial aristocracy were at variance, and they declared against these claims with such unanimity that the counties—usually the stronghold of the Tory party—sent up, as we shall see, an overwhelming majority of representatives favourable to reform. The inhabitants of the country districts shook off the political apathy which usually characterises them, and contributed no less largely to the popular victory than the inhabitants of the towns.

The abuses of which the reformers complained were of no recent origin. Many of them were probably as old as our representative system, which, growing up in ages when anarchy and oppression were struggling together in one weltering chaos, was certain to present a great multitude of anomalies. If some of these were from time to time corrected, others sprang up in their place. In the early periods of our parliamentary history, there seems to have been no fixed rule for the selection of the towns which returned members to the lower house. The king appears to have issued his writs

to such as he thought proper, being usually, though by
no means invariably, guided in his choice by their importance
and population ; and as, in those early times, the lower house
was not an object of jealousy to the crown, but, on the contrary, often proved a useful ally to the sovereign in the contests which arose between him and his barons, there was no
motive for the improper exercise of this power, and little
danger of its being seriously abused. But when the House
of Commons begun to be recognised as a great estate of the
realm, it was felt that bounds must be put to this arbitrary
discretion, and the crown had no difficulty in relinquishing a
prerogative which was of no great advantage to it. Thus, by
the tacit consent of all parties, this discretionary power gradually fell into disuse. It is perhaps to be regretted that it was
not formally transferred to the legislature or to the House of
Commons, instead of being left in such a position that any
step taken by parliament would be regarded as an usurp-
ation of the prerogative of the crown, and any attempt on the
part of the crown to revive its dormant rights would call forth
susceptibilities that were neither unnatural nor unfounded.
A power which ought to have been regulated was prac-
tically destroyed, and the necessary consequence was that
towns which had grown into importance were wholly unrepresented, while others which had fallen into decay still
continued to send members to the House of Commons.
Thus a distribution of the representation, originally made
without much care, but proportioned to the population
with tolerable fairness, had, even in the time of Charles I.,
become so evidently anomalous as to attract the attention of
the Long Parliament, which increased the number of members
returned by the counties and the metropolis—gave representatives to Manchester, Leeds, and Halifax, which even then
were rising into importance — disfranchised a considerable
number of decayed boroughs—and conferred the elective

CHAP. I. franchise on every owner of land whatever might be his tenure. It also enacted that representatives should be sent to the House of Commons from Scotland and Ireland, which was thought a fair and desirable arrangement, and one against which no serious objection would be urged. The civil war prevented the proposed changes from being carried into effect at the time when they were enacted, but the plan was subsequently adopted by Cromwell in summoning the parliament of 1645, and is thus described by Clarendon in his history of that period :—

1645.

"But the time drew near now, when he was obliged by the instrument of government, and upon his oath, to call a parliament ; which seemed to him the only means left to compose the minds of the people to an entire submission to his government. In order to this meeting, though he did not observe the old course in sending writs out to all the little boroughs throughout England, which used to send burgesses (in which there is so great an inequality, that some single counties send more members to parliament than six other counties do), he seemed to take a more equal way, by appointing more knights for every shire to be chosen, and fewer burgesses, whereby the number of the whole was much lessened ; and yet the people being left to their own election, it was not thought an ill temperament, and was then generally looked upon as an alteration fit to be more warrantably made and in a better time. And so upon the receipt of his writs, elections were made accordingly in all places ; and such persons for the moment chosen and returned as were believed to be least affected to the present government and to those who had any authority in it ; there being strict order given, ' that no person who had ever been against the parliament during the time of the civil war, or the sons of any such persons, should be capable of being chosen to sit in that parliament ;' nor were any such persons made choice of."

It is curious to remark how little opposition or objection Chap. I.
this great change in the constitution of the country seems to 1645.
have encountered, especially when we look at the storm raised
by the introduction of the Reform Bill—a measure which,
considering the time at which it was introduced and the
great increase in the anomalies of our representation which
had taken place in the interval, we shall see to be a much less
violent change than that which Cromwell thus boldly carried
out. Clarendon himself, as we have just seen, regarded it
with favour, for he says that " it was not thought an ill temperament, and was generally looked upon as an alteration fit
to be made." The parliament elected under it was certainly
not distinguished by any excess of deference for the Protector.
It begun by questioning his authority, and its whole existence
was one incessant struggle with him,—it took every opportunity of venting its displeasure against him and criticising
his acts; and it was dissolved by him as early as possible,
because it was found to be utterly unmanageable. And yet
no member seems ever to have thought of objecting to the
great reform which the Protector had made in the constitution
of the house. On the contrary, as far as we are able to judge
at this distance of time, not only did they cordially adopt the
change, but proceeded to make further gradual alterations of
the same nature. Thus I find the following entry in White-
lock's Diary :—

" Wednesday, Dec. 6. Debates about disfranchisement of
certain boroughs, and transfer of their franchise to other
places."

From this time the question underwent a long eclipse. Re-appear-
The reaction against Cromwell and the Long Parliament ance of the question
prejudiced men's minds against all changes which had been in 1745.
effected by them, and furnished the opponents of measures
which they had promoted with an argument against them,
which, for a long time, was found irresistible. The consequence

was that the question did not again emerge into distinct daylight until the year 1745. In the October of that year parliament was called together on account of the rebellion in Scotland, and the alarm and consequent distress which attended that event seems to have occasioned a feeling in favour of Parliamentary Reform, which found an utterance in the following amendment to the address, proposed by Sir Francis Dashwood, afterwards Lord De Spencer, and seconded by Sir J. Phillips—" That, for the firmer establishment of His Majesty's throne, on the solid basis of his people's affections, it should be our speedy care to frame such bills as may effectually secure to His Majesty's subjects the perpetual enjoyment of their undoubted right to be freely and fairly represented in parliament, frequently chosen, and exempted from undue influence of every kind."

Foremost among the opponents of this amendment was the elder Pitt. " The amendment," he said, " being offered at a time so exceedingly improper as the present, is fraught with a dangerous tendency. There is only one motive to which this motion can be ascribed, and that is, to make ministers odious in the eyes of the people if they put a negative on it. But I will venture to say that the contrary will be the fact; for although motions of this kind are always popular, yet in this hour of distress and difficulty, when rebellion rages in the kingdom, and an invasion from France is expected, when the people are seriously intent on measures of the highest consequence, they cannot think favourably of those who attempt to draw off their attention from subjects of danger to points of speculation. Shall we employ ourselves in framing bills to guard our liberties from corruption, when we are in danger of losing them, and everything else that is dear to us by the force of arms? Would not this be like a man's amusing himself with making regulations to prevent his servants from cheating him at the very time that

thieves were breaking into his house ? But why are we to
introduce this subject into the address ? No county, nor
city, nor corporation, have requested their representatives
to bring in any such bills ; the people are everywhere engaged
in making subscriptions and forming associations for defending
their sovereign and themselves against those who have
traitorously conspired to rob him of his crown and them of
their liberties. Do gentlemen wish to give a turn to the
spirit of the people, to create a contention about the constitution, that the kingdom may fall an easy prey to the enemy ?
If, sir, I did not know the honourable gentlemen who made
and recorded this motion, I should really suspect their having
some such design.; and, however much I may, from my own
personal knowledge, be convinced that they have no such
design, they may be assured that, if they do not withdraw
their motion, the suspicion will be strong against them
amongst those persons who have not the honour of their
acquaintance." The motion was negatived without a division.

The language employed by Mr. Pitt seems uncalled for.
The adoption of such a motion might and probably would
have had the effect of uniting the people more cordially and
enthusiastically in defence of the throne. Be this as it may,
the terms of the motion were in perfect accordance with the
popular principles which Pitt always professed, and one
is rather surprised to find him reprobating it as ill-timed,
without, at the same time, stating that in the abstract he
cordially approved it. On other occasions he gave utterance
to sentiments entirely in harmony with the amendment
which he now reprobated in such unqualified terms. For
instance, in the year 1766, we find him, in a speech against
the American Stamp Act, making use of the following
memorable expressions :—

"There is an idea in some, that the colonies are virtually
represented in this house. I would fain know by whom an

CHAP. I.
1766.

American is represented here? Is he represented by any knight of the shire in any county in this kingdom? *Would to God that respectable representation was augmented to a greater number!* Or will you tell him that he is represented by any representative of a borough—a borough which, perhaps, its own representatives never saw. *This is what is called the rotten part of the constitution. It cannot continue a century. If it does not drop, it must be amputated.*"

1770.

On the 22nd January, 1770, this great man, now become Earl of Chatham, in supporting a motion of the Marquis of Rockingham, that the House of Lords should take into consideration the state of the nation, made the following remarks on the subject of Parliamentary Reform:—

"Whoever understands the theory of the British constitution, and will compare it with the fact, must see at once how widely they differ. We must reconcile them to each other if we wish to save the liberties of the country; and we must reduce our political practice as near as possible to our principles. The constitution intended that there should be a permanent relation between the constituent and the representative body of the people. Will any man affirm that as the House of Commons is now formed, that relation is in any degree preserved? My lords, it is not preserved; it is destroyed. Let us be cautious, however, how we have recourse to violent expedients.

"The boroughs of the country have, properly enough, been called the rotten parts of the constitution. I have lived in Cornwall and, without entering into an invidious particularity, have seen enough to justify the appellation. But in my judgment, my lords, the boroughs, corrupt as they are, must be considered as the natural infirmity of the constitution. Like the infirmities of the body, we must bear them with patience, and submit to carry them about with us. The limb is mortified, but its amputation might be death.

"Let us try, my lords, whether some gentler remedy may not be discovered. Since we cannot cure the disorder, let us try to infuse such a portion of new health into the constitution as may enable it to support the most inveterate diseases.

"The representation of the counties is, I think, still preserved pure and uncorrupted. That of the greatest cities is on a footing equally respectable, and there are many of the large trading towns which still preserve their independence. The infusion of health which I now allude to would be to permit every county to elect one member more in addition to their present representatives. The knights of the shire approach nearest to the constitutional representatives of the country, because they represent the soil. It is not in the little dependent boroughs, it is in the great cities and counties that the strength and vigour of the constitution resides, and by them alone, if an unhappy question should ever arise, will the constitution be honestly and firmly defended. I would increase that strength, because that is the only remedy we have against the profligacy of the times, the corruption of the people, and the ambition of the crown."

After meeting some objections to his proposal, derived from the terms in which the act of Union between England and Scotland was drawn, he concluded his observations on the subject of Parliamentary Reform, by suggesting that one additional member should be given to every county in England and Scotland. The year following he declared himself a convert to triennial parliaments.

It is hardly necessary to say that the remarks we have cited afford indications of a strong and wide-spread feeling in favour of Parliamentary Reform, even at this period, and render it highly probable that, if that illustrious man had lived, and retained his health, a measure, such as he indicated, would have been carried during the period of

CHAP. I.   discontent and suffering which attended and followed the
1782.   close of the American war.

Mr Pitt's
motion for   The project which the great earl thus announced towards
a select   the close of his glorious career was taken up by his still more
committee.
celebrated son, William Pitt, who, on the 7th of May, 1782,
moved for a select committee on Parliamentary Reform.
His speech, on the occasion, is said to have been warm and
animated; but the only passage which has been preserved is
one in which he thus inveighed against the corrupt influence
of the crown, &c.

"It is an influence, sir, which has been pointed at in
every period as the fertile source of all our miseries—an
influence which has been substituted in the room of wisdom,
of activity, of exertion, and of success—an influence which
has grown with our growth, and strengthened with our
strength, but which, unhappily, has not diminished with our
diminution, nor decayed with our decay."

The motion was seconded by Alderman Sawbridge, a
veteran reformer, and in a house of upwards of 300 members
was lost by only 20 votes, the numbers being—for, 141;
against, 161.

Mr. Burke opposed this motion with characteristic vehemence.   In his great speech on American taxation he had
stigmatised the defects of our parliamentary representation
as "the shameful parts of our constitution," but now he
seemed to think that no change whatever was needed.

1783.   Mr. Pitt renewed his attempt in the following year. This
Mr. Pitt
renews his time, however, he brought forward a specific plan, contained
attempt.   in three resolutions; the first of which was intended to pledge
the house to measures for the prevention of bribery; the
second proposed that whenever the majority of the voters in
any borough should be convicted of gross corruption, the
borough should lose its right of returning a member, and the
uncorrupted minority should become county voters; the third

proposed to give additional members to the counties and to
the metropolis. This proposition was rejected by a much
larger majority than that by which the resolution of the preceding session had been defeated; the numbers being—for,
149; against, 293; majority, 144.

In the year 1785, Mr. Pitt, being then prime minister, made
another and a last attempt to amend the representation. His
plan was to purchase from thirty-six boroughs of small population their right of sending members, and to transfer the seats
thus acquired to counties or populous places; he also proposed to establish a permanent provision for extinguishing,
from time to time, by similar means, the franchise of boroughs
which might have become decayed and depopulated. This proposition, though introduced by a minister who carried almost
all his measures by triumphant majorities, was negatived
by a majority of 74; the numbers being 174 to 248. This
result has thrown great suspicion on the sincerity of his zeal
for Reform; the numbers certainly seem to show that he had
not used any great exertions to secure votes for his motion.
It is not improbable that abuses which he viewed with
abhorrence, while they helped to sustain administrations to
which he was hostile, were regarded by him with more
indulgence when they strengthened his own power. Be
this as it may, he made no further efforts in favour of changes
of which he had once been the zealous advocate, and from the
time of the French revolution he became their uncompromising opponent; instituting prosecutions against men whose
only crime was that they still held the opinions which he had
formerly professed, and used language in advocating them
hardly, if at all, more violent than that which he had once
employed.

This desertion, though it greatly weakened the Reform
party, did not discourage them. The French revolution,
while it terrified many of the aristocratic friends of Reform,

encouraged its supporters among the people, and animated
them to fresh exertions in a cause akin to that which seemed
to be triumphing on the other side of the channel. The
consequence was, that in the year 1793, the question excited
more popular enthusiasm, and met with a more earnest
opposition than on any previous occasion. Mr. Grey, who
had taken up the standard which Mr. Pitt had flung away,
was sustained by demonstrations of popular sympathy such
as had never been made before. On the 2nd of May, petitions were presented to the House of Commons praying
for a reform in the representation of the people, from
Sheffield, signed by 8,000 persons, but rejected on account
of the disrespectful manner in which it was worded; from
Birmingham, signed by 2,720 persons, and from Durham.
On the 6th of the same month a very large number of
petitions were presented, many of which were very numerously signed, and, amongst the rest one from the city of
Edinburgh, the signatures to which were so numerous that
it extended over the whole length of the floor of the house.

Petition
of the
" Friends
of the
People."
But of all the petitions of this time, that which obtained
and deserved the greatest attention was one from "the Friends
of the People," which was presented by Mr. Grey, and which
will be found in another part of this work.* It gives, in
great detail, a most clear and temperate statement of the
abuses and grievances of which the petitioners complained.
Any person wishing to become thoroughly acquainted with
the real views and designs of the reformers of this period,
should carefully peruse this most able document.

Mr. Burke, who in the violence of his recoil from the
excesses of the French revolution, had deserted his old friends
and allied himself with the Tories, whom he almost out-did in
the excess of his antipathy to everything savouring of Reform,

* See Appendix.

objected to the reception of the petition, on the ground that
the residences of the petitioners were not given. Mr. Grey,
in reply, stated that it was not unusual for petitions to have
signatures attached to them unaccompanied by the residences
of the petitioners, and explained that the parties who had
signed the petition were all resident in or near London, and
that it had been drawn up and signed in the metropolis. He
then proceeded at considerable length to advocate and enforce
the prayer of the petition. Referring to that portion of it in
which the petitioners professed their readiness to prove that
upwards of ninety-seven members were actually nominated,
and seventy more indirectly appointed by Peers and the
Treasury, and that ninety-one Commoners procured the
election of one hundred and thirty-nine, so that three hundred and six members, that is, an absolute majority of the
House of Commons were returned by one hundred and sixty
persons, Mr. Grey said, " I assert that this is the condition
of England ; if you say it is *not*, do justice to yourselves by
calling on us for the proof, and expose your calumniators to
reproach ; but if it be the condition of England shall it not
be redressed ?" A long debate followed this speech, in the
course of which the prayer of the petition was supported by
Mr. Erskine, Mr. Francis, Mr. Fox, and Mr. Sheridan, and
was opposed by Mr. Windham and Mr. Pitt. In fact, never
did the question receive a fuller consideration in parliament,
or stir the heart of the country more strongly, until the
occurrence of that great final struggle which it is the more
especial object of this book to record. But the overwhelming
majority of the House of Commons, led by Mr. Pitt, gave the
most decisive testimony to the truth of Mr. Grey's assertions,
by refusing to accept the challenge thus thrown out. The
excesses which followed the French revolution, produced in
this country a strong reaction against Parliamentary Reform,
and a feeling of bitter hostility towards reformers, who were

CHAP. I. supposed to regard that event with favour. The war with
France, which followed, threw the question back for many years.
It was indeed brought forward again by Mr. Grey in 1795 and
1797, but each time with diminished support in the country,
and larger hostile majorities in parliament. Persecuted by the
government, and odious to the mob, the reformers of this
generation were compelled to keep silence, and the question
did not again engage the attention of any great section of
the English people until the conclusion of the peace which
followed the battle of Waterloo.

The Corn
Law.
This peace brought with it but little alleviation of the
distress which the war had produced. Indeed, it had been
preceded by a measure which was calculated to prevent the
people from obtaining their proper share of the benefits which
it was sure to bring in its train. The landed interest had
profited greatly by the war; as long as it continued
they had enjoyed an almost complete monopoly, which caused
a great rise of the profits of the farmer, and the rent of the
landlord. But the peace which followed the first overthrow of
Buonaparte put an end to this monopoly, and the consequence
was an immediate fall of rents and profits, attended by great
agricultural distress. The monopoly had caused a great extension of agricultural operations, the cessation of the monopoly
necessarily produced a collapse. Instead, however, of accepting
this necessity, and endeavouring to accommodate themselves
to it, the dominant landed interest made the prevalent distress
a pretext for protecting, as it was termed, British agriculture,
by duties on the importation of foreign corn. And thus, in
the interval which preceded the last paroxysm of our struggle
with France, was begun that policy of "protection" so long and
so strenuously upheld, and now so universally condemned.

This law relieved the agricultural interest at the expense
of almost every other interest in the nation, and those who
suffered from it were not slow in discovering the cause of

their distresses. In the North of England, where the manu- Chap. I.
facturing interest was already strong, the discontent was great 1816.
and general; but it was felt that it was useless to attack the
obnoxious measure as long as the government of the country
was entirely in the hands of those at whose instigation and
for whose supposed advantage it was adopted, and, therefore,
the old cry of Parliamentary Reform began to be uttered
more and more loudly, and the expedients which were
adopted by the suffering classes to make their wishes and
wants known, soon excited considerable attention and no
little alarm.

Early in the year 1817, the colliers of Bilston had con- 1817.
ceived the idea of making their way to Carlton House, the The Blan-keteers.
residence of the Prince Regent, with two carts of coals,
fondly hoping that they would be admitted to tell their tale
of woe to his Royal Highness, and that the spectacle of their
misery would induce him to do something for their relief.
The Manchester workmen, improving on this idea, determined
that they would walk up to London to make known their
distresses to the authorities there, to ask them to provide
some legislative remedy, and especially to give them the
great panacea of Parliamentary Reform. It was proposed
that each of the petitioners should take a blanket with him,
so that they might sleep on the way in any sheltered place
they might find, and the food which would be required.
They were long remembered by the name of the Blanketeers.
The project of these poor simple-minded men, instead of
exciting compassion, filled the minds of the government and
the upper classes with alarm. It was regarded as an attempt
to overthrow the institutions of the country. The Habeas
Corpus Act being at that time suspended, the leaders of the
proposed expedition were seized and imprisoned. These
strong measures induced the greater part of those who had
intended to join the proposed expedition to abandon their

CHAP. I. design; a few, however, persisted in their intentions; but
1817. troops had been placed along the proposed line of march,
and they were intercepted, searched, and either sent back or
imprisoned. Nothing was found on them to justify these
proceedings, except "two unusually long knives," probably
intended to divide their food.

1819. In 1819, Sir F. Burdett brought the question of Reform
Agitation once more under the notice of parliament. He based his motion
and conse- on the old maxim of the common law, which declares that "the
quent people of England have a property in their own goods, which
alarms. are not to be taken from them without their own consent."
From this ancient dictum Sir Francis inferred that every person paying taxes ought to have a voice in the election of a
representative in the House of Commons. He did not, however, bring forward a specific plan, but contented himself with
moving "That the house should take the subject of the
representation into its consideration early in the next session."
This motion was rejected by a very considerable majority.
Outside the house, and especially in the manufacturing districts, the question found more favour than it did within.
Early in this year an application had been made to the
boroughreeve and constables of Manchester to call a public
meeting of the inhabitants, to petition parliament to repeal
the Corn Bill, but which was really intended to afford an
opportunity of expressing the public opinion in favour of
Parliamentary Reform. Notwithstanding their refusal to
comply with the requisition, it was resolved that the meeting
should be held, and Mr. Hunt, the great Radical agitator and
orator, accepted an invitation to preside over it. He was
accompanied into the town by a great multitude who had
gone out to meet him, and who carried banners on which
were inscribed, among other mottoes, "Hunt and liberty,"
"The rights of man," "Universal suffrage," "No corn laws."
Hunt, on his arrival at the place of meeting, mounted a

waggon, which contained many of the leaders of the movement,
and commenced an harangue on the topics which the meeting
had been summoned to consider. He scouted the idea of
presenting another petition to that House of Commons which
when last assembled had kicked their prayers and petitions
out of doors; and the meeting, at his suggestion, instead of
applying to the parliament, adopted a remonstrance addressed
to the Prince Regent. The example thus given in Manchester
was followed by nearly all the great towns of the empire, and
though the language employed at these meetings was often
very violent, the persons who attended them conducted themselves in an orderly and unexceptionable manner. In many
places the women, as well as the men, took an active part in
the agitation. At Blackburn a *female* Reform Society was
established, and issued circulars to the wives and daughters
of the workmen, inviting them to form "sister societies," for
the purpose of co-operating with the men, and instilling into
the minds of the rising generation a " deep-rooted hatred
of our tyrannical rulers." Attempts were also made to establish a regular communication between the various societies
in different parts of the kingdom, and thus to enable them to
act in concert for the promotion of their common designs.

Unfortunately the government of that day never thought
of enquiring whether there was not some discoverable and
removable cause for the wide-spread and deep-rooted discontent which these proceedings evinced. They never
thought of alleviating the distresses of the people, or converting, by wise legislation, their disaffection into loyalty.
Their only remedies were strong measures of repression,
which exasperated the discontents and increased the sufferings
which produced them. Greatly alarmed by the accounts,
often much exaggerated and highly coloured, which they
received of the proceedings and organization of the reformers,
they resolved to put down the agitation with a strong hand.

CHAP. I. On the 7th of July a circular letter was issued by the
1819.   Secretary of the Home Department to the Lord Lieutenants
July 7.   of the "disturbed" counties, as they were now called, recommending them to take prompt and effectual measures for the
preservation of the public tranquillity, to excite the magistrates to a vigilant and active discharge of their duties, and
to give directions to the yeomanry to hold themselves in
readiness if their services should be required.

The persons to whom this circular was sent fully shared
the alarms of the government, and were only too ready to
adopt the measures which it indicated. On the other hand,
they against whom it was levelled were rather exasperated
than alarmed. At Birmingham a meeting was held on the
12th of July, at which it was estimated that at least 15,000
persons were present. It was there resolved that, without
waiting for the legal enfranchisement of the town, the
meeting would proceed to elect "two legislatorial attornies
and representatives of Birmingham." Their choice fell on
Major Cartwright, a veteran reformer, and Sir Charles
Wolseley. Neither of them was present, but the latter had
sent a letter, in which he apologised for his absence ; and
when informed of his election by a deputation appointed at
the meeting, he accepted the office, and promised that he
would claim a seat in the House of Commons.

A similar meeting was held shortly after at Leeds. But
as no person could be found who was willing and qualified, in
the opinion of the leaders of the movement, to represent the
town in the House of Commons, the election of a delegate
was postponed until a suitable person could be found.

Proceed-   The government lost no time in picking up the gauntlet of
ings of the defiance which the reformers had thus boldly thrown down.
govern-   Sir C. Wolseley was arrested at his own house and carried to
ment.   Knutsford to answer for some words he had used in speaking
at a public meeting held at Stockport. At a Reform meeting

held at Smithfield, a person named Harrison was apprehended
on the hustings, and carried back into Cheshire, on a similar
charge. In revenge for this arrest, the life of Bird, the officer
who effected it, was attempted. Several other arrests of a
similar character were made about the same time. A proclamation was issued in which it was stated that seditious
and treasonable speeches had been delivered to persons
assembled at meetings held to petition for Reform, and that
attempts had been made to bring into hatred and contempt
the government and constitution established in this realm,
and particularly the Commons' House of Parliament. The proclamation further declared that " many wicked and seditious
writings had been printed, published, and laboriously circulated;" and it concluded by charging all persons in authority
to use their best endeavours to repress the disorders of which
it complained, and to bring their perpetrators to justice.

Undeterred by these proceedings, the leaders of the Man- GreatMan-
chester reformers summoned a meeting in that town to choose chester
a representative after the example of Birmingham, but they meeting.
were dissuaded from this design, which the authorities declared to be clearly illegal, by Hunt and some of the more
prudent reformers. It was, however, resolved that a meeting
should still be held for the unquestionably legal purpose of
petitioning for the reform of the House of Commons, and
Hunt consented to attend and speak on the occasion.

This meeting was regarded by both the friends and foes
of Reform as a great crisis in the impending struggle. On
the one hand, the minds of the magistrates were filled with
exaggerated apprehensions, which they communicated to
the government; and, on the other hand, not only were
great exertions made by the reformers to render the demonstration as imposing as possible, but multitudes were drawn
to the spot by curiosity and the expectation of some attempt
on the part of the authorities to prevent the meeting from

being held.   Thus Manchester was filled by an immense crowd of persons from the neighbouring towns, using now and then very strong and absurd language, but really meaning no harm ; while the magistrates and those who acted with them regarded them as a bloodthirsty mob, bent on overthrowing the government, and perhaps on pillaging or destroying the town.   They saw, too, that the movement was becoming day by day more formidable, and they hoped to strike a blow which would put an end to the agitation.

Such were the dispositions on both sides on the morning of the 16th of August, the day appointed for the holding of the great meeting.   From all the surrounding towns and villages clubs came in, many of which marched in military order to the place of meeting,—a large field, near St. Peter's Church, then on the outside of the town, but now in its very heart.   On that field stands the Free Trade Hall, appropriately commemorating the peaceful triumph of a struggle of which its site witnessed the bloody and turbulent commencement.   For though the Reform of Parliament was the means, yet cheap bread, through the repeal of the Corn Laws, was one of the principal ends which the persons attending this meeting proposed to themselves.   Most of the clubs carried flags, and some of them were preceded by bands of music.   Every little circumstance that could serve to inflame the fears of those who dreaded reform and reformers was carefully noted.   It was observed that one of these bodies marched in military style, timing their steps to the sound of a bugle.   Another was preceded by a standard, bearing the motto of William Wallace, "God armeth the patriot."   Other devices inscribed on their banners were—"Annual parliaments," "Universal suffrage," "Vote by ballot."   Among the clubs were two composed of female reformers, one of which numbered 150 members.   There were besides many other females who accompanied their friends to the ground.

Altogether it was computed that at least 80,000 were present;
and when we consider the great population which even then
inhabited the districts around Manchester, the feeling in
favour of Reform that pervaded the bulk of that population,
and the importance attached by both sides to this meeting,
we can hardly think that this estimate of the number of
persons present at this great Reform fête was excessive.
Had this multitude entertained the designs imputed to
them by the anti-reformers, they might unquestionably
have annihilated the handful of soldiers, most of them
very ill disciplined, and of special constables who were
at the disposal of the magistracy, and might have wreaked
on Manchester, or on the portion of its inhabitants that were
obnoxious to their displeasure, any mischief they might have
contemplated. But they harboured no such intentions. They
had come to display their force, not to exert it; and there
can now be no doubt that if they had been permitted to carry
out their proceedings without molestation they would have
quietly returned to their respective homes; but the insolence
and fears of the authorities prevented this happy result.
Before the commencement of the meeting a body of special
constables took up their position on the field, and the multitude opened to afford them a passage. Mr. Hunt, who did
not reach the ground until some time after the hour fixed
for the commencement of the meeting, was received with enthusiastic shouts, and called to the chair by acclamation. He
had not proceeded far with his opening address when the
yeomanry made their appearance and advanced at a brisk
trot, creating much consternation in that part of the crowd
which was nearest to them. They halted for a moment to
re-form their ranks, which had been thrown into disorder by
the rapid movement. No sooner had they recovered themselves, than they drew their swords, which they flourished in
a threatening manner. The multitude replied to this

Chap. I.
1819.
Aug. 16.

demonstration with three cheers. Meanwhile the Riot Act had been read, but in such a manner that it does not appear that a single person in the meeting heard it, nor was any summons then or afterwards addressed to them calling on them to disperse. As soon as tranquillity was in some degree restored, Mr. Hunt resumed his speech, which the arrival of yeomanry had interrupted. He told his hearers that their appearance at this moment was only a trick to disturb the meeting. He was not permitted to proceed. The yeomanry, without regarding the danger to which they exposed the crowd, rode forward to the waggon which served as a platform, and their commanding officer called on Hunt to surrender. Hunt coolly replied that he was ready to give himself up to any civil officer who would produce a warrant for his apprehension. He, at the same time, exhorted the people to behave peaceably, and not to attempt any resistance,—advice which, notwithstanding the irritating and ill-advised conduct of the authorities, they were quite willing to follow. Hunt then gave himself up to an officer, named Nadin, who was then at the head of the Manchester constabulary. Flushed with this first success, the yeomanry then raised the cry of, "Have at the flags," and at once rode on the mob, cutting at them with their swords. They who were thus assailed attempted to escape, but the human mass behind them rendered retreat impossible, and formed a living wall at which the yeomanry rode, cutting their helpless and unresisting victims with their swords or trampling them under the feet of their horses. At length the crowd broke and fled in all directions, followed by the excited yeomanry. A few, in their natural indignation at this cruel and cowardly attack, flung stones and bricks at their assailants, without, however, inflicting any serious injury on them. Altogether between three and four hundred persons were cut or otherwise injured. Mr. Hunt was conveyed to prison amidst the threats and insults

of the yeomanry and special constables, and his life was
in imminent danger from his excited captors, and he
received some slight injuries. This massacre, as it was
termed at the time, greatly embittered the feelings of the
working classes, and produced a feeling of hostility towards
those who were above them in wealth and station, which
continued to work much mischief for many years after.
The affair was never properly investigated, and it is impossible to say whether the magistrates or the yeomanry were
most guilty, but there can be no doubt that both were highly
blameworthy. It was an act of reckless inhumanity to choose
such a moment for the arrest of Hunt and his associates.
It was still more improper to employ in such a service a
body of ill-disciplined yeomanry, when regular troops were
at hand, who would have effected the arrest without the
provoking bravado and ill-temper which the yeomanry displayed. Indeed, nothing could be more striking than the
contrast presented on this occasion between the volunteer
force and the troops of the line. The latter acted with
mingled coolness and firmness, and inflicted no injury whatever on the crowd. Had they been employed to make the
arrest, the meeting might have been dispersed, not, perhaps,
without complaint, but without bloodshed and without engen-
dering that feeling of burning indignation which the conduct
of the yeomanry excited.

Encouraged by their easy victory, the magistrates on the
day following issued a placard denouncing as illegal the practice of military training, which it affirmed to be carried on in
Salford and other places for treasonable and seditious purposes. The magistrates of Cheshire and Lancashire also
issued a joint address, in which they thanked the officers and
men of all the corps which had taken part in the action, and
expressing their gratification at "the extreme forbearance
exercised by the yeomanry when insulted and defied by the

rioters." The military also received the thanks of the Prince Regent for their conduct on the occasion, conveyed in a letter addressed to Lord Sidmouth.

Meanwhile, Hunt and his associates were committed for trial, but were allowed to give bail. Hunt declined to take advantage of this permission, declaring that he would not give bail even though no more than a farthing should be required. The prisoners were therefore sent to Lancaster Castle under the escort of a body of soldiers, but bail having been offered on the following day for Hunt and one of his associates named Knight, they were set at liberty, and returned in triumph to Manchester, accompanied by a large and enthusiastic crowd of friends.

Subscriptions were entered into at London, Liverpool, and other places, for the relief of those who had been injured by the yeomanry, and for the purpose of prosecuting those who had been most conspicuous in the Peterloo massacre, as it was called, "for cutting and maiming with. intent to kill." But the grand juries cut the bills, and subsequently the magistrates refused to commit persons brought before them on this charge.

The effect of these events was to increase the alarm and irritation which prevailed on both sides, and to exasperate the reformers. The government brought into parliament a long array of bills enacting the seizure of arms, the suppression of drilling, the punishment of seditious libels, and otherwise infringing on the liberty of the subject. These bills, notwithstanding the strenuous resistance of the Whig opposition, were carried through all their stages by triumphant majorities, while every motion for enquiry into the causes of the distress of the people was voted down by the adherents of the ministry.

Lord J. Russell's motion.
These untoward circumstances, and the manifest hopelessness of the attempt, did not deter Lord J. Russell from bringing

the question of Reform once more before the House of Commons. His motion was made on the 4th of December, but the resolutions which he moved were withdrawn at the request of Lord Castlereagh, who intimated that the government were disposed to take up the question. He, therefore, contented himself for the present with moving the disfranchisement of Grampound, a borough whose corruption had already been proved, and the transfer of its franchise to some populous town. Even this miserable instalment of reform was denied. The Whigs themselves, either from indifference or despair, supported Lord J. Russell very feebly, and when the post of Prime Minister was filled by Mr. Canning, who, though liberal in his views on some questions, entertained a strong and decided antipathy to a Parliamentary Reform, they allowed the question to be shelved, if not with satisfaction, at all events without serious remonstrance. And certainly the disposition of the people at this moment on the Reform question was not such as to encourage their advocates in the House of Commons. The repressive measures of the government were not without their intended effect; but what was of much more importance, the peace now began to be followed, not, indeed, by plenty, but by a very marked alleviation of the sufferings of the people, and the consequence was that their discontent diminished, and the cry for reform waxed fainter and fainter. If the people were nearly silent, it could hardly be expected that the small band of their friends in the house would continue the hopeless struggle in the face of a hostile and overwhelming majority, and the question was, therefore, allowed to fall into abeyance, or was only raised by proposals so very moderate as to seem like the mockery of reform, but which were, notwithstanding, too violent to be admitted by those to whom the very name of reform was odious. Nor was this feeling of hatred altogether without a cause. Hopeless as the cause then seemed, it was in truth far from desperate. Though

CHAP. I. the agitation slept, it was not dead. The political atmosphere
was charged with electricity, which, though unseen, was felt.
Everywhere there was an uneasy sensation of dread and distrust, as if in apprehension of a coming storm. Ministry after
ministry had fallen, apparently without any adequate cause;
and the king, in calling to the chief place in his councils George
Canning — a man whom he personally disliked — yielded
to a necessity which many felt but none could explain.
Canning, during his exceedingly brief administration, found
himself surrounded by embarrassments and difficulties which
undermined his health, and would probably have dissolved
his administration had not his premature death anticipated
his fall from power. His followers, it is true, still retained
office under the nominal leadership of Lord Goderich, a nobleman of very inferior capacity, but in less than six months his
rickety government fell to pieces through its own inherent
weakness and the dissensions of some of its members.

The Wel-
ling on
adminis-
tration.
This ministry was succeeded by one which gave promise of
stronger vitality, and a longer existence. At its head was
the Duke of Wellington, whose practical good sense, distinguished services, and great military renown, gave strength to
his administration. These advantages were, however, to some
considerable extent counterbalanced by an arbitrary turn of
mind, arising perhaps, rather from the military education and
habits of the new premier than from his natural temper and
disposition, but which led him to exact from his political sub-
ordinates something of that unreasoning obedience which he
properly expected from his military subalterns. This was the
bane of his administration, and the chief cause of its downfall.
But it is a failing which the people of this country had no
reason to regret, because it was the direct cause first of the
concession of the Catholic Emancipation and then of the
Reform Bill, to both which the duke was strongly opposed,
and which might have been long deferred but for the mistakes

which this disposition led him to commit. A short time before
he had declared that he should be mad to aspire to the office
of prime minister, yet he now accepted it, perhaps, we may
say, was forced to assume it as the last possible defender of a
state of things which the king was anxious to maintain, but
which the tide of events was carrying to its inevitable downfall.
The duke was much guided and influenced by Mr. Peel, who
was an excellent administrator, a skilful debater, and, perhaps,
the only man in the House of Commons who could have led that
assembly in conjunction with the duke. Though apparently
subordinate to his chief, he was the real head of the government, because the premier felt that he could not safely stir a
step without his aid and support. In some few matters,
belonging more immediately to his own position as premier,
the duke acted without his advice, and it was when he thus
acted that he took steps which led to the breaking up of that
strong party which had hitherto successfully resisted every
effort at effecting the slightest reform in parliament, and
might, perhaps, have long continued to defy the popular
demands, at the imminent risk of a violent overthrow of our
constitution, but for the events we are now about to narrate.

The duke had introduced into his cabinet several of the Mr. Hus-
friends of Mr. Canning, at the head of whom stood Mr. Hus- kisson's
kisson, a man who did not possess the genius and brilliancy removal
of his chief, but who was a good debater, enjoyed a con- from the
siderable reputation in the house and in the country as a ministry.
financier and political economist, and entertained views on the
subjects of Catholic Emancipation, Reform, and other questions which at that time occupied men's minds, much more
liberal and advanced than those of the prime minister. An
event soon occurred which brought them into direct anta-
gonism.

The borough of East Retford had been convicted of corruption, and the question of the manner in which its franchise

should be disposed of was brought before the House of Commons. On the one hand, it was proposed that the two members which it returned should be given to Birmingham; on the other, that they should be chosen by the hundred in which East Retford is situated. The Duke of Wellington, whose strong antipathy to Parliamentary Reform we shall hereafter see boldly expressed, supported the latter alternative; and the majority of the administration, yielding to his authority, and perhaps partaking his opinions, voted according to his wish. But Mr. Huskisson, who dreaded Parliamentary Reform as decidedly but more wisely than the duke, was pledged to the former proposition, which he had supported on the ground that it was a timely concession which would prevent the necessity for a larger measure. He therefore separated on this occasion from the majority of his colleagues, and voted for the very moderate and reasonable proposition which his chief had resolved to resist. Immediately after doing so he wrote a note to the duke, in which he briefly explained the grounds of his vote, and offered to withdraw from the ministry if his explanation should not be satisfactory. The duke, impatient, as we have already remarked, of all insubordination on the part of his colleagues, especially on the question of Reform, which he was determined to resist to the last, and probably dissatisfied with Mr. Huskisson's views on other questions, treated Mr. Huskisson's letter as a resignation, and at once obtained the king's acceptance of it. Mr. Huskisson disavowed this interpretation of his letter, and offered further explanations. The duke, however, refused to listen to anything but the unconditional withdrawal of the letter; thus placing Mr. Huskisson in the position of either quitting the administration or degrading himself in the eyes of parliament and of the country. He chose, though not without hesitation, the former alternative; and the other members of the Canning party quitted the government with him. His removal from the

ministry gave great dissatisfaction in the House of Commons **Chap. I.**
and out of doors, which was increased when it was known ___1828.___
that Sir G. Murray, a military man, was his successor.

The question which at this moment occupied and almost Catholic
engrossed the attention of the English government was the Emancipa-
state of Ireland. The overwhelming majority of the inhabi- tion.
tants of that country were Roman Catholics, but the whole
political power was in the hands of the Protestant minority,
while the Catholics were excluded from almost every office
of trust and power, and not even permitted to send representatives of their own faith to the Imperial Parliament. A
strong and growing feeling of the flagrant iniquity of this
state of things filled the minds of the oppressed majority,
and many Protestants in Ireland, and a still greater number
in England, were convinced of the injustice and impolicy of
these odious and invidious disabilities. Mr. Pitt, and most
of his successors in office, had been anxious to effect their
removal, but they had been unable to overcome the prejudices and scruples of George III. and George IV., both of
whom considered that they were bound by their coronation
oath to resist any change in this respect, and the latter of
whom had stipulated, with some of those whom he had summoned to form administrations, that this subject should never
be mentioned to him. On this point the Duke of Wellington
shared the opinions of his sovereign. He had on several
occasions declared himself to be the decided enemy of Catholic
Emancipation, and it was probably owing to his well-known
opinions on this point that no such pledge as that which we
have just referred to was exacted from him on his accession
to office. Had it been required he probably would very
readily have given it, and having given would certainly have
adhered to it. Mr. Peel was even more strongly committed
against the Catholic claims. He had assumed a hostile
position towards Mr. Canning's administration, on the express

ground of that gentleman's known desire to remove the Catholic disabilities, though it was known that he was pre-cluded from bringing forward a measure with that object. Indeed Mr. Peel was regarded as the leader and champion of the Protestant party in the House of Commons and in the country; and to that opinion he owed the honour, and at that period it was considered a very great honour, of representing the University of Oxford. Still there was a certain pervading spirit of liberality in his opinions which inspired hope into the Catholics, and an uneasy feeling of distrust into his own followers. Most of the other members of the cabinet shared the sentiments of their chiefs, but their opinions were of comparatively small importance.

Meanwhile the Catholics were not idle. A "Catholic Association" had been formed, and had placed itself at the head of one of the most formidable agitations that had ever been carried on in any country. A semi-military organisation was given to the discontented party, uniforms were made for them, and they increased every day in numbers, in boldness, and in violence. The police, which was necessarily composed of an overwhelming majority of Catholics, shared the passions and the discontent of their countrymen. The Irish soldiers, who formed a large proportion of the British army, and were Catholics almost to a man, were tampered with by the malcontents, and could not be relied on in case of an insurrection.

Daniel
O'Connell.
The leader of this formidable movement was a man well calculated to bring it to a successful termination. Daniel O'Connell possessed a winning and persuasive eloquence, of a kind peculiarly well adapted to stir the passions of the generous and excitable race whose champion he had constituted himself. At one moment he addressed them in terms of the most winning *bonhomme*, at another he denounced the tyranny of their Saxon oppressors, and proclaimed the wrongs of his country in accents of the most withering indignation.

He possessed a rare mixture of audacity and caution, and his
legal education, for he was a barrister, enabled him to go to
the very verge of treason without coming within the grasp
of the law. He possessed in an eminent degree the wit,
humour, and readiness for which his countrymen have always
been remarkable. His talents were of a most versatile nature,
enabling him with equal ease and success to negociate with
the Lord Lieutenant and his government, and guide the
turbulent and impulsive spirits at whose head he was placed,
and whose deliverance he had undertaken to achieve. Most
men, if placed in a similar position, would have been unable
to ride the storm they had conjured up, and would have
become its victims ; but such was the ascendency that
O'Connell had acquired over the lower orders of his fellow-
countrymen, and so unbounded was the confidence they placed
in him, that he was able to goad them almost to madness,
and then, if it suited the purpose of the moment, to restrain
them in the wildest transports of their fury. In a word, he
wielded the wild and excitable millions of the Catholic population with an ease that seemed almost magical. Having it
in his power to throw them into instant rebellion, he took
care that they should exhibit just as much violence as was
necessary to terrify their opponents, without breaking out
into open insurrection, or coming into collision with the force
of the British empire.

The condition of Ireland was the more immediate cause of
the overthrow of the various governments which had, as we
have already stated, succeeded one another so rapidly in England, and it was the great embarrassment of the Duke of
Wellington's administration. Every day the difficulty was
increasing, and the outbreak of an insurrection appeared to
be more and more imminent. We cannot better describe the
operation of the state of things we have mentioned, and the
effect they produced on the administration both in England

and Ireland, than by quoting the words which were employed by Mr. Peel in proposing to the House of Commons
the measure which we shall hereafter find him introducing,
with a view to the removal of the evils which the denial of
justice to the Irish Catholics produced.

" For thirty-five years the state of government in this
country on the Catholic question has been disunion. Lord
Fitzwilliam went to Ireland in 1794, and his government
came to a termination on account of a difference about the
Catholic question. In 1801, Mr. Pitt's government came to
an end, and on the same ground—a difference about the
Catholic question. He resumed the government in 1804,
composing his cabinet in a manner which showed that it was
not formed on the principle of unqualified resistance. After
his death succeeded a new ministry, which endured about
eighteen months and then came to a termination—still, on
the same ground, a difference about the Catholic question. It
was true that during the five years that followed, under the
ministry of Mr. Perceval, government resisted the consideration of this question ; but the resistance did not proceed on
permanent grounds, for during the greater part of that interval Lord Castlereagh and Mr. Canning were members of the
government, and consented to act only in deference to the
conscientious scruples of His late Majesty. So soon as the
restrictions on the Regency had expired, the same parliament
which had been elected in 1807 determined, by a very large
majority, to take the question into consideration. Since then,
up to the commencement of the present session, the Catholic
question has been made what is called a neutral question ;
any member of every government was allowed to take his
own course with respect to it, the consequence of which has
been most unfortunate, though, perhaps, unavoidable. During
the whole of that period the government was divided—sometimes equally; sometimes the proportion was seven to six

against concession; sometimes it was six to seven in favour
of concession. Usually, however, the cabinet was equally
divided. This divided government had been but an apt
representative of the divided opinion of the legislature which
I am addressing. Four out of the five last parliaments have,
at some time or other, come to a decision in favour of the
Catholic question. One House of Commons did resist the
consideration of the question, but that single house, out of
five, resisted its consideration by a majority of only 243 to
241. From a list of the divisions during the last ten years,
I find that in 1819 there was a majority of two against
the question; in 1823 there was a majority of six in its
favour; in 1821 a bill was passed by a majority of nine; in
1822 the bill for the admission of Roman Catholic Peers into
the House of Lords was passed by a majority of five; in 1824
the question was not brought forward; in 1825 a bill was
passed by a majority of twenty-one; in 1826 there was a
general election; and in 1827 the present House of Commons
decided against the question by a majority of four; but in
the last session they had decided in its favour by a majority
of six."

Such was the state of affairs and parties at the time when
Mr. Huskisson and his friends retired or rather were expelled
from the ministry. Among those who had been introduced
into it, in order to supply their places, was the Hon. Vesey
Fitzgerald, member for the County of Clare. His acceptance
of office rendered it necessary that he should go back to his
constituents. He was personally popular with all parties, and,
though a Protestant, was favourable to Catholic Emancipation.
He was therefore supported by almost every man of wealth
and property in the County of Clare. As for the forty-shilling
freeholders, they had always hitherto voted according to the
bidding of the great landed proprietors, who, by long custom,
considered themselves as having a sort of right to command

their votes. His return, therefore, seemed a matter of certainty, and no opposition was anticipated. Nevertheless, the Catholic Association determined to contest the seat, and took the bold and wise step of putting forward as their chosen candidate, Mr. O'Connell himself, who, though according to the then existing law, disqualified from sitting in the House of Commons, might be elected as a representative, and in that capacity protest with greater effect against the injustice with which he and his co-religionists were treated. Every exertion was therefore made to secure his election; and to encourage his supporters he solemnly declared to them, on his reputation as a lawyer, that there was nothing in the state of the law to prevent him taking his seat if elected, and he backed this assertion by the opinion of Mr. Butler, a Roman Catholic barrister of some reputation and considerable learning. His candidature roused the enthusiasm of his countrymen to the highest pitch. From almost every altar in the county the people were solemnly urged to vote for O'Connell as the champion of their church, and they who hesitated were denounced as renegades to their religion and traitors to the liberties of their country. The county was traversed in every direction by agitators who inculcated the same doctrines in language still more inflammatory. The result was that the hitherto irresistible influence of the territorial aristocracy was annihilated; and while the great landowners, almost to a man, supported Fitzgerald, the poor but more numerous freeholders voted with equal unanimity for O'Connell. Mr. Fitzgerald saw from the first that his cause was desperate, and after a five days' poll, on which his opponent had a very decided majority, he withdrew from the hopeless contest.

Effects of
Mr. O'Con-
nell's elec-
tion. This event produced an immense effect throughout the whole empire, but especially in Ireland. The poor miserable half-starved, and less than half-civilised Irish peasant, saw

in it the dawn for him of a social and political millennium.
A first great victory had been gained over his oppressors,
and he hailed it as a guarantee of many future successes.
Henceforth his enthusiasm became wilder, his devotion to
and his confidence in his great leader more unbounded;
and there can be no doubt that had the signal for rebellion
been then given it would have been promptly and generally
obeyed, and a civil war would have ensued, which, though
it might ultimately have been crushed by the superior power
of England, would certainly have assumed very formidable
proportions, and brought misery and massacre on the Irish
adherents of the English government.

On the other hand, nothing could exceed the consternation
with which the Protestants regarded this great defeat of their
party. It revealed to them the full extent of the Catholic
combination, and the intense passion and enthusiasm by
which it was animated. They saw with dismay the hitherto
submissive serfs now rising in a body against their landlords,
and they could not help fancying that the movement, though
now carried on within the limits of strict legality, might end
in an outburst of violence of which they would probably be
the helpless victims. Some of them were cowed by terror,
and either became avowed advocates of Emancipation or
shrunk from all show of opposition to it. Others were
goaded by terror and party spirit into still more violent
resistance to concession. Their exasperation was at its
height, and their imprudent insolence was not unlikely to
lead to conflicts which neither O'Connell nor the Catholic
Association could prevent or restrain. In England, too, the
effect produced was immense, and on the whole highly
favourable to Catholic Emancipation.

O'Connell was not the man to allow his victory to remain
unimproved. He lost no time in following it up by more
vigorous efforts and a hotter agitation. Ireland was traversed

CHAP. I. from one end to the other by the agents and emissaries
1828.   of the Catholic Association, making inflammatory speeches,
organizing threatening demonstrations, and employing every
means that could be devised to embarrass the government and
increase the prevailing disaffection.   O'Connell himself went
over to England to fulfil his pledge of taking his seat in the
House of Commons, but as the session was drawing to a
close, and as nothing was to be gained at the time by pressing
his claim, he prudently deferred the attempt until the commencement of the following session.

Necessity   It was clear that the government could not allow this
of conces-
sion.   state of things to continue without making an effort to put
an end to it.   Blow after blow, humiliation after humiliation
was inflicted on them, and they were unable to do anything.
The Catholic party was daily gaining strength, and they were
becoming weaker and weaker in their means of resisting it.
They were humiliated in the eyes of friends and foes alike.
It was, therefore, becoming more and more necessary that
the agitation should be met either by measures of severity
and repression, or by concession and conciliation.   Either
they must put down O'Connell and the Catholic Association
by force, or they must abate the grievances of which they
complained.   The former course was the one which the ante-
cedents of the chief members of the government seemed to
require, but it was one that involved fearful peril and responsibility.   It was certain to lead to a civil war, which
would produce as its first effect the massacre of those Protestants for whose supposed benefit it was undertaken.   The
foreign relations of the country were far from satisfactory,
and there was reason to fear that the outbreak of an Irish
insurrection would be followed by demands which the government could not grant without humiliation, and could not
resist without extreme danger.   And if a war should arise,
what would be the position and prospects of the government

with England discontented, Ireland holding out her hands
to our enemies, and an army composed in a very great
proportion of disaffected Irish troops. The policy of repression
was not to be thought of, the policy of doing nothing could
not be persevered in much longer—there remained, then,
nothing but the policy of concession. For the sake of the
whole empire, for the sake of Ireland, for the sake, above all,
of the Irish Protestants and the Irish Protestant Church, it
was necessary that something should be done to satisfy the
just demands of the Irish Roman Catholics.

Still, this policy was attended with no small difficulties.
We have already pointed out how strongly the Duke of Wellington and Mr. Peel were committed against Catholic Emancipation, and the decided objection which the King entertained
to it. It seemed, therefore, that the only course which the
duke could honourably and properly take, under the circumstances, was to admit that the policy he had hitherto
upheld could not be any longer maintained, to make way
for his parliamentary opponents, and to support them in
those measures which they felt to be required ; and, perhaps,
if he had adopted this course he would have best consulted his
own reputation, as well as the interests of his party. But
even to this, very plausible objections might be urged.
The cabinet had only been in existence for about half a year,
and it would have been a very serious calamity, after the
many administrative changes which had taken place, that the
only strong government which had existed for some time
should be overthrown, especially in the unsettled state in
which the public mind then was. It would also have the
effect of throwing the king into the hands of the Whig party,
to which in his younger days he had been attached, but with
which he had broken in a manner that did not redound to
his own credit, and which he now regarded with a feeling
of aversion, which would render it very humiliating and

distasteful to him to be compelled to call them in to advise him. The duke, whose loyalty knew no bounds, was ready to make almost any sacrifice in order to save his sovereign from what he regarded as a degradation. The Whigs, too, if called to power, were very likely to stipulate for permission to introduce a bill for the Reform of Parliament; a measure which the duke and the king regarded with even greater aversion than Catholic Emancipation. Besides, the duke and Mr. Peel were sincerely anxious to maintain the Protestant ascendency in Ireland, and they thought that this might be effected by certain securities with which it was intended that the Emancipation should be accompanied, but which their parliamentary opponents would probably object to introduce. Thus the duke felt himself bound by his sense of what was due to his sovereign and his country, to retain the office on which he had so recently entered.

Conces-
sion of
Catholic
Emanci-
pation
resolved
by the go-
vernment.

Such were the circumstances under which Mr. Peel began to feel that his own consistency and the duty he owed to the party of which he had hitherto been the leader, and by which he had been brought into power, must be sacrificed to the higher duty which he owed to his sovereign and his country. The events which were taking place in Ireland convinced him of the necessity of yielding to the demands of the Irish Catholics, and he hoped that the concession might be accompanied by other measures which would tend to remove the danger with which he and his friends believed that the Church of England and Ireland, but especially the latter, was menaced by Catholic Emancipation. He lost no time in imparting to the Duke of Wellington the conviction to which he had been led, and urging him to take the steps which, in his opinion, were imperatively required. At the same time, knowing that his change of opinion would be attributed to a sordid love of pay and power, and justly feeling that he was of all men the most unfitted to propose a measure of

which he had hitherto been regarded as the chief opponent; CHAP. I.
he begged to be allowed to withdraw from the administration, 1828.
promising that, as an independent member of parliament,
he would give his warm support not only to the particular
measures which he thought were required by the circumstances of the times, but also to the general policy of the
government. For the reasons we have already assigned, the
Duke of Wellington was fully prepared to enter into the
views of his colleague, but he too felt the embarrassment of
his position. However, the duke, Mr. Peel, and Lord Lyndhurst, then Lord Chancellor, carefully examined the question
in all its bearings, and the course which it would be advisable
to adopt had been chalked out by them, but no definite resolution had been taken ; and as late as the 11th of December,
the Duke of Wellington wrote a letter to the Roman Catholic
Primate of Ireland, in which he expressed a hope that the
day might come when Catholic Emancipation might be safely
granted, but at the same time intimated that the day was
still at a considerable distance, little thinking, probably, at the
time when he wrote, that in less than a month the measure
to which he referred would have been adopted by himself,
and the government over which he presided. The approach
of the session necessitated a decision, but the subject had
not yet been mentioned to the king. Mr. Peel, however, drew
up, for His Majesty's information, a paper in which he stated
the grounds on which he considered it necessary that Catholic
Emancipation should be conceded without delay, and the
securities by which, in his opinion, it ought to be accompanied,
and which he thought would prevent the dangers which were
apprehended from it. Armed with this document, the Duke
of Wellington succeeded in silencing the scruples, and over-
coming the objections of his master, and in wringing from him
a reluctant consent to the introduction of a measure based
on Mr. Peel's arguments, and accompanied by the securities

CHAP. I.   which he recommended.   Hereupon, Mr. Peel once more
1829.   begged to be allowed to resign, and renewed his promise of
independent support to the government.   The duke, however, felt, and perhaps justly, that he could not hope to carry
the measure unless Mr. Peel, who was its author, would take
charge of it as a minister of the crown.   Amidst all these
negociations, the final decision was only arrived at within a
few days of the opening of the session, and though some
vague rumours of what was in agitation were circulated
through the country, the intentions of the government were
not known until they were revealed by the Royal Speech, at
the opening of parliament, which, on this occasion, was
delivered by commission.

The Catho-
lic Eman-
cipation
Bill intro-
duced.
Accordingly, in the month of March a measure of Catholic
Emancipation was introduced into the House of Commons,
accompanied by two other bills, one of which disfranchised the
forty-shilling freeholders, by whose means, chiefly, Mr.
O'Connell had won his election; the other enacted the suppression of the Catholic Association.   The ministry hoped by
means of these three measures to restore contentment and tranquillity to Ireland, to secure the Church of Ireland, and to put
the Irish Catholics in all important respects on a footing of
equality with their Protestant fellow-countrymen.   The last two
measures encountered no serious opposition ; the Protestant
party, for whose protection they were framed, had no reason
to object to them ; and the Catholics and their friends knew
that by opposing them they might imperil the success of that
great measure of justice for which they had been struggling
so long, and which was now unexpectedly offered to them by
their chief opponents.   But the bill for the Emancipation of
the Catholics encountered a most formidable opposition both
in the house and out of doors.   The great Orange-Tory party,
taken unawares, and complaining, with some show of reason,
that they had been betrayed by their leaders, whose irresolution

certainly wore. the appearance of calculated treachery,
protested bitterly against the haste with which the measure
was pressed forwards, and clamoured loudly for a dissolution,
which would have enabled them to appeal to the Protestant
prejudices of their countrymen, and might very probably
have given them a majority against the bill. They were
absolutely furious, and ready to ally themselves with any
party who would assist them in defeating the measure and
wreaking vengeance on its framers. The clergy opposed it
almost to a man, and used their influence with their flocks
against it. The majority of the Dissenters adopted the
same course.

Nor were these feelings confined to the late supporters of Sir C.
the ministry. They found vehement expression in their own Wetherell.
ranks. The Attorney-General, Sir C. Wetherell, to whom
offers of high office had been made if he would support the
measure, not only refused to follow his colleagues in their unexpected change of opinion, but even to draw the bill. It
might have been expected that the Duke of Wellington, who
had so summarily ejected Mr. Huskisson and his friends for a
much lighter act of insubordination, would not have tolerated
this refusal; but the events that had followed Mr. Huskisson's
dismissal had taught him caution. He knew that if the
Attorney-General were removed, it would be necessary to offer
the post to Sir N. Tindal, who represented the University of
Cambridge, and who might, very probably, lose his seat there
if he accepted office, which would require him to vacate it,
and thus the administration would receive a blow which it could
ill sustain, and the Protestant party obtain a triumph which
at that moment might prove very embarrassing to the government. Sir C. Wetherell was, therefore, permitted to remain
in office, notwithstanding his refusal to draw the bill; and
when it was introduced, it found in the Attorney-General
of the government by which it was proposed, one of its

ablest and most bitter opponents. When it was brought in, he broke forth into a vehement tirade against his ministerial superiors, and especially Lord Chancellor Lyndhurst. "Am I, then," he exclaimed, "to blame for refusing to do that, in the subordinate office of Attorney-General, which a more eminent adviser of the crown, only two years ago, declared he would not consent to do? Am I, then, to be twitted, taunted, and attacked? I dare them to attack me! I have no speech to eat up. I have no apostacy disgracefully to explain. I have no paltry subterfuge to resort to. I have not to say that a thing is black one day and white another. I have not been in one year a Protestant Master of the Rolls, and in the next a Catholic Lord Chancellor. I would rather remain as I am, the humble member for Plympton, than be guilty of such treachery, such contradiction, such unexplained conversion, such miserable and contemptible apostasy." . .

"They might have turned me out of office, but I would not be made such a dirty tool as to draw *that* bill. Let who would do it, I would not defile pen or waste paper by such an act of folly, and so forfeit my character for sense and honesty. I have, therefore, declined to have anything to do with it." Of course, whatever the dangers or embarrassments of government, the man who delivered this harangue could not be allowed to retain his office, and he was at once dismissed, as he had himself anticipated and predicted that he would be.

Indignation of the Protestant party. If such sentiments were expressed in the ministry itself, and by one whose official position afforded him the means of judging the crisis, and the motives by which his chiefs were actuated, we may easily conceive what were the feelings and what the language of those outside, especially among the ignorant, whose prejudices against the Roman Catholics had been industriously fostered and fomented by one-sided histories and speeches, who saw nothing in that religion but a hellish conspiracy against the happiness and liberties of mankind, for the benefit of the priesthood, and who believed that this measure would be the means of restoring their old ascendency, and delivering England, bound hand and foot, into their power. An opportunity for the display of these prejudices was soon afforded. Mr. Peel, though prevented by the peculiar circumstances in which he was placed from withdrawing from the ministry, felt that he was bound in honour to resign his seat at Oxford. Some of his friends, who considered that he had done nothing to forfeit the confidence of the University, resolved to propose him again. The Protestant party, on the other hand, put forward in opposition to him Sir R. Inglis, an upright and honourable country gentleman, but deeply imbued with the prejudices of the party whose chosen champion he was, and in every respect greatly inferior to Mr. Peel. He was returned by a triumphant majority. This was a great blow to the ministry, and it was accompanied by the defection of many of those who had hitherto been their most steadfast adherents, but who now went into bitter opposition to them.

The alienation of their old Tory friends was compensated by the support generously given to the ministry by those who had hitherto been their most formidable opponents. By their aid the bill was rapidly and triumphantly carried through all its stages in both Houses of Parliament. Mr. O'Connell waited for the passing of the measure and then claimed his seat, but the House of Commons, influenced by the ministry, rejected his claim, and declared that as his return had taken place before the passing of the Emancipation Act he was not duly elected; he was, however, re-elected by the county of Clare, and took his seat without opposition.

The ministry succeeded in passing through the session without further difficulty, but they had alienated the old

CHAP. I.   Protestant Tory party, who anxiously waited for an opportu-
1829.   nity of wreaking their vengeance on their former leaders for
what they regarded as an act of the blackest treachery. Actuated by this feeling, many of them became strong reformers,
and in the transient ardour of their new-born zeal outran
most of those who had hitherto taken charge of this question.
On the other hand, the Whig and Catholic parties were but
half satisfied. The former saw that the ministry depended
on them for its existence, and yet that they were entirely excluded from all participation in the framing of their measures or the emoluments of office. Their discontent was
increased as they saw that the government tried every means
of reconciling its old supporters, and of rendering itself independent of those by whose aid it had recently triumphed.
In Ireland the agitation still continued. The Catholic Association, though suppressed by the recent Act, still carried on
its operations under a new name. Meanwhile, all interests in
Distress.   all parts of the kingdom seemed to suffer. Trade, manufactures, agriculture all stagnated. Many parishes were reduced
to such a state of pauperism that the whole of the property
within their limits was insufficient for the maintenance of
their poor ; and assistance had to be sought from neighbouring
parishes already overburdened with the expense of supporting
their own paupers. Landlords could not obtain their rents ;
farmers were impoverished ; the agricultural labourer, whose
wages were often eked out from the poor rates, received just
enough to enable him to procure for his family and himself
the barest necessaries of life. The manufacturing operatives
of Lancashire and Yorkshire were, in many instances, receiving only threepence and fourpence a day for more than twelve
hours' labour. O'Connell stated in the House of Commons
that in Ireland 7,000 persons were subsisting on three-half-
pence a day; and though this statement was perhaps exaggerated, there can be no doubt that great distress prevailed

in that unhappy country, and that the peasantry were reduced to the smallest allowance of the lowest kind of food.

Such was the state of things throughout the United Kingdom at the commencement of the year 1830. Parlia-ment was again opened by commission. In the King's Speech the prevailing distress was indeed mentioned, but in terms which were justly regarded as evincing a very in-adequate sense of the prevailing distress, and which did not disclose any intention on the part of the ministry to introduce measures with a view to its mitigation or removal. Amendments were accordingly moved to this address in both Houses of Parliament, the object of which was to pledge the legislature to take the distress and the means of alleviating it into their serious consideration; but in both, ministers triumphed, though the minority of 105 in the lower house, composed chiefly of old adherents of the administration, showed how unsuccessful had been their efforts to win back those who had been alienated from them by their conduct in respect to Catholic Emancipation.

One of these, the Marquis of Blandford, eldest son of the Duke of Marlborough, moved that the following wholesome admonition to the throne should be appended to the address from the House of Commons:—

" That this house feels itself called upon, in the awful and alarming state of universal distress into which the landed, commercial, and all the great productive interests of the country are at this moment, to take care that your Majesty shall not be the only person in your dominions ignorant of such an astounding fact, as well as of the consequent impend-ing danger to the throne, and other great national institutions established by the wisdom of our ancestors, for the protection and benefit of the people over whom your Majesty has been called to preside.

" That this house is at no loss to indicate the real cause

of this unnatural state of things, and, in justice to your
Majesty and the whole nation, it can no longer hesitate to
proclaim that cause to the world.

" It is a fact, already too notorious, that this house, which
was intended by our ancient and admirable constitution to
be the guardian of the nation's purse, has, from causes now
unnecessary to be detailed, been nominated, for the greater
part, by a few proprietors of close and decaying boroughs,
and by a few other individuals, who, by the mere power of
money, employed in means absolutely and positively forbidden
by the laws, have obtained a ' domination,' also expressly forbidden by Act of Parliament, over certain other cities and
boroughs in the United Kingdom.

" That, in consequence of this departure from the wisdom
of our ancestors, the nation has been deprived of its natural
guardian, and has, in consequence, become so burdened in
the expensive establishments of all kinds, that, in a period
much shorter than the life of man, the taxation has increased
from £9,000,000 to nearly £60,000,000 a year, and the poor-
rate, or parochial assessments, during the same period, have
augmented from £1,500,000 to £8,000,000 annually.

"That to render such a mass of taxation, so dispropor-
tionate to the whole wealth of the kingdom, in any degree
supportable, recourse has been had, either from ignorance or
design, to the most monstrous schemes in tampering with the
currency or circulating money of the country, at one time by
greatly diminishing the value of the same, and at another
time by greatly augmenting such value; and at each and
every of such changes, which have been but too often repeated,
one class of the community after another have been plunged
into poverty, misery, and ruin, while the sufferers, without
any fault or folly of their own, have been hardly able to perceive from what hand these calamities have come upon them.

" That under such circumstances, and with this knowledge

before its eyes, this house would consider itself lost to every
sense of duty towards your Majesty, and guilty of treason
towards the people, if it did not seize this opportunity of
declaring to your Majesty its solemn conviction that the state
is at this moment in imminent danger, and that no effectual
means of salvation will or can be adopted, until the people
shall be restored to their rightful share in the legislation of
the country—that is, to their undoubted right, according to
the true meaning of the constitution of choosing the members
of this house."

The great body of the reformers refused to support a
motion which they considered to be more calculated to embarrass the government than to lead to any practical results,
and only eleven members voted for it, while ninety-six voted
against it.

But, though the Whigs generally aided the ministry, and
often saved them from their former friends—now become
their bitterest opponents—they were not disposed to continue
this support unless the government was willing to adopt their
views, and Sir F. Burdett distinctly intimated, in the course of
the debate on Lord Blandford's motion, that ministers must
enter into a closer connection with the Whigs if they desired
a continuance of the support thus afforded them.

The Marquis of Blandford, undeterred by the signal The Mar-
failure of his first attempt, took the first opportunity of Bland-
renewing it, and on the 18th of February he brought forward ford's
a measure of Parliamentary Reform in accordance with the Bill.
indications of his rejected motion. It was entitled "A bill to
regulate abuses in the elections of members of parliament,"
and was designed to restore the fundamental principles of
representation which, as its author contended, had been
established in the days of Henry III. and the three Edwards.
He proposed that a committee should be chosen by ballot, to
make a review of all the boroughs and cities in the kingdom,

CHAP. I. and to report to the Home Secretary those among them
which had fallen into decay, or had in any manner forfeited
their right of representation on those principles of the English
constitution which, as he maintained, had been anciently
recognised by national and parliamentary usage. The Home
Secretary was to be bound to act immediately on this report,
and to relieve such places from the burden of sending members to parliament. He proposed that the franchises of these
places should be transferred to large unrepresented towns.
The qualification of a vote under the bill was to be the payment of scot and lot. Copyholders and leaseholders were
also to have the right of voting conferred upon them. He
likewise proposed that members of parliament should receive
payment for their services during the session of parliament—
county members at the rate of £4 per day, and borough
members at the rate of £2 per day. In Scotland the representation was to be placed on the same footing as that of
England. The members were to be chosen from the inhabitants of the places which they represented. No compensation
was to be given to the proprietors, as they were called, of the
disfranchised boroughs; but Lord Blandford stated that if the
passing of his measure could be facilitated by that means he
was willing to introduce a clause providing for their compensation.

This measure was decidedly opposed by the government,
and very coldly received by the opposition. For most of
them it went too far. Besides, the sincerity of its proposer
was suspected, and of his indiscretion there was no doubt.
Lord Althorp, therefore, as the leader of the Whig party in
the house, moved, as an amendment to the motion for leave
to bring in the bill, the following resolution:—"That it is
the opinion of this house that a reform in the representation
of the people is necessary." Both the amendment and the
original motion were negatived.

The case of East Retford was again brought before the
House of Commons by Mr. Calcraft, a member of the government, who, on the 11th of March, moved for leave to bring in
a bill to enlarge the constituency by giving the franchise to
the freeholders of the adjoining hundred of Bassetlaw. It
was met by a counter motion for leave to bring in a bill "to
exclude the borough of East Retford from electing burgesses
to serve in parliament, and to enable the town of Birmingham
to return two members in lieu thereof." Mr. Huskisson and
his friend Mr. C. Grant strongly supported this latter proposition. On the other hand, Mr. Peel, on behalf of the
government, supported the original motion. He did not
deny the desirableness of giving members to large towns;
he reminded the house that he had himself voted for the
transfer of the franchise from Penryn to Manchester, and had
at the same time stated that if on any future occasion a
majority of the inhabitants of any borough should be convicted of bribery and corruption, he should not object to the
transfer of the franchise of that borough to a large town,
with the understanding that there should be a division of
the franchises, so at the disposal of parliament, between the
landed, commercial, and manufacturing interests. He saw
no reason to change that opinion, but thought that there
were circumstances in the case of East Retford which should
induce parliament to extend the franchise to the adjoining
hundred. One element in the case which weighed with him
was, the consideration that the county of Nottingham sent
only eight members to parliament, and he saw no good reason
why that number should be reduced to six. He promised,
however, that if the house should come to a decision contrary
to his own opinion, he would not oppose any vexatious delays
to the passage through the house of the bill which would in
that case be brought in. The proposal, which was supported
by the ministry, was carried by a majority of twenty-seven;

CHAP. I.   the votes being one hundred and twenty-six for the original
            motion. and ninety-nine for the amendment.

                Lord Howick followed up this debate by the following
            motion :—

Lord   "That bribery has been repeatedly and habitually em-
Howick's   ployed to influence the election of members of parliament.
motion.   That this fact has been often established, never denied, and
            was especially proved at the bar of this house, in the first
            session of the present parliament, in the case of Penryn and
            East Retford.   That it is notorious that a similar practice is
            openly resorted to in many of the cities and boroughs of the
            United Kingdom.   That the recent disfranchisement of
            Grampound does not appear to have in any degree diminished
            the prevalence of the evil.   That this house, therefore, finding
            that the passing of specific bills directed against particular
            cases, has neither had the effect of removing the existence or
            arresting the progress of corruption, is of opinion, that its
            character may best be vindicated by abandoning these useless
            and expensive proceedings, in order to adopt some general
            and comprehensive measure, as the only means of effectually
            checking so scandalous an abuse."   These resolutions were
            negatived by a majority of ninety-nine.

Petition   The question of Reform was also raised, in an indirect
from   manner, by a petition from some of the electors of the
Newark.   borough of Newark ; in which it was complained that the
            Duke of Newcastle had employed his influence, as proprietor
            of a large portion of the town, in an improper manner, and
            had, in effect, nominated the member for Newark.   It was
            asserted that he had expelled from their tenancies all those
            who had voted against the candidate whom he supported;
            and that he had done this, not only on his own property, but
            also on some other property in and near Newark, which he
            held by lease from the Crown, and that when remonstrated
            with on the subject, he had cut the matter short by

replying—"May I not do what I will with my own?" A Chap. I.
motion to refer this petition to a select committee produced
a long debate, but was finally rejected by a majority of 194
to 61. The affair, however, produced a strong impression
throughout the country, and aided materially in increasing
the desire already felt for a Reform of the House of
Commons.

Undaunted by these repeated failures, and the hostility Lord J.
Russell's
motion.
of the overwhelming majority to every project of Reform,
Lord J. Russell asked leave to bring in a bill to give members to Manchester, Birmingham, and Leeds, the three largest
unrepresented towns in England. In this proposal he was
warmly seconded by Mr. Huskisson, who avowed that he
would have preferred the plan of transfer; but as the house
had rejected it, he was ready to accept in its place that which
was now proposed. At the same time he distinctly declared
that he was not prepared to go any further in the way of
Parliamentary Reform. The motion of Lord J. Russell was
negatived by 188 to 140. Another bill, which Mr. O'Connell
asked leave to introduce, and which embraced triennial
parliaments, universal suffrage, and the ballot, only found
support from 13 members in a house of 332.

On the whole, then, the Reform question, though decidedly making way, did not wear a very promising aspect.
While the more extreme, or crotchety, propositions were
rejected by overwhelming majorities, even the most moderate
and the most acceptable were in a decided minority, and it
was little expected, on any side of the house, that within less
than a year from the time that Lord J. Russell failed to
obtain leave to bring in a bill for the very moderate measure
of Reform which he proposed, he would, as a minister of the
Crown—without a division, and almost without a negative
voice—obtain leave to bring in a bill to make a most necessary change in the national representation. But two events

CHAP. I. which occurred in the course of this year placed the question
of Reform and its advocates in a much more favourable
position than they had hitherto occupied.

Death of   The first of these events was the death of George IV.
George IV. While young, he had manifested a sympathy for liberal
opinions, and had attached himself to the Whig party, and
they entertained great hopes when he became Regent, that
he would put the administration of affairs into their hands.
But these expectations were completely disappointed. From
that moment he gradually detached himself from them, and
during the later years of his life he manifested a deep-rooted
aversion both to their principles and their persons, and
especially to Earl Grey, who had become their leader. We
have already seen with what reluctance he yielded to an
imperious necessity, in consenting to the introduction of
the Catholic Emancipation Bill; and there can be no doubt
that his opposition to any measure of Parliamentary Reform
would have been even more obstinate and decided.

William   On the other hand, his brother, William IV., who succeeded
IV.   him on the throne, was supposed to be not unfavourable to
the Whigs, and was known to have a personal grudge against
the Duke of Wellington, who, greatly to his honour, had
refused to sacrifice a respectable officer, Sir G. Cockburn, who
had incurred the displeasure of the new monarch, then Duke
of Clarence and Lord High Admiral, by a refusal to obey
orders from His Royal Highness that were inconsistent with
his duty. The consequence of the Duke of Wellington's firmness on this occasion was, that the Duke of Clarence resigned
the office of High Admiral, for which he was ill qualified, and
in which he was doing great mischief. Nevertheless, on his
accession, the new monarch declared to his ministers that he
approved their policy and would give them his support. He
was, probably, sincere in making this declaration, but his
feeling towards them could not have been very cordial. The

Whig party, however, were in high spirits, and no longer Снар. I.
disposed to continue the support they had thus far given to
the government. They knew that, if not actually favoured
by the new sovereign, they were, at all events, not personally,
obnoxious to him. They were confident that a general election, which must shortly take place, would give them great
additional strength, for they were highly popular in the
country, and the ministry very unpopular. They saw that
the ministry were determined to recover, if possible, the confidence of their old supporters, and to estrange themselves
more and more from those by whose aid they had been
enabled to carry the Catholic Relief Bill, and to maintain
themselves in office since the passing of that measure. The
Whigs now began to exchange their position of independent
supporters of the ministry, for an attitude of determined and
uncompromising opposition. They took every opportunity
of contrasting them with their new sovereign, speaking of
the latter in courtly, and sometimes highly adulatory, terms;
while they declaimed strongly against the former. The Duke
of Wellington, seeing that the approach of the dissolution of
parliament diverted the attention of the members of the
House of Commons from the measures of the government,
wisely resolved to dissolve as speedily as possible. The opposition, on the other hand, sought by all means in their power
to delay the dissolution, and insisted on first settling the
appointment of a regency, in case of the king's decease before
the re-assembling of parliament. On this question they
divided both houses against the government, but in both
they were defeated by large majorities. On the 23rd of July
parliament was prorogued with the usual formalities, and on
the following day was dissolved by proclamation.

Thus the government found themselves, on the eve of the
general election, in presence of two powerful and bitterly hostile parties :—the Tories, who were still exasperated against

Position of
the go-
vernment
on the eve
of the
general
election.

CHAP. I. them on account of their conduct in reference to the Catholic question ; and the Whigs, who disapproved their present policy, and hoped to replace them in the government of the country. The former were strong for electioneering purposes in their wealth, their property, the number of boroughs which were under their control, and the violent prejudices against the Roman Catholic religion, which had long prevailed in this country, and which were carefully fostered by the ultra-Protestant party. The Whigs, on the other hand, besides a large amount of property and borough influence which was at their disposal, enjoyed the support of the great majority of the people, who looked to them as the party by whose aid their political redemption was to be wrought out, and who, though at that time very inadequately represented, were by no means altogether without a voice in the choice of members of the House of Commons; nay there were at that time some places, such as Preston, in which the suffrage was more nearly universal than it is at present. It was true that there was an immense amount of bribery, corruption, and intimidation, but these practices were resorted to quite as much by the opponents of the ministry as by their supporters, and they were less influential in times of great popular excitement, such as were those during which the present election was carried on. Thus the anti-Reform influence of the immense number of close boroughs was to some extent neutralized, and an anti-Reform ministry was assailed by means of the very system of which they were the last possible upholders.

Revolution in France. Such was the state of things, and such the aspect of affairs, when an event occurred which resounded throughout the world, and exercised on the elections, which were just on the eve of their commencement, an influence which proved fatal to the Wellington administration. The French government, urged forward by their king, and finding that each successive election produced a chamber of deputies more unfavourable to their views, and more opposed to the royal authority—that the press were becoming more and more violent and audacious in their assaults on the government— and that changes of great importance, and in their eyes likely to lead to an overthrow of the government, were otherwise inevitable, issued a body of ordinances, which fundamentally changed the constitution, as determined by the charter, and destroyed the liberty of the press. The publication of these ordinances produced an insurrection, for which the French government had made no adequate preparation, and after three days' fighting in the streets of Paris, during which the troops were almost without food, the city was evacuated and left in the hands of the populace. The king abdicated in favour of his grandson; but the condition was disregarded, and the Duke of Orleans was appointed; first, lieutenant-general and then king. The dethroned monarch fled to England, and it was for some days doubtful whether the monarchical form of government would be preserved in France, or a republic established. The white flag, the symbol of French royalty, was discarded, and the tri-color flag, then regarded as the emblem of revolution and republicanism, was substituted for it.

This event produced an immense sensation throughout Europe. In Brussels the popular enthusiasm issued in an insurrection, which ended in the separation of Belgium from Holland, and its erection into an independent kingdom. But nowhere was sympathy with the popular victory in France more warmly felt and manifested than in England, where, as we have seen, the general election was just on the point of commencing, under circumstances of peculiar gravity. Had the monarch been at that moment unpopular, he would probably, like Charles X, have been hurled from his throne. Fortunately, however, the new king, by his affable de- meanour, his sailor-like bluntness, his dislike of ostentation, and his supposed liberal leanings, was highly popular throughout the nation, but especially in the metropolis. Therefore the feelings which might, under other circumstances, have been directed against the sovereign, were turned against his ministers, who were not supposed to stand very high in his favour, and these feelings found a ready vent in the electoral struggle. The result was that the elections, which, before the Reform Bill, were almost invariably carried on amidst tumult and disorder, especially in the large towns, were scenes of greater confusion than ever, and resulted, almost in every place where the constituency was really free to elect its own representatives, in the triumph of the advocates of Parliamentary Reform over the ministerial candidates. In county after county the latter were defeated, in some cases by ultra-Tories, bent on avenging themselves on the government for its supposed treachery in conceding Catholic Emancipation; in others by their Whig opponents. Of the defeats which the ministry thus sustained, the most remarkable and the most damaging was that which they experienced in Yorkshire, where their great opponent, Mr. Brougham, though entirely unconnected with the county, was returned without serious opposition. The government, greatly to its credit, abstained from using the means at its disposal for influencing the election, and which had usually been employed by preceding administrations to procure the return of their supporters. Thus the result of the general election was, that the ministry was weakened by about fifty votes in the House of Commons, besides the damaging moral effect produced by the number, and still more by the character of these defeats.

Opening of the new parliament. The new parliament assembled on the 26th of October, but the session was not open till the second of November, the interval having been occupied in swearing in the members. On the last-mentioned day, the king came to the house with great pomp, and delivered his speech in person. The

address in reply passed both houses without a division,
but in the upper chamber a debate arose upon it, which
was remarkable on account of the declaration of the prime
minister on the subject of Reform; and as this declaration
is supposed to have been the immediate cause of the fall
of the administration, and of the consequences to which that
event led, we place it before our readers at full length.
Referring to some remarks on the subject of Reform which
had been made by Earl Grey, the duke said:—

　" The noble earl has alluded to something in the shape Declaration of the
Duke of
Welling-
ton
against
Reform.
of a Parliamentary Reform, but he has been candid enough
to acknowledge that he is not prepared with any measure of
Reform; and I have as little scruple to say that His Majesty's
government is as totally unprepared as the noble lord. Nay,
on my own part, I will go further, and say that I have never
read or heard of any measure, up to the present moment,
which could in any degree satisfy my mind that the state of
the representation could be improved, or be rendered more
satisfactory to the country at large than at the present
moment. I will not, however, at such an unreasonable time,
enter upon the subject or invite discussion, but I shall not
hesitate to declare unequivocally what are my sentiments
upon it. I am fully convinced that the country possesses, at
the present moment, a legislature which answers all the good
purposes of legislation, and this to a greater degree than any
legislature ever has answered in any country whatever. I
will go further, and say that the legislature and the system
of representation possess the full and entire confidence of the
country, deservedly possess that confidence, and the discussions in the legislature have a very great influence over the
opinions of the country. I will go still further, and say that
if at the present moment I had imposed upon me the duty
of forming a legislature for any country, and particularly for
a country like this, in possession of great property of various

CHAP. I. descriptions, I do not mean to assert that I would form such a legislature as we possess now—for the nature of man was incapable of reaching it at once—but my great endeavour would be to form some description of legislature which would produce the same results. The representation of the people at present contains a large body of the property of the country, in which the landed interests have a preponderating influence. Under these circumstances, I am not prepared to bring forward any measure of the description alluded to by the noble lord. I am not only not prepared to bring forward any measure of this nature, but I will at once declare that, as far as I am concerned, as long as I hold any station in the government of the country, I shall always feel it my duty to resist such a measure when proposed by others."

The wisdom of this declaration has often been assailed, and certainly not without reason. But when its impugners add, as they generally have done, that if the duke had at this time conceded the transfer of the franchises of a few corrupt nomination boroughs, such as Penryn and East Retford, the people would have been satisfied, and the changes which form the subject of this work might have been deferred for a long time, we must demur to the statement. Believing, as we do, that the diminution of the predominance of the landed interest, through the Reform of the House of Commons, was a moral and political necessity, that it was rapidly becoming, to a large portion of the nation, a question of bread or no bread, we also believe that changes which had no tendency to remove the evils which were felt, and which would have produced no visible alleviation of them, would not have satisfied a demand for Reform which owed its force to far other causes than a mere sentimental disapproval of abuses, and, therefore, it seems to us that, viewing the matter from the duke's standpoint, he was quite right in resisting changes which were not likely to prevent but rather to produce a demand for further

changes in the same direction. But in every point of view
this frank and uncompromising declaration was highly
impolitic. It proved that Reform was more than ever hopeless
under the Wellington administration, and showed the Whigs,
if they were not already convinced of the fact, that they could
not obtain office in any other way than by overturning it.
The duke was now fairly at bay; he turned on his assailants
with the same steady tenacity which he had displayed at
Torres Vedras and Waterloo, but he took up his ground with
far less skill and with very different fortune.

Closely on this declaration there followed another event,
of very little importance in itself, but which served still further
to increase the unpopularity of the ministry, and to encourage
its opponents in their assaults upon it. Their majesties had
been invited to dine at the Guildhall on the 9th of November, and the invitation had been accepted. A few days
before the intended dinner, Mr. Peel, the Home Secretary,
received information from various quarters, and particularly
a communication from Mr. Key, the Lord Mayor elect,
warning him that some ill-disposed persons were likely to take
advantage of the occasion to create a disturbance; and, though
the Duke of Wellington was the person against whom these
designs were more particularly directed, it was thought that
even if he absented himself on the occasion some disturbance
might take place, which, in the crowded state of the streets
which the king's visit was certain to produce, might cause
terrible confusion and even loss of life. Under these circumstances ministers resolved to advise the king to postpone his
visit to the city. The announcement of this resolution, which,
considering the state of the popular mind, was perhaps prudent, produced great disappointment in the metropolis and
consternation throughout the country. As the visit was coun-
termanded at the last moment, expensive preparations had
been made. The most sinister rumours were in circulation.

CHAP. I   In the first moments of panic it was thought that London
was going to follow the example of Paris, and that a revolution was imminent.   The funds, which the declaration
of the Duke of Wellington had brought down from 84 to 80,
now fell to 77.   As these apprehensions were soon seen to be
entirely groundless, terror was promptly succeeded by ridicule
and censure.   Ministers were now accused of having allowed
themselves to be alarmed, and of having terrified the country
without any good reason, and having, through fears originating
entirely in their own unpopularity, prevented the most popular monarch who had ever occupied the throne from receiving
the homage of a loyal and enthusiastic people.

Unpopu-   In fact, never perhaps before or since had any adminis-
larity of
the go-   tration become so odious to the people as was the government
vernment.   of the Duke of Wellington at this moment.   Abuse, ridicule,
argument, invective, calumny, in fact every species of assault
was directed against them from every quarter.   The shops,
not only of the booksellers but of the linen drapers, were
filled with caricatures of them ; in the case of the latter they
were stamped on handkerchiefs and other articles of linen or
calico.   The duke was usually represented in the dress of an
old hackney coachman, while Sir R. Peel figured as a rat-
catcher ; the old Tories were entirely alienated, and though
most of them dreaded Reform, they distrusted a ministry
which in their opinion had already betrayed them, and
might be expected to betray them again.   They remembered
that if the duke now declared strongly against Reform, he
had formerly declared just as strongly against Catholic Emancipation.   Besides, they were so blinded by passion and indignation that they were ready to run any risks in order to take
vengeance on the supposed treachery of their old leaders.
Little did they think that there was any danger of such a
measure of Reform as we shall speedily see proposed and ultimately carried.   Little did they dream of the utter shipwreck

of their party which was close at hand. Others again, as we
have already seen, like the Marquis of Blandford, had become
reformers, hoping that the people, who were strongly imbued
with anti-Catholic prejudices, might, if admitted to the franchise, elect men who would retract the concessions made to the
Catholics, or at all events, prevent any further legislation in
that direction, and punish the authors of the hated measure
with political annihilation. The Whigs, who had now completely broken with the government, clearly saw that their
only chance of power was in its overthrow. The friends of the
ministry supported it without enthusiasm; its enemies were
open and vehement in their attacks on it, and many, foreseeing
its approaching downfall, were preparing to desert it. The
king, who was very fond of popularity, did not choose to risk
the loss of it by sustaining a ministry evidently odious to his
people, and which he himself had no great reason to love. The
opposition encouraged these feelings by the most unbounded
adulation of the patriot king, whom they took every opportunity of eulogizing at the expense of his government. The
ministers themselves began to see that their fall from power
was inevitable, and to pave the way for a future return to it.

Nor was that fall long deferred. On the fourteenth of
November a motion was made by Sir H. Parnell "for the
appointment of a select committee to take into consideration
the estimates and amounts proposed by command of His
Majesty, regarding the civil list." This motion was carried
by a majority of 29, in spite of the strenuous opposition of
the government. The defeat was not of a nature to render
a resignation absolutely necessary, according to constitutional
usage, and the government might very probably have tried
their fortune again, if they had not been prevented from
doing so by the fear of placing themselves and the party
they represented in a worse position. Mr. Brougham, during
the Yorkshire election, had pledged himself to the electoral

body of that county to take the earliest opportunity of bringing forward a bill for the reform of the representation. He
had accordingly, as soon as the house assembled, and before
the Speaker had even read the speech from the throne, given
notice of his intention to introduce a bill to carry out this
pledge. His plan had been submitted to a large meeting of
members, and had been approved by them. He proposed
to give votes to all copyholders, leaseholders, and householders; to give members to Manchester, Glasgow, Leeds,
Sheffield, and other large towns; to deprive each nomination
borough of one of its representatives; to disfranchise the out-
voters in towns but not in counties; to allow freemen in towns
to vote if they had resided for six months; to reduce the time
of elections to a single day; and, perhaps, to limit the number
of members in the house to five hundred.

Such was the plan which Mr. Brougham had undertaken
to introduce into the house on the evening following that on
which Sir H. Parnell's motion was carried. The success of
that motion shewed the ministers that they had lost the
confidence of the house, and that their fall could not be
much longer delayed. It was highly probable that they
would suffer another defeat on Mr. Brougham's motion, which
the Duke of Wellington's declaration pledged them to resist,
and to which most if not all of them were strongly opposed.
Should this prove to be the case, they would be compelled to
resign on the question of Reform, and this would necessitate
the appointment of a ministry pledged either to carry Mr.
Brougham's plan, or bring forward another of its own.
This danger they hoped to elude by resigning at once.
Besides, by quitting office on the civil list question, they
placed their opponents in a very embarrassing position. The
king very strongly objected to any interference with the civil
list, which he regarded as an invasion of his prerogative, as
well as likely to lead to a reduction of his own appointments,

or at least to unpleasant investigations.   By resigning on this Chap. I.
question they placed their opponents in the position of assail- Resigna-
ants of the Royal prerogative, and themselves in that of Welling-
martyrs on account of their devotion to it.   Influenced by ton admin-
these considerations, the ministry tendered their resignation
on the morning after their defeat on Sir H. Parnell's motion.
The resignation was accepted by the king, and communicated the same evening to both houses.   Mr. Brougham,
though really unprepared to introduce his measure, which he
knew must be deferred, professed great reluctance in consenting to its postponement at the earnest request of Lord
Althorp and several other political friends, adding, at the
same time, " as no change that may take place in the administration can possibly affect me, I beg to be understood that,
in putting off this motion, I will put it off to the 25th of this
month and no longer."

CHAPTER II.

Chap. II.

Influence of freedom of speech and of the press on measures of parliament.

It may be thought that a House of Commons, of which the majority were, as we have seen, representatives of a few individuals, or close corporations who generally sold their right of nominations for a valuable consideration, would be of little real use, and would never be likely to admit a Reform which remedied abuses so profitable to the proprietors of the nomination boroughs. There were, however, two things which served to counteract, to a very great degree, the defects of the representation, and to give public opinion a very considerable influence over its measures. The first of these was the right of free speech, which was enjoyed by all its members; the second was the publicity given to its debates by the newspaper press.

The freedom of speech, which had from the earliest ages been enjoyed to a great extent by the members of the legislature, was now as fully admitted and as firmly established as could be desired. Every member, however unpopular might be his opinions, could command the attention to which his abilities entitled him. He might bring forward any proposal he thought fit, or introduce any arguments he pleased in supporting or opposing the propositions of other members, and might exercise his right by protesting as strongly as he pleased against the conduct of the government and the measures of parliament. And though he might be in a most insignificant majority, or even might stand alone, yet if he had truth and right on his side he generally, at length, found support; and if he did not himself always witness the success Chap. II. of his endeavours, he bequeathed his cause to others, who took it up and carried it forward to ultimate victory.

But there was another principle now fully established which constituted an important and necessary supplement to the freedom of speech enjoyed by the house, and that was the right, now fully accorded to the press, of reporting and commenting freely on the proceedings of parliament, by which means the English people assisted, as it were, at the discussions of their representatives, and many a man whose views were not listened to in the house, produced a great impression in the country. Thus, every man who could read the periodical press might form his own opinions on the questions brought before the legislature, and every man who could write might publish his thoughts, and might suggest new arguments in favour of, or in opposition to, the measures brought under discussion ; and if his arguments were worthy of attention, they were pretty sure to find their way through some channel or other into the great legislative arena in which the decisive struggle was carried on. Hence, everything that could be urged in favour of or against measures proposed was sure to be brought forward, and so the progress made, though slow, was safe and well considered ; and though public opinion was long in getting itself recognized, yet when once fully and firmly formed, its success was only a question of time. Still the process was extremely slow, and it often happened that while public and legislative attention was occupied with one class of questions, abuses grew up in other quarters and multiplied unchecked. And this was necessarily and especially the case with regard to abuses inherent in the legislature itself, and which many of its members had a strong interest in perpetuating. Of the truth of this statement, the great struggle on the history of which we are now entering is an instance and an illustration. The

CHAP. II. abuses which it ultimately removed had grown up almost
unheeded during a long period, and when at last public
opinion was directed to them, more than half a century of
fruitless discussion—fruitless, at least, so far as any immediate
result was concerned—was carried on before the final effort
which we are now to record.

Earl Grey
accepts
office.
On receiving the resignation of the Duke of Wellington
and his colleagues, the king sent for Earl Grey, who, from his
age, his abilities, his consistent advocacy of Parliamentary
Reform, his high worth and integrity, occupied the foremost
position in the Whig party, and was the man whom all
naturally expected to take the place vacated by the duke's
resignation. In accepting office he stipulated that the Reform
of parliament should be made a cabinet measure. From that
moment the question assumed a new position. Hitherto it
had figured in the Whig programme as one among the many
measures of improvement which they deemed necessary. At
the late election it had appeared on the banners of the party
side by side with "retrenchment," "triennial parliaments,"
"civil and religious liberty," and the "abolition of colonial
slavery;" and, though it was supported by the masses, their
want of education and direct political power prevented their
wishes from having much influence, and their partiality for the
measure was in some degree prejudicial to it on account of
the recollection of the excesses which the lower classes of the
neighbouring country had committed in the first French revolution. But from the moment that it became known that the
measure had been adopted by the government it assumed a
paramount importance, all other questions seemed to sink into
insignificance, and the whole nation formed itself into two
hostile parties of reformers and anti-reformers. The first,
composed of the great mass of the nation, and especially of the
youthful ardour and progressive spirit of the nation ; the
other comprehending the aged, the wealthy, the cautious, and

the interested, who all combined in organising resistance to an Chap. II. innovation which they feared would reproduce in this country the terrible scenes which accompanied the first French revolution.

The support of the great majority of the nation facilitated the task which Earl Grey had undertaken, and enabled him to construct his ministry without much difficulty. The most serious impediment he encountered was that which was created by the position of Mr. Brougham. He was a man of transcendent ability, great diligence, extraordinary mental and physical energy, and indisputably the first orator of the day. Though not the nominal he was the real leader of the Whig party in the House of Commons ; and he had a number of followers quite large enough to make him the absolute arbiter of the fate of any ministry that Lord Grey might form. But what was much more than all this, he had in his hands the question of Reform, the question on which the whole strength of the ministry must depend, and without which it could not hope to cope with the Tories, now thoroughly alive to their danger, and ready to restore their allegiance to the leaders whom they had assisted to overthrow. The fate of the new government was evidently in his hands, and he felt it and so did all parties. We have already seen how he declared that under no circumstances could any change in the ministry affect him, and there is not the least ground for believing that he was insincere in this declaration, or that he made it, as was afterwards insinuated, in order to extort higher offers from his political associates. Throughout life he has gloried in his office of member for Yorkshire, to which he had been elected by the largest constituency in the empire, entirely on public grounds. The position which he occupied at that moment at the bar and in the House of Commons, seemed to render it certain that he must make a very large sacrifice of wealth and of real power in accepting office, which at that

CHAP. II. time seemed likely to be of very precarious and uncertain
1830.   tenure.   Earl Grey began by offering to him the office of
Attorney-General, which he rejected, not, as was asserted at
the time, rudely and peremptorily, but calmly and courteously
stating the reasons of his refusal.   Earl Grey next suggested that the Mastership of the Rolls should be offered
to him, with the understanding that he was to retain his
seat for Yorkshire.   This offer was one that Mr. Brougham
was prepared to accept, but it is stated to have been objected
to by the king, on the ground that, as member for Yorkshire
and with the Reform question in his hands, he would be too
strong for the ministry and the king together.   It is hardly
likely that this objection could have originated with William
IV.; it was probably suggested to him by some of those
with whom he privately conferred.   The statement, however,
that the objection was made by the king, rests on the
authority of Earl Grey himself.

"But," rejoined the premier, "how am I to carry on the
government if he remains in the House of Commons, with
the feeling that he has been slighted and ill-used by the
party to whom he has rendered such great services, and to
which his support is so essential?

"Let him be Lord Chancellor," replied the king.

"Your majesty has just objected to his appointment to
the inferior office of Master of the Rolls, and therefore I
should not have ventured to suggest his name for the higher
office of Lord Chancellor; nevertheless, if such is your
majesty's pleasure, I will offer him the office."

Accordingly the chancellorship was offered to Mr. Brougham,
and the king, in allusion to what passed on this occasion,
frequently said to him afterwards, "Remember you are *my*
Lord Chancellor."

Mr.   Mr. Brougham was, however, in no haste to accept even
Brougham. this splendid offer.   His professional income at the bar was

much greater than that which he would derive from the chancellorship—an office which he might lose in a few months, in which case he would retire with a pension of £4,000 per annum. Besides, having hitherto practised at the common law bar, he was ill-acquainted with the mode of procedure in Chancery, and could only hope to discharge creditably the duties of an equity judge by exertions from which even his gigantic energy and powers of application might well shrink. Moreover, if he gained in dignity he would lose in real power, for he would relinquish the lead of a great party in the House of Commons for the more splendid but less influential position of Chancellor. These considerations disposed Mr. Brougham, in the first instance, to decline the chancellorship. Lord Grey, however, requested him, before giving a final answer, to talk the matter over with some of his proposed colleagues. At this meeting he stated to his political friends the reasons above assigned, and they agreed that they could not fairly expect him to make the sacrifices which the acceptance of the chancellorship would involve. When the rest had gone, Lord Althorp remained, and said to him, "Remember that our party has been out of office for twenty-five years, and that your refusal to join us will, in all probability, prevent the formation of a ministry, and keep us in opposition for another quarter of a century. Mr. Brougham yielded to this appeal, the new ministry was constituted, and the names were soon after announced.*

---

* The following is the list of the new ministry :—

Earl Grey . .	First Lord of the Treasury.
Mr. Brougham . .	Lord Chancellor (created Lord Brougham & Vaux).
Viscount Althorp .	Chancellor of the Exchequer.
Marquis of Lansdowne	President of the Council.
Lord Durham . .	Lord Privy Seal.
Viscount Melbourne ,	Secretary for the Home Department.
Viscount Palmerston	Secretary for the Foreign Department.
Viscount Goderich .	Secretary for the Colonies.
Sir J. R. Graham	First Lord of the Admiralty

CHAP. II.
1830.
Nov. 22.
Earl
Grey's ex-
planationsOn the 22nd of November, Earl Grey, in his place in the House of Lords, gave a brief explanation of the policy of the new administration. He thought that government should at once consider the state of the representation, to correct those defects which had been occasioned by the operation of time, but he would not support universal suffrage, nor any of those fanciful and extensive plans, which would lead not to Reform but to confusion. Government had succeeded to the administration of affairs in a season of unparalleled difficulty, and he promised that the state of the nation should have the immediate, diligent, and unceasing attention of the cabinet. It was their intention to repress outrages with severity, and to reduce all

Lord Auckland	Master of the Mint.
Mr. Charles Grant	President of the Board of Trade.
Duke of Richmond	Postmaster-General.
Lord Holland	Chancellor of the Duchy of Lancaster.
Earl of Carlisle	

(The above formed the cabinet.)

Mr. C. W. W. Wynn	Secretary at War.
Sir James Kempt	Master General of the Ordnance.
Duke of Devonshire	Lord Chamberlain.
Marquis Wellesley	Lord Steward.
Earl of Albemarle	Master of the Horse.
Marquis of Winchester	Groom of the Stole.
Lord John Russell	Paymaster of the Forces.
Mr. G. J. W. Ellis	First Commissioner of Land Revenue.
Mr. C. P. Thompson	Treasurer of the Navy and Vice-President of the Board of Trade.
Sir Thomas Denman	Attorney-General.
Sir W. Horne	Solicitor-General.

IRELAND.

Marquis of Anglesea	Lord-Lieutenant.
Lord Plunket	Lord Chancellor.
Sir J. Byng	Commander of the Forces.
Hon. E. G. Stanley	Chief Secretary.
Mr. E. Pennefather	Attorney-General.
Mr. P. Crampton	Solicitor-General.

Anti-reformers pointed out with triumph, and reformers observed with regret, that Lord Grey had placed six or seven relatives and connexions in his administration.

unnecessary expense with an unsparing hand. "My lords," Chap. II.
he said, in conclusion, "the principles on which I stand are: 1830.
amelioration of abuses—promotion of economy—and the en-   Nov. 22.
deavour to preserve peace, consistently with the honour of the
country. The administration stands before you and the public.
You know the persons,—you have heard our principles, for the
maintenance of them we throw ourselves upon the confidence
and support of our sovereign, the house, and the country."

Some time necessarily elapsed before those members of Proroga-
the administration, who were also members of the House of tion of par-
liament.
Commons, could be re-elected. They were all, however,
returned without difficulty, except Mr. Stanley (now the Earl
of Derby), who was defeated at Preston by Radical Hunt.
This defeat was owing to the refusal of Mr. Stanley to support
the ballot, a measure very popular at this time. After the
business requiring immediate attention had been despatched,
parliament was prorogued on the 22nd of December to the
3rd of the following February, in order to allow ministers
time to prepare the measures they intended to bring forward,
and especially their plan of Parliamentary Reform.

Earl Grey assigned the task of framing this important Committee
measure to a committee composed of Lord Durham, Lord to frame a
Reform
Duncannon, Lord J. Russell, and Sir J. Graham. To this Bill
committee Lord Durham and Lord J. Russell both brought
outlines of the schemes which appeared to them best calculated to meet the expectations of the nation and the requirements of the times. Lord Durham proposed that the country
should be divided into electoral districts. Lord J. Russell,
whose plan was sketched on a small piece of note paper,
proposed that fifty of the smallest boroughs should be totally
disfranchised, that fifty more should in future return one
member instead of two ; that the seats thus gained should be
transferred to counties and large towns; that the qualification for voting should be the payment of a certain rental,

the amount of which was left blank, in order that it might
be the subject of future deliberation, and which, as we shall
see, was subsequently fixed at £10. Lord J. Russell's plan
was adopted by the committee, but in deference to the opinion
of Lord Durham, it was so far modified, that instead of the
arbitrary number of fifty being selected for disfranchisement
or semi-disfranchisement, it was determined that all towns
which by the census of 1821, had fewer than 2,000 inhabitants should be disfranchised entirely; and that all towns
having a population of between 2,000 and 4,000 persons
should be disfranchised partially. Finding that the amount
of disfranchisement would be pretty nearly the same on this
system as on his own original plan, Lord J. Russell assented to
this modification, not, however, without some misgivings, which
were abundantly justified by the event. In the discussions
which subsequently took place he had repeated reason to
repent that he had not more strongly resisted this suggestion,
which was eventually set aside in favour of one nearly identical with that which he originally suggested. The plan agreed
on by the committee was submitted to the cabinet, by whom
it was received, not only with unanimity but with enthusiasm.
Many of them, if we may judge by the opinions they had
previously expressed on the subject, must have regarded
the proposed measure as excessively violent and pregnant
with danger. But they probably felt that there was quite as
much peril, under existing circumstances, in not going far
enough as in going too far; that it was desirable that the
subject should be dealt with broadly, boldly, and, for the time
being, finally, and that consequently they must be prepared
to yield and even to risk a good deal rather than disappoint
the highly raised expectations of the people. Besides, the
state of the nation at that moment was such as required
strong measures of some sort. The popular discontent had,
for the moment, been allayed, but a disappointment of the

hopes that had been raised would soon cause it to revive, and,
therefore, it was evident that either the causes of their dissatisfaction must be removed, or a lamentable and continually
widening estrangement must take place between the government and the governed.

Nor were these discontents without reason. The people
of this country had for some time past been suffering cruelly,
and had been forcing themselves on the attention of their law-
givers in an altogether unpleasant and unsatisfactory manner.
Statements of agricultural distress, mining distress, and manufacturing distress were made, and echoed and re-echoed.
Sometimes they were met by qualified assent, sometimes by
vehement contradiction, but they still continued to be made,
though with no practical result. But let governments and
members of parliament say what they will, there *was* distress,
and very serious and terrible distress too. Agricultural
labourers were found starved to death, having tried in vain to
support nature with sorrel and other such-like food. In vain
did landlords abate their rents, and clergymen their tithes,
wages continued to fall, and had at length reached such a
point of depression that they did not suffice to support existence,
and required to be supplemented by poor-rates. Nay, we find
that in the division of Stourbridge, in the county of Dorset,
the magistrates published the following scale, according to
which relief was to be given :—

When the standard quartern wheaten loaf is sold at	d. 12	d. 11	d. 10	d. 9	d. 8	d. 7
The weekly allowance, including earnings, is to be made up to—	s. d.	s. d.	s. d.	s. d.	s. d.	s. d.
For a labouring man	3 1	2 10	2 7	2 4	2 1	1 10
For a woman, boy, or girl, above 14 years old	2 4	2 2	2 0	1 10	1 8	1 6
For a boy or girl of 14, 13, or 12	1 11	1 9	1 7	1 5	1 3	1 1
For do 11, 10, or 9	1 7	1 6	1 4	1 3	1 2	1 0
For do under 9	1 5	1 5	1 3	1 2	1 1	1 0

At the time to which we refer the quartern loaf cost 10d. Let us suppose a family, consisting of a man, his wife, one boy or girl of fourteen, one boy or girl of eleven, and one little child. For these five persons there are eight shillings and ninepence altogether. That is to say, there are ten and a half quartern loaves, or forty-three pounds of bread to divide among the five, which gives a little more than eight pounds of bread for each to live on for a week, or rather more than a pound of bread per day for each to live and work on, and that without allowing anything at all for rent, fuel, drink, clothing, or washing. And to this condition the agricultural labourer was rapidly sinking everywhere; for if in some counties the allowance was on a somewhat more liberal scale, in others it was even lower than in Dorsetshire. It was clear that such a state of things could not be allowed to go on. Something must be done, and that speedily. Political economists might demonstrate that it was unavoidable, but flesh and blood will rebel. It is not, therefore, very surprising, though it puzzled legislators and justices of the peace a good deal, that agricultural labourers who were thus provided for took the matter into their own hands; that they assembled in an altogether unlawful manner ; nay, compelled others, though not very much against their own will, to join them, and go about in a tumultuous way demanding increase of wages ; and when this demand was not complied with, as we may be sure it

Machine breaking and incendiary fires. generally was not, then they began to break threshing and other agricultural machinery, which they believed to be the chief, as it certainly was the apparent, cause of their distress. The farmers, thoroughly frightened, referred their labourers to the clergyman or landlord to ask for a reduction of tithe or rent, and thus to enable them to pay better wages. However, these proceedings, as might be expected, produced little or no benefit, and things were rapidly going from bad to worse. The peasantry finding no more machines to break, or forcibly prevented from breaking them, began CHAP. II. secretly to set fire to stacks of corn or hay, and soon, through twenty-six counties, night after night, the sky was reddened with the blaze of the nation's food, going up in flame and smoke. The peasantry who beheld these sad scenes often stood with folded arms grimly smiling at the work of destruction, Nay, they sometimes cut the hose of the fire-engines brought to extinguish the conflagration, and in other ways obstructed the firemen. Never, perhaps, had this country been in a more deplorable condition, never had so deep a sadness weighed on the minds of all classes of the population as towards the close of this year, 1830. Terrible imaginations magnified tenfold the terrible reality. The political atmosphere seemed to be charged with electricity. Members of the government, members of the legislature, well-to-do country gentlemen, substantial and unsubstantial farmers were all sorely distressed, puzzled, bewildered, and affrighted. All sorts of reports were in circulation. All sorts of explanations were given of the supposed causes of these fires. There were stories of foreigners, of elegantly-dressed gentlemen riding on horses or in post-chaises, who had come down to instigate the peasants to fire the ricks, or who fired them with their own hands. Then Cobbett, who often employed very unmeasured language in his efforts to draw attention to the sufferings of the labouring classes and the causes of their distress ; and who, notwithstanding a great deal of violence and a great deal of crotchety nonsense about bank paper. saw clearly and told plainly what required to be done, was accused most unjustly of being the instigator of the outrages committed by the labourers. Then, again, there was a mysterious " Swing," with whose name many of the threatening letters were signed, who was supposed by many to be at the bottom of all the mischief. Old Lord Eldon assured the House of Lords that he was informed that the gaols contained

CHAP. II. great numbers of persons who were not natives of this country; and Lord Sidney, in a long and intemperate letter, made the same statement. But there was no shadow of foundation for these assertions. The plain and simple fact was that wars, national debt, increase of population, corn laws, and other legislation or hindrance of legislation, had reduced the great mass of the people, and especially the agricultural labourers, to the verge of starvation and despair. They were going mad with misery, and in their madness they did mischief by which they themselves were sure to be the first and greatest sufferers. We know that it has been maintained that the condition of the people at this period was grossly misrepresented, for party purposes, both by Whigs and Tories, and that, in spite of partial distress, the people were really well off. Now we hold this to be a capital error, and one which, if entertained, must lead to a very erroneous view of the nature of the Reform struggle, and prevent those who entertain it from doing justice to the government by which the Reform Bill was proposed, and the House of Commons by which it was carried. Were the people goaded on by suffering to demand Reform, or were they incited to it by the arts of a party ? This we hold to be the question of questions in reference to our subject, and, in order to assist the reader in solving the problem, we present, and strongly recommend to his attention, a picture of the state of this country in this year, 1830, not drawn by us, but by the people themselves. Innumerable petitions from every county of England were presented to the House of Commons in the course of this year, 1830, one hundred and eighty-five of which the author of this work has examined, and from which he has extracted descriptions of the distress which they allege to prevail in every part of the kingdom, and in every branch of industry.

State of the country.

Bedfordshire.

The petition of the gentry, clergy, and freeholders of the county of Bedford states—"That the rates levied for the

maintenance of the poor-law, are becoming annually more Chap. II.
burthensome upon the occupiers of the land in England, inasmuch as in many instances their actual amount has increased,
while in almost all parishes they absorb the proceeds of a
greater proportion of the productions of the soil, by reason of
the reduction of prices.   .   .   It could be shown that there
are parishes, purely agricultural, where there are at some
seasons from fifty to ninety able men who, destitute of other
work, are employed by the parish, and receiving four shillings
per week, or less, for unmarried men; and scarcely even as much
as ten shillings per week for the most numerous families."

Mr. Macqueen, the late member for the county of Bedford, thus describes the state of the labouring classes in that
county :—

"In January, 1829, there were ninety-six prisoners for
trial in Bedford gaol, of whom seventy-six were able-bodied
men, in the prime of life, and chiefly of general good
character, who were driven to crime by *sheer want,* and who
would have been valuable subjects, had they been placed in
a situation where by the exercise of their health and strength
they could have earned a subsistence."

From different accounts which Mr. Macqueen gives at
length, it appears that the lowest annual expenses of a culprit
in prison is in Worcester gaol, where he costs £28 per annum ;
the highest Milbank Penitentiary, where he costs £56 per
annum ; his allowance as an honest man being £7. 10s.

In a letter to the Duke of Wellington, January 13, 1830, Berkshire.
the magistrates of Berkshire assembled at the general quarter
sessions, "express their concern and alarm at the great increase
of crime," which they attribute to "the almost unprecedented
state of distress under which all persons at this time suffer."
Mr. Dundas, the chairman, grieved to hear that in some
places the weekly payments to single men had been as low
as 2s. 8d.—*Times,* Jan. 21, 1830.

CHAP. II.

The petition of the mayor and inhabitants of the borough of Newbury, states that "the labourer is often reduced to $2\frac{1}{2}$d. a day for his subsistence; while it is found by committees of magistrates, acting under the advice of medical men, that felons in our gaols cannot be subsisted under six shillings a day, besides the cost of their bed clothing and apparel of the value of threepence a day."

Buckinghamshire.

The magistrates, clergy, owners, occupiers of land, and tradesmen, in the three hundreds of Newport, view "with feelings of intense anxiety the utter inability of the farmer to find employment for the peasantry."

The petition of Ashenden states that "many have contracted disorders by eating the flesh of animals that die naturally, and other unwholesome food: their health suffers for want of fuel," &c.

Lord Nugent in presenting this petition affirms and offers to prove by evidence, that in the district in which he lives, by "the wicked and illegal system of paying labourers out of the poor rates, the weekly rate of wages for our able-bodied unmarried labourer has been reduced to 3s. or 3s. 6d., and even this sum was, during the late dreadful winter, no less than three weeks in arrear.

Cambridgeshire.

The petition of the owners and occupiers of land in the county of Cambridge and Isle of Ely states that "distress to an unprecedented degree pervades every branch of the agricultural interest of this county."

The petition of the owners and occupiers of land in the hundred of Ely and south part of the hundred of Witchford states that the labourers are "now no longer able to maintain themselves by the sweat of their brow, they are driven to the scanty pittance derived from the parish funds, and which is doled out to them, not according to the labour received in return, but to the extent of their families; congregated in roads and in gravel pits, their spirits have become

broken, and they are constantly repining at their hard Chap. II.
condition, and inciting each other to vicious courses, while 1830.
their employers are regarded as taskmasters, and the ties of
attachment to the land of their birth become gradually torn
asunder."

The freeholders and inhabitants of Cornwall, in county Cornwall.
meeting assembled, " declare that the present embarrassment
of the county threatens, unless timely averted, to dissolve all
bonds and endanger all orders of society."

The petition of the inhabitants of Camelford complains of
"the appalling pecuniary difficulties and distress which per-
vade all classes in that district of England."

The petition of the sheriff of Cumberland in behalf of the Cumber-
land.
nobility, gentry, and freeholders, duly convened in county
meeting, alleges that "distress is not confined to one branch of
productive industry, but at the same time and with equal
pressure, weighs down the landholder and the manufac-
turer, the shipowner and the miner, the employer, and the
labourer."

The inhabitants of Alston attribute the lowness of wages,
of which they complain, "not to any want of feeling on the
part of their employers, but purely to their employers receiving no benefit, or next to none, from their labours "

The shipowners of Maryport state that they "have long
suffered and are still suffering under difficulties and privations, which far from being alleviated by the hand of time, or
by some legislative interference of the house, have gone on
progressively increasing, until the petitioners are at this time
reduced nearly to insolvency."

A large number of magistrates, clergy, freeholders, and Derby-
shire.
farmers of the county of Derby, intimate to the Duke of
Wellington "with melancholy reluctance, their personal knowledge of rents greatly reduced, and still in arrear—of tenants
ruined, of labourers unemployed, of farms thrown out of

CHAP. II.   cultivation, and of sales forcibly effected of produce infinitely
1830.   below the cost of production."

Durham.   The occupiers and owners of land in the district of
Norham and Islandshires state that "they have for some
years been labouring under great distress in their farming
concerns, having now nearly consumed all their capital, and
are unable to fulfil their pecuniary engagements."

The shipowners of Sunderland are "labouring under
serious difficulties."

The county meeting complains "that the whole of the
agricultural, commercial, and trading community, are labouring under hardships without parallel in their severity and
injustice."

Essex.   The owners and occupiers of land, merchants, and tradesmen residing in the Eastern division of the county of Essex,
state "that the agriculture and commerce of the county are
labouring under peculiar and unprecedented difficulties, which
appear to increase so rapidly that the petitioners look forward
to the future with the most anxious fears, apprehending that
some dreadful crisis may occur. They beg to declare that the
pressure is not confined to one class only, but that all classes
alike suffer; commerce is embarrassed, and confidence destroyed, not in the integrity of men, but in their ability to
fulfil their obligations."

Glouces-   The freeholders and inhabitant householders of the town
tershire.   and parish of Dursley state that the whole of the agricultural,
commercial, and trading community labour under unparalleled
distress.   "The petitioners, while they view with extreme
commiseration the hardships and privations of the lower
classes of the town and neighbourhood, dragging on an existence, barely supported by the scanty allowance which parish
relief affords, which in no instance exceeds the sum of one
shilling and threepence per week to each individual pauper
for his weekly parish labour, cannot but be sensibly alive to

their own situation, when they find their capitals daily wast- Chap. II.
ing, the middle classes falling into the list of paupers, and the 1830.
amount of the poor rates in many instances equalling, in
others actually exceeding, the gross yearly rental of their
lands and tenements."

In North Nibley "the petitioners are living in a parish in
which, from a population of 1,600 persons, upwards of 800
are receiving parochial relief, and by far the greater proportion
of those who do not receive relief are incapable of paying
their quota towards the poor rates." In 1823 the poor rates
amounted to £840, in 1829 they had reached £2,100.

The county meeting of Hampshire alleges "that the pro- Hants.
ductive classes of society in this kingdom are suffering under
distress the most alarming, both in degree and extent, and is
now become so notorious as no longer to remain a matter of
doubt to the nation at large or the house in particular."

The owners and occupiers of land within the division of
Kingsclere state "that the deepest distress pervades every
class of His Majesty's subjects. The labourers are destitute
of employment, or starving on insufficient wages; the farmers
are cultivating without profit, and often at a loss; and the
proprietors are equally suffering from the extreme depression
of the times."

The petition of the parishioners of Leominster asserts Hereford-
"that after fifteen years of profound peace, and without any shire.
great national calamity, there are millions of people who
cannot by any honest means obtain the most common necessaries of life, although these necessaries are to be had at a
price far below that of remuneration to those who supply
them. . . . The petitioners are far from wishing
to occupy a station in life above their proper sphere; all they
wish, all they implore, of the house is to place them in a
situation in which they may obtain an honest living by the
sweat of their brow."

CHAP. II.   The nobility, gentry, clergy, and freeholders, assert "that
Hertford-   the most alarming distress pervades the agricultural, manu-
shire.
             facturing, and commercial classes of this country."
Kent.
                 The petition of a county meeting declares the distress to
             be "grievous and unexampled," and affecting "all branches
             of productive industry throughout the country."

                 The owners and occupiers of land, tradesmen and free-
             holders of Romney Marsh, beseech the house "to give their
             serious and immediate attention to the unparalleled distress
             which pervades all classes of society in that district;" they
             add "that from causes entirely beyond their control they
             have already seen their property and capital reduced one
             half in value, and that even at the present ruinously depressed
             prices, they can neither procure market for their produce nor
             sale for their commodities; that from causes equally beyond
             their control, the charges and burdens on their property of
             all descriptions are immensely increased, that their poor rates
             are overwhelming, and that, notwithstanding their most
             earnest and unremitting endeavours to remedy this evil, the
             able paupers are in general most unproductively employed,
             or unemployed altogether. With the melancholy certainty,
             therefore, that the ruin which has already overtaken many of
             them must soon involve them all, unless effectual relief is
             granted them, they now most humbly implore the immediate
             attention of the house to their grievances."

                 The parishioners of Offhan and Addington "are wholly
             unable to pay their rents, rates, and taxes, and to employ
             labourers on their lands, and yet, such is the unfortunate
             situation of them, that in proportion as their means diminish
             their burdens increase, they are obliged to maintain as paupers
             those to whom they can offer no profitable employment as
             labourers; that such is the general want of employment and
             distress amongst agricultural labourers in particular, that
             pauperism, crime, loss of moral character are most rapidly

increasing, so much so as to threaten the very frame and
existence of society."

The inhabitants of Tunbridge and its vicinity testify to
"the inability of the agriculturists and others to employ a
requisite number of labourers, or to afford them wages sufficient to enable them to procure the necessaries of life for the
support of themselves and their families."

In presenting this petition, Lord Torrington stated that
the distress that pervades the agricultural classes cannot be
imagined by those who have not witnessed it; that, to his
own knowledge, many farms had been thrown up by parties
who had no longer the means to work them, and this too in
that district which was called the garden of Kent.

The owners, occupiers, and other inhabitants of the parish
of High Halden, "are suffering under ruinous and overwhelming distress." The population of the parish consists of
616 inhabitants, of which 324 receive parochial relief, and
only 86 persons contribute to the rates, which amount to
13s. 6d. in the pound on the rack rents.

Labourers, owners, and occupiers of land of the parishes
of Leybourne and Snodland, "firmly believe that a large
proportion of the occupiers of lands are either ruined or on
the brink of ruin, and that the consequent want of employment amongst the labouring classes has led to a state of
unexampled want, and misery, and crime."

The parishioners of Cranbrook assert "that the state of
the occupiers of land, the trade, and the labouring population is such as has never before been witnessed; that, unless
some speedy and effectual remedy is applied, one total ruin
must involve the whole."

The inhabitants of Yalding, Hunton, East Peckham,
Barming, Maidstone, and their respective vicinities, "view
with feelings of horror and dismay the present frightful and
overwhelming distress." The petitions from this county,
conceived in a similar spirit, are very numerous.

The Lord Mayor, Aldermen, and Liverymen of London, in Common Hall assembled, the 5th day of April, 1830, declare in their petition "that the general and overwhelming distress which now pervades all classes of the community, (except those who have fixed incomes, annuitants, and those who live upon the taxes,) is now universally admitted by every one but such persons whose interest it is to misrepresent and delude the people."

The shipowners of London represent "that, in the general distress which affects all classes of the empire, there exists none more intense and unmitigated than that of the shipowners."

The merchants, traders, manufacturers, shipowners, and others, "feel themselves called on to represent to the house the great depression, and consequent distress, that now exists in the mercantile, trading, manufacturing, and shipping concerns of the city of London and the metropolis, which bears with peculiar severity on the industrious and labouring classes."

The inhabitants of St. Leonard's, Shoreditch, in public vestry assembled, state "that they are involved in great and unheard-of distress; that tradesmen and shopkeepers are becoming bankrupts and insolvents, and the virtuous, frugal, and industrious are on the verge of ruin, and that the labouring class are reduced to a state of misery and degradation."

The retail dealers of Salford "are suffering to an extent they never before experienced, and instead of being able to support themselves and their families on the profits of their business, are forced to make daily inroads on the capital which is to carry it on."

The petition of a town's meeting at Manchester, having ten thousand signatures, states "that the great manufacturing districts, of which that town is the centre and mart, notwithstanding the unwearied attention to business, and incessant labour of its inhabitants, is suffering under a pressure of distress which is wholly unexampled in its extent and severity."

The retail dealers of the same town " have for a series of
years been suffering from a diminution of their profits, and are
now, in consequence of the poverty of all classes of their custo-
mers (so far from being able to support their families out of
those profits), scarcely able to pay the rents of their shops, and
the heavy government and local taxes to which they are liable."

The inhabitants of Colne and its vicinity affirm that " the
difficulties and distresses which they have experienced and
witnessed for several years, have reduced to beggary and
pauperism a great proportion of the labouring classes, and
effected the insolvency and ruin of tradesmen, manufacturers,
farmers and others, to an extent beyond all precedent."

The operative cotton weavers of Preston and its vicinity,
assert that their misery " is without parallel in the annals of
history," and that they are reduced "to work from twelve to
fourteen hours in the day, for tenpence, and in thousands of
cases, a man, together with his family of four to six persons,
are compelled to subsist on that small pittance."

The petition of the inhabitants of Lincoln speaks of the Lincoln-
" overwhelming distress which pervades the agricultural and shire.
manufacturing classes."

The inhabitants of the county of Lincoln " call upon the
house to give their undivided attention to the unspeakable
distress which pervades the country."

The gentry, clergy, owners, occupiers and tradesmen in
the town and neighbourhood of Louth, are reduced "to a state
of poverty unparalleled; landlords, rents, and tradesmen's bills
are unpaid, farmer's capital is fast disappearing, labourers are
without employment, crime increases, the bonds of society
are loosened, and from the peer to the peasant, all classes are
rapidly approaching to ruin, misery, and starvation."

A county meeting represents " the great distress, priva- Northamp-
tions, and difficulties which affect the agricultural, commer- tonshire.
cial, and manufacturing interests of the county,"

The owners and occupiers of land, maltsters, and others of the town and neighbourhood of Daventry, state that "the difficulties under which the cultivators of the soil have laboured, have of late increased to an alarming extent."— "The present posture of affairs, as evincing the depressed condition of agriculture, is truly appalling."

Norfolk.

The gentry, clergy, yeomanry, &c., of the county of Norfolk, assembled at a county meeting, "feel and lament the general distress which pervades almost every class of the community."

The inhabitants of the city of Norwich "perceive everywhere amongst them the rapid inroads of distress and ruin; their trade is either sinking into decay, or rendered unprofitable by destructive competition; the earnings of the artisan are reduced to the lowest scale; pauperism is overspreading and desolating the face of the land; the burthen of the poor rates is increasing, as the means of supporting it decline; confidence is universally destroyed, and the whole energy and spirit of the nation are completely paralyzed."

Nottinghamshire.

The owners and occupiers of land represent "in the strongest terms the great and overwhelming distress in which the agricultural and commercial interests of this once opulent county are now involved."

Northumberland.

"The nobility, gentry, clergy, and freeholders of Northumberland, duly convened in county meeting, beg leave to represent to the house the great distress, privation, and difficulties which affect the agricultural, commercial, manufacturing, and shipping interests of the county of Northumberland, apparent in the diminution of rent to the landlord, and the absence of profit to the tenant, in the decreased comforts of the labouring classes, in the general stagnation of trade, in the want of remuneration in freights, and in the great depression of price on every article of productive industry."

Rutlandshire.

The county meeting of Rutlandshire "see with pain that

themselves, and more especially the labouring class, are in a Chap. II.
state of unprecedented distress, and they fear that, should the _____
house continue to disregard the urgent prayer of the people, 1830.
they may be driven to acts which may place the country in
a state of great peril."

The nobility, clergy, gentry, freeholders, and inhabitants Suffolk.
of the county of Suffolk, assembled on the 6th of February,
1830, in full county meeting, call attention "to the causes
which are bringing our agricultural population and its dependents in all trades to pauperism and ruin."

Merchants, traders, and other principal inhabitants of the
town of Bury St. Edmunds, "find themselves in a situation
of much pecuniary embarrassment and distress, owing to
their sources of trade having in a great measure fallen off;
the credit and confidence are rapidly decreasing between
man and man, and bankruptcy and insolvency making rapid
strides among them, that the immediate cause of the present
situation of the petitioners, and of their unpropitious prospects, has, as it appears to them, mainly arisen from the
almost unexampled state of depression of that highly valuable
portion of the community commonly denominated the manufacturing interest."

Another petition from the same neighbourhood states
that "the farmers cannot continue to pay the rent, or to
employ labourers in the cultivation of the soil."

Proprietors and occupiers of land in the hundred of
Hoxne testify "that they have for some time past seen proprietors of land become occupiers only, the occupiers paupers;
and unemployed paupers, from the number of thirty to ninety
in each parish, subsisting on a pittance barely sufficient to
procure them bread only."

The county meeting expresses its "deep sense of the Surrey.
grievous distress which oppresses every class of the inhabitants of this once happy and prosperous country."

CHAP. II.
1830.

Freeholders, farmers, tradesmen, and others, residing in Croydon and its vicinity, "can no longer endure to see their fellow-countrymen, who are born to the lot of labourers, starving under their eyes."

Sussex.

Inhabitants of the town of Rye speak of "distress of an unprecedented and most alarming nature as at present prevailing, which is shown "by the numerous bankruptcies in the *Gazette,* by the number of small farmers who have been reduced from a comparative competency to want and misery, many having to subsist on the charity of their friends, and others reduced still lower, being compelled to work on the public roads, or end their days in a workhouse. That the distress of the latter may be shown in their altered appearance, in their being no longer able to obtain meat or beer, being compelled to satisfy their hunger with a dry crust, and their thirst with water."

The gentry, clergy, freeholders, and inhabitants of the rape of Hastings "approach the house under the deepest dismay and apprehension, arising from the distress which having for years past, with more or less severity, continually pressed on the great body of the people, now overwhelms them with an accumulated force."

Shropshire.

Gentry, clergy, yeomanry, and tenantry of the parish of Middle, in Shropshire, and its neighbourhood, "call the immediate attention of the house to the distress acknowleged in parliament last session, which now unhappily continues."

Somersetshire.

Inhabitants of the town and neighbourhood of Frome Selwood state "that thousands of those who have been usually supported by manufacture, are now, from want of employment, obliged to subsist on rates collected for the poor; and from various causes there is no prospect of a return of employment, that the poor are consequently in a wretched state of dependance for the necessaries of life."

In presenting the above petition, the Bishop of Bath and

Wells, who has "always taken a great interest in the con- Chap II.
dition of the poorer classes," says " I saw, with my own eyes, ___
multitudes who could obtain no work and were starving; 1830.
others yoked together like oxen, drawing coals from the pits
of the neighbourhood! But notwithstanding all this immense
distress, I have not known, and I say it with pleasure, a single
instance in which the poor sufferers have had recourse to
violence."

The inhabitants of the liberties of Longton and Lane-end, Stafford-
in the Potteries, " call the attention of the house to the un- shire.
precedented state of distress which oppresses the manufacturing, agricultural, commercial, and working classes of
society; they do not pretend to know the cause of this
national calamity, but they feel it to be a duty incumbent
upon them to state to the house that unless immediate relief
be afforded, the impending consequences to all classes of the
community will be dreadful."

The inhabitants of Birmingham refer to the "want of Warwick-
employment for labourers, the general reduction of the wages shire.
of labour, the general deficiency of profit in every branch of
productive industry throughout the country, and the positive
losses which attend the employment of capital and industry
in the most important branches of trade, together with all
the distresses which now afflict the country."

Gentry, clergy, yeomanry, and tradesmen of the borough
of Warwick, state " that the general distress which prevails
amongst all the agriculturists of this kingdom, has brought
many of the labouring poor into a state of deplorable suffering, from the total inability of the farmers to employ them."

Manufacturers, shopkeepers, tradespeople, and inhabitants
of the city of Coventry, "have for some time past beheld
with feelings of the most painful interest, the silent
work of destruction which is proceeding with such amazing
rapidity among all classes of the agricultural, manufacturing,

CHAP. II. .trading, and labouring population of this once flourishing and
1830.   happy kingdom."

Worces-   "The freeholders and other inhabitants" of the county of
tershire.
Worcester "know and feel that the distress is general and
unprecedented, that all interests are suffering to a most
alarming degree, and that the retail trade in particular was
never in so depressed and ruinous a state·as at the present
time."

The manufacturers, shopkeepers, mechanics, artizans, and
other inhabitants of the town and neighbourhood of Dudley,
refer to "the lamentably distressed state of trade, manufactures, commerce, and agriculture."

Wiltshire.   The inhabitants of the county of Wilts "represent that
the most alarming distress pervades both the agricultural and
manufacturing districts of the county."

York-   Landowners, farmers, and others interested in agriculture,
shire.
in and near the borough of Doncaster, beseech the house to
take measures "to alleviate the distress, which, if continued,
will inevitably issue in the most disastrous consequences to
the community at large."

"The shipowners of the port of Scarborough" ask for "a
committee to take into consideration the increasing sufferings
of the shipowner." Those of Whitby urge that "the consequences of the distress are not felt by the shipowner alone,
but that all the numerous residents in a populous seaport,
who are completely dependent on shipping for employment,
are of necessity in an equal state of embarrassment and distress. That previous to the year 1826, there were eight
different ship-building establishments and seven graving
docks, generally in full operation, giving employment to
upwards of one thousand men; and since that period three
of these establishments have been given up, two others are
on the point of being abandoned, and the remainder must
inevitably share the same fate, unless some measure can be

adopted by the house to restore prosperity." Similar representations are made from Hull.

Bankers, merchants, manufacturers, and others, inhabitants of the borough of Leeds, plead " that the present state
of the country is one of severe and general distress, affecting
in a greater or less degree, all the productive classes of
society. That the profits of capital are reduced extremely
low, and in many cases annihilated, and that the wages of
labour are proportionably depressed."

"Inhabitants of the district of Craven," who "have for
several years been employed in the manufacture of lead,"
state " that owing to the extreme depression of the price of
lead, and the consequent burden of increasing stocks, the
petitioners, in common with all others concerned in lead
mining, are reduced to great difficulty and distress, and, if
the present low prices continue, a great proportion of their
works must be abandoned, their capital destroyed, and numbers of workpeople deprived of support."

The petitions from which these selections have been
made, with scarcely a single exception, breathe an ardent
spirit of loyalty and attachment to the institutions of the
country. Agreeing in the existence and the extremity of
the distress, they ascribe it to different causes; some to
excessive taxation, some to the malt tax, some to the East
India Company, some to the state of the currency, to paper
money, machinery, or the corn laws, and of course the prayers
of the petitioners are as various as their opinions. But the
French revolution, and the events at home which followed it,
had greatly changed the spirit of the working classes, and
especially of the lower and more ignorant portion of the agricultural labourers. Finding that the people of a neighbouring
country have risen in insurrection and overthrown their government, having thus discovered that the ruling few, with all their
politics, are no match for the misgoverned many, when they

combine in their fury and despair, they resolve that they will have bread or that none else shall have it. If they cannot raise themselves from the abject misery into which they have sunk, they will at least pull down those whom they regard as the authors of their calamities to the level of their own wretchedness. Such were the feelings, and such the designs, which distress and misery have engendered, and we have already seen what crimes and follies they have produced. But now light has come to the sufferers. Glad tidings have reached them that the hated government of the Duke of Wellington has been overthrown, and has been succeeded by a new government, composed of "friends of the people;" that the changes from which they have been taught to expect the removal or the alleviation of their misery are to be carried out, and, above all, that the great measure of Reform which they have come to regard as the grand panacea for all their sufferings is about to be carried. That they have, too, now a "PATRIOT KING," who honestly desires the welfare of his people ; who is the friend of Reform, who has chosen a Reform ministry, and is determined to give it every kind of support. From that moment hope revived ; the tumultuous assemblages ceased; the incendiary fires became less frequent; trade began to recover and distress to diminish, and a proclamation issued by the new government, condemning the outrages and directing their prompt suppression, finds the people already contrite and submissive. The Reform government, however, are determined to show that though friends of the people they are no friends of their excesses. Special commissions are issued for the trial of the offenders who have been apprehended in great numbers, and by a mixture of judicious lenity and judicious severity, the last remnants of insubordination are almost entirely extinguished.

The distress in the manufacturing districts, though less severe than in the agricultural counties, is as the above cited

documents shew, far from being inconsiderable, and manifests
itself in strikes, disturbances, and assassinations. But, in this
case, the suffering is less and the situation is better understood. The manufacturing population, too, on the whole, are
more patient, because they have more hope of the speedy
removal of their distresses, and see more clearly how it is to
be obtained.

In Ireland, as has been already mentioned, a very extensive failure of the potato crop had brought the western
districts of that country, which were almost always close down
upon starvation point, to actual famine. The consequence
was a fearful increase of those outrages and assassinations,
which were so common at all times as to be regarded by
English statesmen as the chronic and irremediable malady of
that unhappy country.

In all these cases the ministers, feeling themselves strong
in the confidence of the people, acted vigorously and wisely,
and their bitterest opponents were obliged to confess that
they had manifested more firmness than their predecessors in
office. They did what they could, which was but little, to miti-
gate the immediate sufferings of that unhappy and long-mis-
governed people; they vindicated the majesty of the law by
putting down and punishing crime as far as it was possible
to do so; O'Connell, who had now commenced an agitation
for the repeal of the Union with England, was prosecuted and
convicted, though he was ultimately allowed to escape punishment, and all that the state of the law and the state of society
in that country admitted of being done to repress violence
and restore order was done by the government.

Such was the aspect of affairs when parliament re-assem- Re-assembled on the 3rd of February, 1831, the day to which they had blage of
parlia-
adjourned before Christmas. Earl Grey, after presenting ment—the
numerous petitions in favour of Reform, announced that a Reform
Bill an-
measure on that subject had been framed, which would be nounced.

CHAP. II.   effective without exceeding the bounds of a just and well-
1831.   advised moderation. He added, that it had received the
unanimous consent of the whole government, and would be
submitted to the other house of parliament at as early a
period as possible.

In the lower house a similar announcement was made by
Lord Althorp, who added, that the bill would be introduced
Lord J.   on Tuesday, the 1st of March, by Lord J. Russell, the pay-
Russell.   master of the forces, who, as we have already seen, was the
real author of the scheme to be submitted. He was not
at this period a member of the cabinet but was introduced
into it subsequently. Lord Althorp, after making the
above announcement, added that the noble lord had been
selected by the government for the discharge of this important duty, in consequence of the ability and perseverance he
had displayed in advocating Parliamentary Reform in days
when it was unpopular. "Now, therefore," said Lord Althorp,
"that the cause is prosperous, the government think that on
account of his perseverance and ability, the noble lord should
be selected to bring forward a measure of full and efficient
Reform, instead of the partial measures he has hitherto proposed." It was evident from this declaration, that whatever
the provisions of the coming bill might be, it would at least
go far beyond the measures which had before been advocated
by the Whig party, and to which the majority of them had
given a very feeble and doubtful support. This intimation
was received with lively satisfaction by a large party in the
house, and by an overwhelming majority out of the house,
who evidently desired a strong and sweeping Reform.

The selection of Lord John Russell to introduce the bill
was not only a wise, but an almost necessary choice on the
part of the government. Lord Althorp, good-natured, courteous, thoroughly honest, a sincere, tried, and enthusiastic
reformer, but feeble and incapable as a legislator, and as a

speaker so hesitating, tedious, and embarrassed, that it was Chap. II.
painful to listen to him, was no match for such antagonists 1831.
as Sir Robert Peel, Sir C. Wetherell, Mr. Croker, and other
able debaters, who sat on the opposite side of the house, and
were sure to offer the most pertinacious opposition to the
intended measure. Other members of the cabinet rather
accepted the bill as a concession to the demands of the people
that could no longer be safely denied, than as a measure
desirable on its own account. Others, again, had not the
weight and the moderation which the task required. It,
therefore, devolved almost inevitably on Lord John Russell,
whose connection with the house of Bedford, identified with
most of the great struggles for English liberty in modern
times, gave him great weight, whose known courage, patience,
and perseverance, and tried attachment to the cause of Reform,
but above all, whose virtuous and noble character pointed
him out as pre-eminently fitted to take charge of the measure
on which the government deliberately staked its existence,
and on the strength of which it claimed and received the
support of the great body of the nation. And the result
proved the propriety of the selection. Probably no other
member of the ministry would have exhibited the same combination of steady resolution and firmness throughout the
whole of the long and vexatious struggle which ensued, or
would have steered his way through the two great dangers
that were continually impending—that of a serious mutilation of the measure on the one hand, or of a violent popular
outbreak on the other.

This selection of Lord J. Russell was not, however, allowed
by the opposition to pass unchallenged. In referring to it,
Sir C. Wetherell fastened on the fact that Lord J. Russell
was not a member of the cabinet, and insinuated that the
measure was committed to him because it had not the support
of the whole government. This insinuation Lord Althorp

CHAP. II. vigorously repelled, declaring that every member of the
1831.   cabinet was favourable to the bill, and that it would be regarded as a government measure.   In justification of the
arrangement, he reminded the house that the celebrated East
India Bill was brought forward by Mr. Burke, who, like Lord
J. Russell, was paymaster of the forces, and not a member of
the cabinet.*

Financial   The most serious difficulties and the greatest perils which
embar-
rassments the new ministry encountered, arose out of their financial
of the go-
vernment. measures.   On this subject the expectations of their followers
had been highly raised.   At the last general election
"retrenchment" had figured on their banners, side by side
with "reform."   On every hustings their candidates had
exaggerated and inveighed against the extravagance of pre-
ceeding administrations, and had led the people to expect that
the accession of the Whig party to power would be at once
followed by an enormous reduction in the expenditure of the
government and the burdens of the people.   Moreover, the
new government had come into office through the success of
Sir H. Parnell's motion on the civil list.   It was, therefore,
confidently expected by the supporters of the ministry, both
in and out of parliament, that very considerable reductions
would be made; that the civil list, in particular, would be at
once brought under the control and supervision of the house,
and many items of expenditure which it contained would be
struck out.   The government, however, found themselves

---

* On the precedent thus adduced, Mr. Roebuck remarks, "the plan proposed by Burke was his own, and Lord J. Russell was not Mr. Burke." But
as we have already stated, the Reform Bill, in all its principal outlines, was
Lord J. Russell's plan, just as much as the India Bill was Mr. Burke's; and
to say that Lord J. Russell was not Mr. Burke is quite irrelevant to the question at issue, which did not relate to his competence or want of competence,
but simply to the fact of his not being a member of the cabinet. One thing, at
least, must be admitted, which is that Lord J. Russell succeeded in carrying
through the measure intrusted to him; while Mr. Burke, with all his transcendent abilities, signally failed.

very much embarrassed by the expectations which had certainly contributed in no small degree to place them in office.
William IV. was quite as tenacious of his supposed right to
control the civil list expenditure, and quite as much opposed
to any parliamentary interference with that fund, or any
reduction of it, as the most unreforming of his predecessors.
And now it became manifest how skilfully the late ministry
had chosen their ground in resolving to resign on the civil
list question. They had thus made themselves the cham-
pions, and almost the martyrs, of the interests and prerogatives of the crown, while their successors came in as the
triumphant assailants of both. This, probably, laid the first
foundation of that gradual estrangement of the king from
the new ministry, which began to be manifested at a very
early period of the Reform struggle, and which led at length
to the recal of the Duke of Wellington. The new government were most anxious to propitiate the sovereign, but they
could not altogether ignore the pledges they had virtually
given, nor the circumstances under which they had obtained
office. Again, when they turned their eyes from the civil list
to the general expenditure of the country, they found that
they succeeded a very frugal administration, which had
already made almost all the reductions they were prepared
for, and in some respects had carried them further than, considering the present circumstances of the country, they considered safe or prudent. Added to this, they were almost, or
altogether, new to office, and were to a great extent in the
hands of subordinate officials appointed by preceding governments, men who hated the names of reform and retrenchment, and who, though obliged to work under the government, were little disposed to suggest reductions, or to assist
in carrying them out. Besides, Lord Althorp, with all his
amiability and personal popularity, was a wretched Chancellor of the Exchequer. The consequence was that the

CHAP. II. financial measures of the government signally failed, and
1831. great was the disappointment of the nation when the budget
was brought forward on the 11th of February. The only
important changes the ministry effected were to wring from
the reluctant monarch a withdrawal of a claim for an outfit
for the queen, and to make some portions of the civil list, in
which the sovereign had no direct interest, a little more subject than before to the control of parliament. They also
proposed some unimportant reductions and a few changes in
the incidence of taxation, most of which were afterwards
withdrawn, as being admitted on all hands to be undesirable,
but nothing at all commensurate with the expectations that
had been raised. The nation saw, with considerable surprise
and displeasure, that the pension list was untouched, the
army increased by 7,000 men, and the navy by 3,000, that
an annuity of £100,000 was voted to the queen in case she
should survive her husband. Had the Reform measures of
the government disappointed the expectations of the nation
nearly as much as their measures of retrenchment, the fate
of the Whig party would have been sealed; but the hope of
a good Reform Bill reconciled the people to the disappointment of their expectations of retrenchment, and it was soon
forgotten in the general joy and enthusiasm which the provisions of the ministerial measure of Reform excited. In the
meantime, the press did great service to the government. It
pointed out the difficulties in which the ministry were placed,
in a parliament filled with the nominees of boroughmongers.
It asked whether a patriotic and reforming king was to be
treated less liberally than his unreforming predecessors. And
it reminded the country that a reformed House of Commons
would speedily enable the ministry to deal with financial
questions with a more vigourous and unsparing hand. By
these and other arguments it palliated, if it could not altogether
cover, the financial failure of the ministry.

Indeed, had matters been even worse than they were, the Chap. II.
country was not disposed to brood over the budget. All men 1831.
were now looking forward with excited curiosity to the appearance of the coming measure of Reform. As yet the secret
had been completely kept. Meetings were being held in such
numbers that the newspapers favourable to Reform could
scarcely find space for the enumeration of them; and from
all parts of the country, petitions for Reform came pouring
into the two houses, and gave rise to frequent discussions,
which tended to keep up the feverish excitement that prevailed
on the subject. Great numbers of these petitions asked for the
ballot, universal suffrage, annual or triennial parliaments.
Still there was a general disposition to wait for the promised
measure of the government, and to give it a fair and candid
consideration.

At length the long-expected first of March arrived. The March 1.
state of the house and of all its approaches testified to the inten- Appearance pre-
sity of the public feeling. Never before had there been so great sented by
the
a desire to witness the proceedings; never had the avenues House of
leading to the house been so thronged with persons anxious Commons.
to obtain admission. The lobbies, the staircases leading to
the galleries, were all crowded. The business on which the
house was engaged caused the opening of the doors, by which
the public were admitted, to be delayed till nearly five o'clock.
No sooner were they thrown open than a tremendous struggle
for admission took place, attended by so much noise and
violence, that the Speaker threatened to order the galleries
to be cleared if the tumult were not at once suppressed.
This menace put a stop to the disorder, and the fortunate
few who had succeeded in fighting their way into the gallery,
had leisure to look around them. Only about a hundred
members were present at the time, but every bench in the
body of the house and in the side galleries had its back
labelled with the name of some member, who had adopted

CHAP. II. this means of securing a seat for the debate. As the hour of
1831.   six approached the house filled rapidly, and before it arrived
scarcely a single unoccupied place was discernible.   The
clock was on the stroke of six when Lord J. Russell entered
His appearance was welcomed with a tremendous cheer.

Introduc-   And now we have reached the commencement of that
tion of the unparalleled war of tongues, which continued with some
Reform
Bill.   intervals, night after night, from this first of March, 1831, to
the fifth of June, 1832. Its word battles, intensely interesting
to a nation in a state of violent political ebullition, would be
insupportably tedious to the cool and unexcited reader,
even in the most condensed form.   Nevertheless, they must
ever constitute the surface of our history, nay to some considerable extent its pith and substance, affording, as they do,
insight into the great conflict of social forces that was going
on behind them, and of which these debates were the parliamentary outcome.   Our undertaking, therefore, imposes on us
the necessity of giving the reader some account of them, and
particularly of this first discussion, more notable than any of
those that succeeded it, because it was the first, and because,
though it led to no decisive result, it pretty nearly exhausted
all the arguments for and against the leading features of the
measure. We shall, therefore, try to put before the reader not
the speeches themselves, but their distilled essence. We shall
first allow Lord J. Russell, who excelled in statement, to unfold and explain his plan at some length, though still in a considerably condensed form; then we shall give, with much more
condensation, the speeches of some of those who delivered their
reasons for supporting or opposing the bill. We have selected
only those who were representative men, that is to say, men
who expressed not only their own feelings and opinions, or
those of a select circle of friends, but men who spoke the
sentiments and views of large bodies of their countrymen.
For this reason we pass over not only the Smiths, Twisses,

Shelleys, Walls, Newarks, Darlingtons, &c., but we also omit CHAP. II.
the eloquent and scholarly dissertations of Macaulay,* and 1831.
the polished plausibilities of Croker. In every case we shall
preserve the style, and, as far as the exigencies of great
abbreviation will allow, the very words of the different
orators. In this way we hope to give the reader as good a
notion as we can, in the smallest possible compass, of the
na.ure and extent of the proposed changes, and of the manner in which they were regarded. Of the subsequent debates
our account will be much more brief, though probably quite
full enough for the patience of the reader.

Lord J. Russell had no sooner entered the house than he
was called on by the Speaker, and after a short interruption,
arising from its crowded state, he proceeded, amidst breathless and expectant silence, but in a low voice and somewhat
deprecatory manner, to unfold his plan.

"The object of ministers," he said, "has been to produce Lord J.
a measure with which every reasonable man in the country speech.
will be satisfied—we wish to take our stand between the
two hostile parties, neither agreeing with the bigotry of those
who would reject all Reform, nor with the fanaticism of those
who contend that only one plan of Reform would be wholesome or satisfactory, but placing ourselves between both, and
between the abuses we intend to amend and the convulsion
we hope to avert.

"The ancient constitution of our country declares that no
man should be taxed for the support of the state, who has not
consented, by himself or his representative, to the imposition
of these taxes. The well-known statute, *de tallagio non
comedendo*, repeats the same language ; and, although some
historical doubts have been thrown upon it, its legal meaning

* Another reason for the exclusion of Macaulay's speeches is that they
are printed in the well-known collection of his speeches.

CHAP. II. has never been disputed. It included 'all the freemen of
1831. the land,' and provided that each county should send to
the Commons of the realm, two knights, each city two burgesses, and each borough two members. Thus about a
hundred places sent representatives, and some thirty or forty
others occasionally enjoyed the privilege, but it was discon-
tinued or revived as they rose or fell in the scale of wealth
and importance. Thus, no doubt, at that early period, the
House of Commons did represent the people of England;
there is no doubt likewise, that the House of Commons, as it
now subsists, does not represent the people of England.
Therefore, if we look at the question of right, the reformers
have right in their favour. Then, if we consider what is
reasonable, we shall arrive at a similar result. A stranger,
who was told that this country is unparalleled in wealth and
industry, and more civilized, and more enlightened than any
country was before it; that it is a country that prides itself
on its freedom, and that once in every seven years it elects
representatives from its population, to act as the guardians and
preservers of that freedom,—would be anxious and curious to
see how that representation is formed, and how the people
choose those representatives, to whose faith and guardianship
they entrust their free and liberal institutions. Such a person
would be very much astonished if he were taken to a ruined
mound, and told that that mound sent two representatives
to parliament—if he were taken to a stone wall, and told
that three niches in it sent two representatives to parliament
—if he were taken to a park, where no houses were to be
seen, and told that that park sent two representatives to parliament; but if he were told all this, and were astonished at
hearing it, he would be still more astonished if he were to
see large and opulent towns, full of enterprise, and industry,
and intelligence, containing vast magazines of every species
of manufactures, and were then told that these towns sent no

representativeş to parliament. Such a person would be still
more astonished, if he were taken to Liverpool, where there
is a large constituency, and told, 'here you will have a fine
specimen of a popular election.' He would see bribery employed to the greatest extent and in the most unblushing
manner ; he would see every voter receiving a number of
guineas in a box, as the price of his corruption; and after
such a spectacle, he would no doubt be much astonished that
a nation whose representatives are thus chosen, could perform the functions of legislation at all, or enjoy respect in
any degree. I say then, that if the question before the house
is a question of reason, the present state of representation is
against reason.

"The confidence of the country in the construction and
constitution of the House of Commons is gone. It would be
easier to transfer the flourishing manufactures of Leeds and
Manchester to Gatton and Old Sarum, than to re-establish
confidence and sympathy between this house and those whom
it calls its constituents. If, therefore, the question is one of
right, right is in favour of Reform; if it be a question of
reason, reason is in favour of Reform; if it be a question
of policy and expediency, policy and expediency are in favour
of Reform.

"I come now to the explanation of the measure which,
representing the ministers of the king, I am about to propose
to the house. Those ministers have thought, and in my opinion
justly thought, that no half measures would be sufficient;
that no trifling or paltering with Reform could give stability
to the crown, strength to parliament, or satisfaction to the
country. The chief grievances of which the people complain
are these. First, the nomination of members by individuals;
second, the election by close corporations; third, the expense of
elections. With regard to the first, it may be exercised in two
ways, either over a place containing scarcely any inhabitants,

and with a very extensive right of election; or over a place of wide extent and numerous population, but where the franchise is confined to very few persons.   Gatton is an example of the first, and Bath of the second.   At Gatton, where the right of voting is by scot and lot, all householders have a vote, but there are only five persons to exercise the right.   At Bath the inhabitants are numerous, but very few of them have any concern in the election.   In the former case, we propose to deprive the borough of the franchise altogether. In doing so, we have taken for our guide the population returns of 1821; and we propose that every borough which in that year had less than 2,000 inhabitants, should altogether lose the right of sending members to parliament, the effect of which will be to disfranchise sixty-two boroughs.   But we do not stop here.   As the honourable member for Boroughbridge (Sir C. Wetherell) would say, we go *plus ultra;* we find that there are forty-seven boroughs of only 4,000 inhabitants, and these we shall deprive of the right of sending more than one member to parliament.   We likewise intend that Weymouth, which at present sends four members to parliament, should in future send only two.   The total reduction thus effected in the number of the members of this house will be 168.   This is the whole extent to which we are prepared to go in the way of disfranchisement.

"We do not, however, mean to allow that the remaining boroughs should be in the hands of a small number of persons, to the exclusion of the great body of the inhabitants who have property and interest in the place.   It is a point of great difficulty to decide to whom the franchise should be extended.   Though it is a point much disputed, I believe it will be found that in ancient times every inhabitant householder resident in a borough was competent to vote for members of parliament.   As, however, this arrangement excluded villeins and strangers, the franchise always belonged to a

particular body in every town;—that the voters were persons
of property is obvious, from the fact that they were called
upon to pay subsidies and taxes. Two different courses seem
to prevail in different places. In some, every person having a
house, and being free, was admitted to a general participation
in the privileges formerly possessed by burgesses : in others,
the burgesses became a select body, and were converted into
a kind of corporation, more or less exclusive. These differences, the house will be aware, lead to the most difficult, and
at the same time the most useless, questions that men can
be called upon to decide.* I contend that it is proper to get
rid of these complicated rights, of these vexatious questions,
and to give the real property and real respectability of the
different cities and towns, the right of voting for members of
parliament. Finding that a qualification of a house rated at
£20 a year, would confine the elective franchise, instead of
enlarging it, we propose that the right of voting should be
given to householders paying rates for houses of the yearly
value of £10 and upwards, upon certain conditions hereafter to be stated. At the same time it is not intended to
deprive the present electors of their privilege of voting, provided they are resident. With regard to non-residence, we
are of opinion that it produces much expense, is the cause of
a great deal of bribery, and occasions such manifest and
manifold evils, that electors who do not live in a place ought
not to be permitted to retain their votes. With regard to
resident voters, we propose that they should retain their right
during life, but that no vote should be allowed hereafter,
except to £10 householders.

* The author believes the following to be a tolerably complete list of the
voting qualifications for boroughs before the passing of the Reform Bill:—
Householders, resident householders, householders paying scot and lot, inhabitants, resident inhabitants, inhabitants paying scot and lot, burgesses, capital
burgesses, burgageholders, freeholders, freemen, resident freemen, corporations,
potwallopers, payers of poor's rates.

CHAP. II.   " I shall now proceed to the manner in which we propose
1831.   to extend the franchise in counties.   The bill I wish to introduce will give all copyholders to the value of £10 a year,
qualified to serve on juries, under the right hon. gentleman's
(Sir R. Peel's) bill, a right to vote for the return of knights of
the shire ; also, that leaseholders, for not less than twenty-
one years, whose annual rent is not less than £50, and whose
leases have not been renewed within two years, shall enjoy
the same privilege.

" It will be recollected that when speaking of the numbers
disfranchised, I said that 168 vacancies would be created.
We are of opinion that it would not be wise or expedient to
fill up the whole number of those vacancies.   After mature
deliberation, we have arrived at the conclusion, that the
number of members at present in the house is inconveniently
large.   Besides, when this house is reformed, as I trust it will
be, there will not be such a number of members who spend
their moneys in foreign countries, and never attend the house
at all.   We propose, therefore, to fill up a certain number of
the vacancies, but not the whole of them.   We intend that
seven large towns should send two members each, and that
twenty other towns should send one member each.   The seven
towns which are to send two members each are as follows :—

> Manchester and Salford.
> Birmingham and Aston.
> Leeds.
> Greenwich, Deptford, and Woolwich.
> Wolverhampton, Bilston, and Sedgley.
> Sheffield.
> Sunderland and the Wearmouths.

The following are the names of the towns which it is proposed should send one member each to parliament:—

Brighton.	Bolton.
Blackburn.	Stockport.
Wolverhampton.	Dudley.

South Shields and Westoe.
Warrington.
Huddersfield.
Halifax.
Gateshead.
Whitehaven, Workington,
and Harrington.
Kendal.

Tynemouth and North
Shields.
Cheltenham.
Bradford.
Frome.
Wakefield.
Kidderminster.

It is well known that a great portion of the metropolis and its neighbourhood, amounting in population to 800,000 or 900,000, is scarcely represented at all, and we propose to give eight members to those who are thus unrepresented, by dividing them into the following districts:—

Tower Hamlets . . . population, 283,000.
Holborn . . . . „ 218,000.
Finsbury . . . . „ 162,000.
Lambeth . . . „ 128,000.

Next, we propose an addition to the members of the larger counties — a species of Reform always recommended, and which, I believe, Lord Chatham was almost the first to advocate. The bill I shall beg leave to introduce will give two members to each of the three ridings into which Yorkshire is divided—the East, West, and North—and two additional members to each of the following twenty-six counties, of which the inhabitants exceed 150,000 :—

Chester.
Derby.
Durham.
Gloucester.
Lancaster.
Norfolk.
Somerset.
Suffolk.
Wilts.

Warwick.
Cumberland.
Northampton.
Cornwall.
Devon.
Essex.
Kent.
Lincoln.
Salop.

Stafford.
Sussex.
Nottingham.
Surrey.
Northumberland.
Leicester.
Southampton.
Worcester.

"I now beg leave to direct the attention of the house to that part of the plan which relates to the expense of long protracted polls, and which, while it removes that evil, also greatly facilitates the collection of the sense of the elective body. We propose that all electors in counties, cities, towns, or boroughs, shall be registered, and for this purpose, machinery will be put in motion similar to that of the Jury Act—that is to say, at a certain period of the year (I now speak of boroughs), the parish officers and churchwardens are to make a list of persons who occupy houses of the yearly value of £10. This list of names will be placed on the church doors, we will suppose in September, and, in October, the returning officer will hold a sort of trial of votes—where claims made and objections stated will be considered and decided. On the first of December the list will be published, every person who chooses may obtain a copy of it, and it will be the rule to govern electors and elections for the ensuing year. The means of ascertaining who are the electors being thus easy, there is no reason why the poll should be kept open for eight days, or, as in some places, for a longer period; and it is proposed that, nearly according to the present law, booths shall be erected in the different parishes, so that the whole poll may be taken in two days. For my own part, I may say that I expect the time will come when the machinery will be found so simple, that every vote may be given in a single day; but in introducing a new measure, it is necessary to allow for possible defects. Attempts might be made to obstruct the polling, and I therefore recommend two days, in order that no voter may be deprived of the opportunity of offering his suffrage.

"As to the counties, the matter may be somewhat more difficult. We propose that the churchwardens should make out a list of all persons claiming the right to vote in the several parishes, and that these lists shall be affixed to the

church doors; a person, to be appointed (say a barrister of a
certain standing) by the judge of assize, shall go an annual cir-
cuit, within a certain time after the lists have been published,
and he will hear all claims to vote and objections to voters.
Having decided who are entitled to exercise the privilege he
will sign his name at the bottom of the list, and will transmit
it to the clerk of the peace, and it will then be enrolled as the
list of the freeholders of the county for the ensuing year.

"Everybody knows and must have lamented the enormous
expense to which candidates are put in bringing voters to the
poll.   In Yorkshire, without a contest, it costs nearly
£150,000; and in Devonshire, the electors are obliged to
travel forty miles, over hard cross roads, which occupies one
day, the next is consumed in polling, and the third in returning home.   The whole, a manifest source of vast expense and
most inconvenient delay.   We propose, therefore, that the
poll shall be taken in separate districts, those districts to be
arranged according to circumstances by the magistrates in
quarter sessions, and not changed for two years.   The sheriffs
will hold the election on a certain day; if a poll is demanded,
they will adjourn the election to the next day but one, and
the poll will be kept open for two days.   On the third day
the poll will be closed, and on the sixth day an account of
the number of votes will be published.   It shall be so
arranged, that no voter shall have to travel more than fifteen
miles to give his vote.   It is also proposed that the number
of polling places in each county shall not exceed fifteen, as the
multiplication of places for receiving the votes would give rise
to great inconvenience.   We propose that each county should
be divided into two districts, returning each two members to
parliament.   There will be some difficulty in adjusting these
districts, but I propose that His Majesty shall nominate a
committee of the privy council, to determine their extent
and direction.   In some of the boroughs to which the right

of representation will be continued, the number of electors is exceedingly small. We shall therefore insert in the bill a clause, giving power to the commissioners nominated under that bill to enable the inhabitants of the adjoining parishes and chapelries to take part in the elections, when the number of electors in such borough shall be below 300. That these are extensive powers I shall not attempt to deny, and if any gentleman in the house will suggest a better, safer, and more constitutional mode of effecting the object, His Majesty's ministers will have no hesitation in adopting that mode and waiving their own.

" I have now only one thing more to say with regard to the representation of England. In all those new towns to which we propose to give the right of sending members to parliament, all persons who are entitled by their property to vote shall be excluded from the right to vote for the representatives of the county; but it is not intended to interfere with the franchise of those freeholders who are at present entitled to vote. With respect to the right of the forty-shilling freeholders, I do not think that there should be any alteration."

In obedience to the loudly expressed wish of the house, Lord J. Russell then read, amidst great laughter and much cheering, the list of the boroughs which the bill proposed to disfranchise, as having fewer than 2,000 inhabitants, according to the population returns of 1821; as well as that of the boroughs to be semi-disfranchised, as having a population under 4,000, according to the same census.* He then proceeded as follows:—

" Scotland needs Reform even more than England, as in

* Subjoined is the list read by Lord J. Russell, to which we have added the prevailing influence in each borough, and the number of the constituency:—

Place.	Prevailing Influence.	No. of Constituency.
Aldborough	Duke of Newcastle	60
Aldeburgh	Marquis of Hertford	80
Appleby	Earl of Thanet and Earl Lonsdale	100

that country no such thing as popular representation is CHAP. II.
known. There we intend to give the suffrage to every copy- 1831.
holder to the annual value of £10, and to holders of leases
for ten years, not renewed within two years previous to the
election, and paying £50 a year rent. The counties are to be
settled as follows :—Peebles and Selkirk to be joined, and to
elect one member together; Dumbarton and Bute, Elgin and
Nairn, Ross and Cromarty, Orkney and Shetland, Clackman-
nan and Kinross, with certain additions, to do the same. The
remaining twenty-two counties are each singly to return one

Place.	Prevailing Influence.	No. of Constituency.
Bedwin . . .	Marquis of Aylesbury	80
Beeralston . .	Earl of Beverley	100
Bishop's Castle	Earl Powis	60
Bletchingley .	Mr. M. Russell	80
Boroughbridge	Duke of Newcastle	50
Bossiney . .	Lord Wharncliffe and Mr. Turmo . .	35
Brackley . .	R. H. and J. Bradshaw . . .	33
Bramber . .	Lord Calthorpe and the Duke of Rutland .	20
Buckingham . .	Duke of Buckingham	13
Callington . .	Mr. A. Baring	50
Camelford .	Marquis of Cleveland	25
Castle Rising .	Marquis of Cholmondeley and Hon.F.G.Howard	50
Corfe Castle . .	Mr. H. Bankes	50
Dunwich . .	Lord Huntingfield and Mr. Barne . .	18
East Looe . .	Mr. Hope	50
Eye . . .	Sir E. Kerrison	100
Fowey . .	Mr. Austin and Mr. Livey . . .	70
Gatton . .	Lord Monson	5
Haslemere .	Earl of Lonsdale	60
Heden . .	Money	830
Heytesbury .	Lord Heytesbury	50
Higham Ferrers	Lord Fitzwilliam	145
Hindon . . .	Lord Grosvenor and Lord Calthorpe . .	240
Ilchester . .	Disputed between Lord Cleveland and Lord Huntingtower	70
Lostwithiel .	Earl of Mount Edgcumbe . . .	94
Ludgershall .	Sir G. Graham and Mr. Everett . . .	70
Malmesbury .	Mr. Pitt	13
Mawe's, St. .	Duke of Buckingham	20
Michael, St. . .	Lord Falmouth and Mr. J. H. Hawkins .	32

CHAP. II. member. The burghs are to be as follows:—Edinburgh to
1831. have two members; Glasgow to have two; Aberdeen, Paisley,
Dundee, Greenock, and Leith (with the addition of Porto-
bello, Musselburgh, and Fisherow), each singly to return one
member. Thirteen districts of burghs to return one member.
By the proposed alterations there will be an addition of five
new members to the representation of Scotland, making the
total number fifty, instead of forty-five as at present.

Place.	Prevailing Influence.	No. of Constituency.
Midhurst	Mr. John Smith	18
Milborne Port	Marquis of Anglesea	90
Minehead	Mr. Luttrell	10
Newport, Cornwall	Duke of Northumberland	62
Newton, Lancashire	Mr. Legh	60
Newton, Isle of Wight	Lord Yarborough and Sir F. Barrington	40
Okehampton	Money	250
Orford	Marquis of Hertford	20
Petersfield	Colonel Joliffe	140
Plympton	Mr. Trehy and the Earl of Mount Edgcumbe	210
Queenborough	Money *versus* Ordnance	270
Romney, New	Sir E. Dering	150
Ryegate	Earl of Hardwicke and Lord Somers	200
Saltash	Mr. Buller	36
Seaford	Lord Seaford and Mr. J. Fitzgerald	—
Steyning	Duke of Norfolk	110
Stockbridge	Lord Grosvenor	106
Tregony	Mr. J. A. Gordon	180
Wareham	Right Hon. J. Calcraft	20
Wendover	Lord Carrington	140
Weobly	Marquis of Bath	90
West Looe	Mr. Buller	55
Whitchurch	Lord Sidney and Sir S. Scott	70
Winchelsea	Marquis of Cleveland	40
Woodstock	Duke of Marlborough	400
Wootton Bassett	Earl of Clarendon and Mr. Pitt	100
Yarmouth	The Holmes Family	50

The following was the list of boroughs which would return one member
of parliament each :—

Amersham	Mr. W. Drake	125
Arundel	Money	450
Ashburton	Lord Clinton and Sir L. V. Palk	170

"In Ireland we propose to give the right of voting to all
holders of houses or land to the value of £10 a year. There
are some places in that country which have not their due
share in the representation; of these the principal are Belfast,
Limerick, and Waterford, to which we propose to give representatives so as to add three to the whole number of members
for Ireland. The arrangement which I now propose will be
eminently favourable both to Ireland and Scotland, and to
Ireland particularly so, for as the number of the present
members in the house representing places in England is to be
reduced, and their places are not to be supplied, the Irish
members will become of greater relative importance.

Place.	Prevailing Influence.	No. of Constituency.
Bewdley	Lord Littelton	13
Bodmin	Marquis of Hertford and Mr. D. G. Gilbert	36
Bridport	Money	340
Chippenham	Mr. Neald	135
Clitheroe	Earls Howe and Brownlow	45
Cockermouth	Earl of Lonsdale	180
Dorchester	Earl of Shaftesbury and Mr. R. Williams	200
Downton	Earl of Radnor	60
Droitwich	Lord Foley	12
Evesham	Bribery	600
Grimsby	Money	300
East Grinstead	Earl De la Warr	30
Guildford	Lord Grantley	250
Helston	Duke of Leeds	36
Honiton	Money	350
Huntingdon	Earl of Sandwich	240
Hythe	Corporation and patronage	150
Launceston	Duke of Northumberland	15
Leominster	Money	700
Liskeard	Earl St. Germain	105
Lyme Regis	Earl of Westmorland	30
Lymington	Sir H. B. Neale	70
Maldon		2,000
Marlborough	Marquis of Aylesbury	21
Marlow	Mr. O. Williams	285
Morpeth	Earl of Carlisle and Mr. W. Ord	200
Northallerton	Earl of Harewood	200

" The result of all the measures comprehended in this bill, as affecting the number of members in this house, will be that of the present number of 658—168 being taken off by the disfranchisement of the boroughs—400 will remain. To that number five being added as the increase of members for Scotland, three for Ireland, eight for London, and 142 for the rest of England and Wales, making the future number of members of the united parliament 596. The decrease of the present number will accordingly be sixty-two. The number of persons who will be entitled to the suffrage under this bill, not previously possessing that right, will, I suppose, be in the counties, 110,000; in the towns, 50,000; in London, 95,000; in Scotland, 50,000; in Ireland, about 40,000; and it is my opinion that the measure will add to the constituency of the Commons' House of Parliament about half a million of persons, all connected with the property of the country, having

Place.	Prevailing Influence.	No. of Constituency.
Penryn	Money	400
Richmond	Lord Dundas	270
Rye	Dr. Lamb	25
St. Germains	Earl St. Germains	70
St. Ives	Mr. Wellesley	200
Sandwich	Money	955
Shaftesbury	Lord Grosvenor	300
Sudbury	Money	800
Tamworth	Lord Townshend and Sir R. Peel	300
Thetford	Duke of Grafton and Mr. A. Baring	31
Thirsk	Sir F. Frankland	60
Totnes	Corporation	58
Truro	Earl of Falmouth	26
Wallingford	Money	180
Westbury	Sir E. A. Lopez	70
Wilton	Earl of Pembroke	20
Wycombe	Corporation and Sir J. D. King	65

In most of these boroughs the seats were sold by the proprietors. Sometimes they themselves or some of their relatives or dependants were nominated to represent them. Bribery was also practised with little or no reserve or concealment where it was necessary, but in many instances the constituency was so dependent on the proprietor that no expenditure of this kind was requisite.

a valuable stake amongst us, and deeply interested in our
institutions. They are persons on whom we may depend in
any future struggle in which the nation may be engaged, and
who will maintain and support parliament and the throne in
carrying that struggle to a successful termination. I think
this measure will further benefit the people by inciting them
to industry and good conduct. For when a man finds that,
by industry and attention to his business he will entitle
himself to a place in the list of voters, he will have an additional motive to improve his circumstances and preserve his
character. I think, therefore, that in thus adding to the constituency, we are providing for the moral as well as for the
political improvement of the country.

"Language has been held as if I had said that the institutions of the country could, by their own indirect strength,
defend every attempt at sedition if no Reform were adopted.
In my opinion the question has little to do with sedition or
rebellion. The question is, whether, without some large
measure of Reform, the government, or any government, can
carry on the affairs of the country with the confidence and
support of the nation. If this cannot be done, then it may
become a question whether Reform can be resisted, but there
can be no question that in such a case the British constitution must perish. The House of Commons, in its unreformed
state, has nothing to look to but public confidence, and the
sympathy of the nation for its support. It appears to me that
if Reform is refused all such sympathy and confidence will
soon be withheld. I ask whether, when the ministers of the
crown consider that Reform is necessary, when the sovereign
has permitted them to lay before the house their proposition,
and when they come with that proposition to declare, in the
most unequivocal manner, that they consider Reform to be
indispensable, and when people out of doors, by multitudes
of petitions and millions of voices, are calling for the same

thing, is it for the House of Commons to say—'We are the
judges of our own purity; we equally despise the ministers
of the crown and the voice of the people; we will keep our
power against all remonstrances and all petitions; and we
will take our chance of the dreadful consequences?' I appeal
to the gentry and the aristocracy of England. In my opinion
they were never found wanting in any great crisis of the
country. When war was carrying on against the national
enemy, they were always the foremost to assert the national
honour; and when great sacrifices were to be made, and great
burdens to be supported, they were as ready to bear their
proportion as the rest of their fellow-subjects. I ask them
now—now that a great sacrifice is to be made for the public
safety and the general good—will they not show their gene-
rosity, will they not evince their public spirit, and identify
themselves in future with the people? I ask them to come
forward under these circumstances and give stability, political
strength, and peace to the country. Whatever may be the
result of the proposition I have made to the house, I must
say that His Majesty's ministers will feel that they have
thoroughly done their duty in bringing the measure forward;
neither seeking for the support of particular classes nor the
applause of the multitude. When they have felt it their
duty to resist popular feelings, they have not hesitated to
encounter and withstand them by a firm and vigorous enforcement of the law, by which many disturbances have been
prevented or suppressed, I trust permanently. By their
vigorous enforcement of laws passed before they entered
office, agitation has been made to subside and peace has been
re-established. In no case could it be said that ministers
have wavered in their duty by bending to popular clamour,
or by seeking to ingratiate themselves in popular and transient favour. I have a right to say that, in submitting the
present proposition to the house, they have evinced an interest

in the future welfare of the country. They think that what
they propose is the only thing calculated to give permanence
to the constitution, which has so long been the admiration of
foreign nations on account of its free and popular spirit, but
which cannot exist much longer except by an infusion of new
popular spirit. By these means the house will show to the
world that it is determined no longer to be an assembly of
the representatives of small classes and particular interests,
but that it is resolved to form a body of men who represent
the people, who spring from the people, who have sympathies
with the people, and who can fairly call upon the people to
support their burdens in the future struggles and difficulties
of the country, on the ground that they who ask them for that
support are joining hand and heart with them, and, like themselves, are seeking only the glory and welfare of England."

Lord J. Russell then sat down, amidst loud and prolonged
cheering from all sides.

The motion which he made for leave to bring in the bill
was briefly seconded by Sir J. Sebright.

The first man who rose to oppose the motion was Sir R. Sir R. H.
H. Inglis, member for the University of Oxford, an elegant Inglis.
scholar, a thorough gentleman, a worthy and honest man ;
he admirably represented the opinions and prejudices of the
country gentlemen and clergy of the day. Nobody in the
house was more deservedly popular and respected, none more
strongly resisted every proposed alteration of the existing
institutions of the country. His opposition to the measure
might certainly be reckoned on, and his opinion on it was all
the more important, because it was sure to be the opinion of
the two great classes of which he was at once the representative and the *beau ideal.* After some preliminary observations,
he thus proceeded to deal with the arguments which the proposer of the motion had advanced in favour of the bill :—

"We are not sent here for the particular spot which we

CHAP. II. represent, but to consider the affairs of the country and the
1831. good of the church. When a member is returned to this
house, he ceases to be responsible to his constituency. It is
at the end of the period when he has to serve them in parliament that he again comes before them, and it is then only
that he is accountable to them. In the United States, in
France, or in Belgium, where there are changes from day to
day, such changes—such a proposition of the noble lord—
might find favour; but in England the case is very different.
I know there are such men as Delolme and Montesquieu,
who have taken on themselves to talk of representation being
founded on the basis of population and taxation, but I can
find no trace of such a principle in any of the ancient times
of our constitution. If it can be shewn that places were
returned to send members which were neither parishes nor
market towns, I presume it will be admitted that those places
could not be very considerable. Now there are Haslemere
and West Looe, which have never been one or the other, and
yet they have been called on to send representatives to parliament. And not only have small towns been called on to
send representatives, but large towns have been left unrepresented ; and this is a most important point in answer to those
who pretend that they only ask for the restoration of the constitution. Can the noble lord shew that any town or borough
has been called into parliamentary existence because it was
large or populous, or excluded from it because it was small ?
The noble lord has tried to make much of the instance of
Old Sarum. In one and the same year, the 23rd Edward I.,
a writ was issued to both Old and New Sarum, and in neither
case was it conferred on account of population or taxation.
On the contrary, I believe it was given, in the first instance,
to oblige some Earl of Salisbury, by putting his friends into
the house. And in an account of the borough, it was stated
that it had lately been purchased by Mr. Pitt, the possessor

of the celebrated diamond of that name, who has obtained an
hereditary seat in the House of Commons, as much as the
Earl of Arundel possessed one in the House of Peers by being
the owner of Arundel Castle.   How, then, can it be said that
according to the constitution of the country, noblemen are not
to be represented and their interests regarded in this house ?
The cause of the creation of many boroughs is, I believe,
obscure; but, on the other hand, some were as clear and as
well ascertained as possible.   It is known that two writs to
return members were issued by Elizabeth, at the desire of
one of her favourites, Sir Christopher Hatton ; and Newport,
in the Isle of Wight, had received its franchise to please Sir
George Carew.   This is the history of many of the small
boroughs ; and all the Cornish boroughs were formed in that
manner.   Fifteen Cornish boroughs had at one time received
the right of representation, some of which were small villages,
and none of them entitled to rank as considerable among the
towns of England.   It is in vain after this to talk of the
purity of representation in former times.   I defy the noble
lord to point out any time when the representation was
better than it is at present.   I say, therefore, that what is
proposed is not restorative.   The house and the country may
judge what it is, but I will state, in one word, that it is
REVOLUTION ; — a revolution, that will overturn all the
natural influence of rank and property.

"I have omitted to observe in the proper place, that many
of the towns to which the noble lord proposes to give the
elective franchise, were considerable places at the period
when the right of representation was given to other places,
and yet they were omitted.   Halifax, three hundred years
ago was known to have a population of 8,400 ; Wakefield was
a most considerable town at the same time ; and Manchester,
according to tradition, had not less than 5,400 inhabitants for
two hundred years before the year 1580 ; and, at all events it

CHAP. II. was certain that, at the latter period, it possessed the amount
1831.   of population I have just mentioned.   But can it be said in
          answer to this, that no boroughs have been created after that
          time, and that therefore it had not been possible to do justice
          to such considerable places ?   Just the reverse of this is the
          fact ; for, after the date to which I have referred, with respect
          to Halifax, fifty-one boroughs have been summoned to send
          representatives to parliament; and after the date with respect
          to Manchester, fourteen boroughs had received writs.   But I
          have another objection to that part of the proposition of the
          noble lord, in which he would have taxation and representa-
          tion go hand in hand.   There are individuals who only come
          into this house by a casting vote.   In such cases the minority
          is all but equal to the majority, and yet they are to have
          no representation.   If this principle of the noble lord is worth
          anything, it is worth this—that no person of such minority
          would be bound to pay the taxes or obey the laws that
          were enacted, as his representative had no share in their
          formation.

          "The great benefit of the constitution of the House of
          Commons, as it now exists (though if the noble lord's plan is
          adopted, that benefit will cease) is, that it represents all
          interests, and admits all talents.   If the proposed change
          takes place, it will be almost entirely confined to one interest,
          and no talent will be admitted but the single one of mob
          oratory.   Many of those who sat for 'close and rotten
          boroughs,' as they have been designated for the first time by
          a member of the government, have constituted the chief
          ornaments of the house and the support of the country, but
          would, if this plan had been adopted in their days, never have
          been received into the house.   I ask the noble lord by what
          means the great Lord Chatham came into parliament ?   By-
          the-bye, the first borough for which that great man sat was
          Old Sarum itself.   Mr. Pitt sat for Appleby.   Mr. Fox came

in for a close borough, and when rejected for a populous place, CHAP. II.
he again took refuge in a close borough. Mr. Burke first sat 1831
for Wendover ; and when, by that means, he became known,
he was transposed in his glory to Bristol, as Mr. Canning,
who also first sat for Wendover, was transposed to Liverpool.
When their talents became known, they were the honoured
representatives of large towns; but would such places ever
have thought of selecting Mr. Canning, Mr. Burke, or Lord
Chatham, if they had not previously had an opportunity of
showing their talents in the house ? It is only by this means
that young men who were unconnected by birth or residence
with large towns, can ever hope to enter this house, unless
they are cursed—I will call it cursed—with that talent of
mob oratory which is used for the purpose of influencing the
lowest and most debasing passions of the people."

Passing by Mr. Twiss and Lord Althorp, we come to Mr. Mr.Hume
Hume, the member for Middlesex, and the leader of the more
moderate and reflecting portion of the Radical party. He
frankly declared that, " Radical reformer as he was, the plan
proposed much exceeded his expectations, and that, with all
his disposition to put confidence in ministers, he was not prepared to find them come forward with so manly a measure."
" They have," said he, " fully redeemed their pledge, and
though, in my opinion, the omission to shorten the duration
of parliament and to introduce the ballot are deficiencies,
yet, as they are points on which a large number of members
have not made up their minds, ministers have acted wisely in
not encumbering the present measure with them, as they can
be brought forward at any time as separate questions.   .   .
I can assure the house, that all those with whom I have con-
versed, are satisfied with the measure.   Many whom I know
to be the strongest reformers in England, allowed that they
have the utmost reason to be delighted.   .   .   .   I have
no doubt that many think the qualification too high, but

there is too much sense in the British community not to feel that vast good will result from this measure, though some may not immediately participate in its benefits."

Mr. Hunt. The next speaker we shall select will be our old acquaintance Orator Hunt, now sitting, as we have seen, for the town of Preston. His approbation of the measure was much less warm than Mr. Hume's, and as the discussion proceeded, it became icy cold; in fact, was changed into something very nearly approximating to opposition. He acknowledged that the measure went beyond his expectations, but declared that he had not heard a single word, in the course of the debate, that was new to him. "All," said he, "that has been said in this house has been said twenty years ago by the weavers of Lancashire. As the bill does not touch the rights of my constituents, I will give it my support, but I am sorry that so little is said about the ballot and the duration of parliaments. The suffrage is not widely enough extended if the rabble, as they are called, are not to have votes. My opinions are well known to the country. I have fearlessly and manfully advocated the rights of the people, and I should be unworthy of a seat in this house if, on an occasion like the present, I did not advocate the same sentiments here. I have always contended for the right of every one to have a share in the elective franchise, because I have been taught that, according to the constitution of England, representation and taxation go hand in hand, and that no man ought to pay taxes unless he has a share in the representation. Am I to be told that the people who have fought the battles of the country, the lower orders, whom I call the useful classes of society, are to be called on to pay taxes on every article of human subsistence, and afterwards denied the right of choosing representatives? I plainly tell the house, and I speak the voice of millions, that such an exclusive doctrine will give no satisfaction out of doors. I am delighted to hear that the

rotten boroughs are to be sacrificed. Some honourable members have called the measure proposed by the noble lord, not
Reform, but revolution, and an alteration in the constitution.
Now, I will admit that statement to be correct, the moment
it is proved that rotten boroughs are a part of the constitution.   When the honourable member for Calne (Mr. Macaulay) talked of the *rabble*, he looked very hard at me." These
words were received by the house with shouts of laughter.
" I understand," continued Mr. Hunt, "the meaning of that
laugh, and I am only sorry that the honourable and learned
member has not remained in his place, that I might have
looked in the same way at him.   How is this house constituted ? How are many honourable members elected ?   Look
at the borough of Ilchester, and the boroughs of Lancashire
and Cornwall, and see what classes of men return members
to this house.   I will tell the house a fact which has come to
my knowledge, and which bears on that particular point.   In
the borough of Ilchester, where I was sent to gaol for two
years and six months, (great laughter,)—I understand the
meaning of that laugh again—but I repeat that in Ilchester
many of the voters are of the most degraded and lowest
class, who can neither read nor write, and who always take
care to contract debts to the amount of £35 previous to an
election, because they know that those debts will be liqui-
dated for them.   Is that, then, the class of men which the
house is told represents the property of the country ?   I am
one who think that this house ought to be what it professes
to be—the Commons' House of Parliament, representing the
feelings and interest of all the common people of England.   I
do not stand up to approve the disfranchisement of any persons, because I have always contended for the right of the
whole people of England to have a share in the representation.   I am fully convinced that the people of England are
competent to choose proper representatives.   I have been in

CHAP. II. the habit, for many years past, of attending large public
1831. meetings, composed of persons whom the honourable and
learned member for Calne has chosen to call the rabble; but
I will undertake to say that they are a much more intelligent
rabble than the electors of Calne. That *Calne* is one of the
most degraded of rotten boroughs; and I wonder by what
chance the ministers have overlooked that most rotten and
stinking hole of corruption in their sweeping measure of
Reform. We have been told by the honourable and learned
member for Calne that if the present measure is not conceded
to the middle classes, we shall have revolution and massacre.
What sort of massacre is it that the hon. member has alluded
to? I remember that when the people of Manchester assembled together in 1819, as legally and as peaceably as the hon.
members are now assembled in this house, for the purpose
of petitioning for a Reform in parliament and a repeal of the
corn-laws, and their petitions were couched in much more
respectful and moderate language than many petitions which
have been lately presented to this house; then, indeed, there
was a massacre. (Cries of 'No, no.') I say yes. The
meeting was constitutionally and peaceably assembled, and
what was the result? Why, a drunken and infuriated yeomanry — ('Order,' 'order,' 'question,' 'question,') — with
newly-sharpened sabres — ('question,' 'question,') — rushed
among the people and chopped them to pieces. ('No, no,'
'order,' 'order.') They slaughtered to death fourteen,
('No, no,') cut and badly wounded six hundred and eighteen."
(Here the excitement and outcries became so great, that
Mr. Hunt was unable to proceed; nothing daunted,
however, by the interruption, he lifted up his powerful voice above the tumult, and exclaimed, in his most sten-
torian tones,)—" Where is the man who says no? I repeat
that this infuriated yeomanry murdered fourteen, wounded
and slaughtered six hundred and eighteen of as peaceable

and well disposed subjects of His Majesty as any I see around me at the present moment. At that meeting I was advocating the cause of Reform. And I was astonished to hear the noble lord, the paymaster of the forces, say, in bringing forward the present measure, that the government had not taken up the question before because the people of England had not called upon them in a manner to justify the interference of government. The people of England have for many years past been anxious for Reform, and in the years 1816, 1817, 1818, 1819, loudly expressed their wishes for some measure to amend the state of the representation. . . . ;
I certainly thought that the scene which was exhibited in the house yesterday, when the noble lord brought forward the Reform measure, had never been equalled since the time of the revolution, when Cromwell came into the house and took away the bauble of the mace. When I was tried, condemned, and sentenced to suffer two years and six months' imprisonment in a dungeon—(Here Mr. Hunt was interrupted by laughter and loud cries of ' question.') I think it is very hard, that while some members, in urging the question of Reform, have gone back to the time of Edward III., I am not allowed to refer to transactions which have taken place within the last twenty-nine years." (Here renewed interruption occurred.) "Well, then," exclaimed Mr. Hunt, "I will tell the people of England that the man whom they have sent to this house to advocate their right is not allowed to be heard. (' No, no.') But I say, *yes, yes !* I repeat," continued the imperturbable orator, "when I was condemned to suffer two years and six months' imprisonment in a solitary dungeon, for advocating that question which is now advocated by so many honourable members in this house, I little expected to see a measure of Reform proposed by government ; though I knew that Lord Chatham had said that if Reform did not come from within, it would come from without with a vengeance.

The honourable member for Calne has said that none but a few crazy Radicals in the street would ever dream of invading the rights of the throne.   I ask that honourable and learned member where any of those Radicals are to be met with ?   I am as thorough-going a Radical as ever paced the Strand, but I defy the hon. and learned gentleman to prove that I have ever proposed to attack the privileges of the Crown, though I have often enough protested against the extravagance of the family on the throne, and the misconduct of that house which has brought the institutions of the country into disrepute."

He expressed his determination to support the bill.   He regretted that he had been compelled to address the house before the hon. members for Tamworth and Boroughbridge. Hitherto he had heard nothing in the course of debate that he was not familiar with in the proceedings at the meetings of the Lancashire weavers.

Lord Morpeth and Sir Charles Wetherell rose together. There was a loud call for the latter, but the Speaker decided in favour of the former, who spoke very briefly in favour of the measure, and was then succeeded by Sir
C. Wetherell, the comical member of the house, and withal one of the ablest, the darling and champion of the high Tory party.   He began by bespeaking, in those tones of mock solemnity which he could assume with a most powerful effect on the risible muscles of his fellow members, the favour of the house, as he was now making his last dying speech as member for the condemned borough of Borough-bridge.   Referring to Mr. Hunt's speech, he proceeded to insinuate that Calne had been spared because it was a Whig borough, and called upon ministers to rise and defend themselves from the imputation of partiality, to which the preservation of this borough rendered them obnoxious. Coming then to the subject immediately before the house, he said "I am aware that in long debates elegance is too apt to

run away with accuracy." (Here a cry of "hear" and "question"
was raised.) The hon. gentleman paused, and addressing himself directly to the interrupting member, exclaimed "Does the
hon. member who never speaks himself desire to withhold me
from a digression of five minutes ? Does the hon. member who
cries 'hear' and 'question,' and says nothing else, and never
affords others an opportunity of reciprocating the same cries—
Does the hon. gentleman behind the chair ('oh!') suppose—
but I will not pursue the subject.   It appears then by this
bill of the military paymaster, sixty boroughs are to be
deprived of their franchise, and of the right of sending one
hundred and twenty members to parliament ; and that forty-
seven are to lose one member each ; and that in the whole,
one hundred and sixty-eight members are to be ejected from
this house.   I do not wish to call this by an offensive term,
but as a great man, Mr. Locke, has said that things should be
called by their right names, I call this 'corporation robbery.'
But then there is to be a sort of restitution made, 'except
that there are sixty members less in the house than there
are now.'   But does this make the robbery less ?   Is it less
a measure of robbery and pillage, if you take from A. B. and
C. D. and give to E. F., and if the house is to be composed of
sixty members less than at present.   The present cabinet of
Althorp and Co. seem to have proceeded upon the precedent
in the history of England, which was given by Cromwell,
Fairfax, Milburne, and Co.   This plan of cutting off the
boroughs and diminishing the number of members has not
the merit of originality, for it is almost the same in form,
in substance, and in principle, as the radical system of
Reform which was introduced by the regicides, when
they established a Commonwealth in England.   Yet it
is said, that the object of the measure is to preserve our
ancient institutions.   Conservatism is to be the rule of the
system.   It is to prevent certain inconveniences, and to

establish a system of representation consistent with the prerogatives of the Crown, the Church, and the Constitution;
the exercise of the functions of the House of Lords, and without danger to the property of the country. Yet, this plan tends
to destroy all these things. Gentlemen on the other side say—
'Those who oppose this bill must be prepared to negative all
possibility of Reform.' I am one of those who oppose this
bill, but I never said that there was no possibility of improving
our representative system. I never said that we could not
improve our election law, or introduce any practical amendment into the system in general. I never said that this
could not be done by a legal and gradual course of dealing
with cases as they occurred. Do gentlemen recollect how
many experimental governments are now afloat. Do they
recollect that there is a smithy of political blacksmiths, where
constitutions are continually on the anvil, which is at work
in making experimental governments for all Europe? That
there is a question to settle as to a constitution for Greece?
Another as to a charter for Portugal? That in Belgium, the
relations of the president and the representative government are yet unsettled? Do gentlemen recollect what has
taken place in France? Do they recollect that in South
America, for the last seven or eight years, new governments
are continually appearing, and that, nowithstanding, they have
no government there yet? As I am politically, *in extremis*,
let me be permitted to utter the last dying wish of an expiring
man, which is, that Great Britain may not be added to the
catalogue of experimental states; and that these visionary
projects of His Majesty's government may not be realized.
Is this a time, when Europe is in disorder, when everything is
at sea, to hoist the flag of innovation, and to sail on an
experimental cruise in search of a new constitution? Why is
the experiment to be made now?" Returning to his charge of
"corporation robbery," the honourable gentleman proceeded:—

"I defy the whole cabinet and all its deputies, military and civil, to cite a case of any corporation having its chartered rights abrogated at one fell swoop, without a case of delinquency having been even insinuated against it,—without any form of trial, without any pretext palliative of such monstrous conduct, without any shadow of argument—unless, forsooth, the telling us that we are bigotted adherents of the laws and usages of the constitution were received as argument. The course which the present consolidated and unanimous cabinet propose to themselves to follow is not only opposed to every recognised principle of law and justice, but to every precedent of parliament. I will tell them again and again that their measure is one opposed to every principle of law and justice—a measure which no cabinet with which the history of this country has made us acquainted could have sanctioned. It is a measure which only some Cromwellian band, ruthless of all law and of all those usages which the constitution has preserved for ages, could have ventured to propose as a remedy for any complaint of the public mind."

After proceeding in the same strain at great length, the honourable gentleman thus perorated:—

"I have now performed, and I trust within reasonable limits, the duty which I owe to myself, to the British public, and the House of Commons, in making the observations on this bill which I have found myself compelled to make, and I have now but a few more words to utter. There existed in Cromwell's time a purge of the House of Commons. (Laughter.) That purge was called Colonel Pride's purge. (Laughter and cheering.) The gentlemen on the opposite side of the house are close imitators of the Cromwellian system; not only of his system of Parliamentary Reform, but also of his sanitary and purgative system, for they are prepared to expel, by one strong dose, no fewer than one hundred and sixty-eight members from

the house.   I do not know what name should be attached to
this specific, for I did not conceive it possible that the country
would see a repetition of such a process.   Within the last
three days, however, the house has been promised a purge,
to which, as no name has been attached, I will attach the
name of 'Russell's purge.'   (Roars of laughter and great
cheering for some time.)   I say that the principle of the bill
is republican at the basis; I say that it is destructive of all
property, of all right, of all privilege; and that the same
arbitrary violence which expelled a majority of members
from that house at the time of the Commonwealth, is now,
after the lapse of a century from the revolution, during
which the population has enjoyed greater happiness than has
been enjoyed by any population under heaven, proceeding to
expose the House of Commons again to the nauseous experiment of a repetition of Pride's purge."   The cheering which
followed the delivery of this speech was very loud, and lasted
for several minutes.

The
Attorney-
General.
    The opposition had already adopted that Fabian policy
which we shall afterwards find them carrying to great
lengths, and were seeking to prolong the debates as much as
possible, in the hope that some contingency might arise
which might diminish the popularity of the measure in the
house or in the country, and enable them to get rid of it.
This was evident in many of the speeches already delivered
from the opposition side of the house, and in none more so
than in that of Sir C. Wetherell, which, able as it was, contained a good deal of repetition, which we have got rid of in
our report of it, and was evidently intended to occupy as
much time as possible.   When, therefore, the Attorney-General
(Sir T. Denman) rose to reply on the part of the government,
although it was not yet half-past twelve o'clock, and though he
had been very pointedly alluded to, and in some sort chal-
lenged in the preceding speech, his rising to reply was the

signal for loud cries of " adjourn" from the opposition, which
were continued during a great part of the honourable gentleman's address.   He however persevered, and spoke for an
hour, replying to the various points which had been raised
by the preceding speaker.

The next speech which we shall notice is that of Lord
Palmerston, the representative of the party of the late Mr.
Huskisson and Mr. Canning—a party which had hitherto
been almost as strongly opposed to Parliamentary Reform as
the Duke of Wellington himself.   A considerable part of his
speech was taken up with justifying and defending the policy
of the administration to which he belonged.   Coming at
length to the question immediately before the house, he
said :—

" What is it which for years has produced so much mis-
government, so much disregard of public opinion ?   The gross
bribery practised at elections, by means of which parties
come into parliament, and undue influence at elections for
members of that house, by means of which so many of them
come in, either without constituents, or only with those whom
they have purchased and may sell again.   When then, by
such practices, the people were driven to tear aside the veil
of sanctity with which hereditary respect had invested even
the imperfections of the constitution, it was impossible that
they whose limited propositions of Reform had been rejected,
would not be led to demand wider and more extensive
changes.   There are many men in this house who wish
things to remain as they are, and who are willing to bear
the faults of the constitution for the sake of its many
excellencies.   I will tell them, that if they are now driven to
the necessity of choosing between a change which they fear
and the evil consequences which would arise from the refusal
of that change, the blame must rest on those who three years
ago refused to make even the smallest concession to public

CHAP. II.
1831.

feeling. If, three years ago, advantage had been taken of
the conviction of corrupt boroughs, to bring gradually into
connection with this house the great unrepresented towns,—
if instead of drawing nice equations between the manufacturing and agricultural interests, they had turned reformers
on even a moderate scale, the house would not now have been
discussing a plan of general Reform, proposed by my noble
friend, His Majesty's Paymaster of the Forces. I supported
all these plans of limited Reform, because I thought them
good in themselves, and because I saw that if they were
refused, we should be obliged to have recourse to wider and
more extensive changes. But my predictions were condemned and disregarded by the gentlemen opposite. For
reasons similar to those for which I then supported those
limited propositions of Reform, I am now prepared to support
the more extensive measure which has been proposed by my
noble friend. Taunts were thrown out in the course of last
night's debate against those who, like myself, were admirers
of Mr. Canning. We have been taunted with abandoning
the principles which that great man had adopted with respect
to the important question of Reform. I think that the
events which have taken place in this house since the
lamented death of that illustrious person, might have taught
those who indulged in such taunts, that public men might
change their opinions on questions of national concernment
without being influenced by any but honest and honourable
motives. What Mr. Canning's opinions on the question of
Reform would now have been, had he lived to the present
day, it is not for me to say ; but they are bad expounders of
Mr. Canning's opinions who look for them in the particular
sentiments expressed at particular times, and do not scruti-
nize the principles by which his public life was guided. If
any man took a great and enlarged view of human affairs,
without doubt that eminent man did, and I venture to say

that had Mr. Canning lived in the present day, and stood in CHAP. II.
the circumstances in which I stand, his great genius would at 1831.
once have comprehended the necessity on which the opinions
of the government were founded, and would have stated to
the house, in my belief, the sentiments which I am now
expressing."

The next speaker was Sir R. Peel. Admirable in tact, in Sir R. Peel.
talent, and in the management of details, he was unable to
conceive or accept a great and organic change. His temper,
cautious even to timidity, led him generally to yield before it
was too late, but never to yield too soon. The Reform Bill,
however, involved far too large a stride for his mind to take at
once, and though he afterwards profited by the mistake he
made on this occasion, he resisted it with all his power, and
to the very last. He began his speech by declaring that
he was not one of those who joined in taunting Lord Palmerston on account of the change of his opinions, and begged
to assure him that his character, conduct, and views, afforded
a sufficient guarantee for the purity of his intentions. He
replied to some charges which Lord Palmerston brought
against the late administration. Referring to the manner
in which the name of the king had been used in favour
of the measure, he said :—

"I thought the king had been the fountain of grace and
favour ; but it seems as if this plan of extreme disfranchisement is to be received by the house and not dissented from,
under the terror of its being introduced with the king's
express sanction, if not at the king's suggestion. Then the
house is menaced with dissolution. The chances of dissolution are as strong if the measure is carried, as if it fails. I
care not if the house is dissolved, or not ; nor should I be fit
for the performance of a single legislative duty if I permitted
such a menace to influence me. I care not whether I am
returned again or not ; but if I felt any anxiety on that head,

I would go to my constituents with the bill in my hand, and would place my special ground to their renewed confidence on my determined opposition to it. I will go to a community, whose numbers, by the returns of 1821, were not more than 4,000, and I would tell them that this bill had been brought in without any allegation of necessity, or without any case being made out against them, and that I opposed it. I know that they have never abused their right, that the humblest man amongst them never obtained or asked a bribe for the vote he gave. They received me when I had been subjected to the indignity of expulsion for what I conceived to be a special act of duty, even to the church of which I am a humble member. They then returned me as their representative, and till the necessity of the measure is established by more cogent arguments than I have yet heard, I will not consent to deprive them of their right. But I am told that I must adopt this measure, as the alternative is civil commotion. I, at least, have not been one who industriously excited the stormy wave of the multitude,—who employed all my faculties to create dissatisfaction and discontent. I, at least, never uttered the language of the noble lord, in 1827, who found the people peaceful, quiet, and contented, and complained that he could not rouse their indignation against the constitution of the House of Commons,—who grieved that they were so apathetic, as to 'prove deaf to the voice of the charmer, charm he never so wisely.' I, at least, never called for a list of the names of 113 privy councillors, in order to direct against them the full torrent of popular displeasure and resentment, on account of the remuneration afforded to their services. Neither have I ever instituted any invidious comparison between great naval commanders and the civilians who presided over the Admiralty. Neither have I instigated or encouraged any body of men to display, under the very window of the seat of government, a foreign emblem of revolution. I have never been the person to excite the people to a pitch of frenzy, to spur their lazy indifference to an emulation of revolutionary clamour. If, therefore, this extraordinary measure, (which common prudence would have forborne introducing at such a crisis in our foreign and domestic relations, when fresh causes of excitement ought to have been avoided,) if, I say, this extraordinary measure should be defeated, I can never allow that the responsibility of the disappointment could attach to me, or to any other individual member of this house. It is the inevitable tendency of this bill to sever every link of connection between the poorer classes and that class from which their representatives are usually chosen. Now, this severing of the ties which connect the highest and the lowest class is opposed to the practical workings of the present system of representation—a great characteristic recommendatory feature of which is, that it enables every class in the community, in some way or other, to have a voice in the election of the members of this house. Now, I do not mean by this to say that the franchise should be extended to all the members of all the classes of the community, but that the constitution works well, from having here and there an entrance channel for the broadest principle of popular representation. If, to make myself better understood, it was proposed to me to make a selection between the franchise in force in Windsor, and that in force in Preston, I should not hesitate to prefer the former; but I would not therefore abolish the Preston franchise, and assimilate it to that in Windsor. All that I would do would be to take care not to take it as the model of my plan of extending the franchise to other places. But not so the noble lord's bill. It would disfranchise all those open boroughs, the voters of which are not rated at £10—though no reason had been, or could be, adduced for depriving the freemen of Coventry, or the potwallopers of Preston of their franchise. I put it to the noble lord and the house, to consider whether the effect of this disqualifying principle would not be the affixing a political stigma on those not eligible to vote under the £10 qualification? I could not consent to the measure, were it only on this ground—for I could not consent to a stigma on from 200 to 300, which this bill would disfranchise."

Applying himself to the arguments which had been employed against the close borough system, Sir Robert then proceeded :—

"It is usually, and as it appears to me, most convincingly argued, that these boroughs are advantageous, by affording the means of access to the house to men who have no claims beyond their ability. Two objections have, in the course of this debate, been urged against that argument. The one—which, I must say, came with a very bad grace from the hon. member for Westminster (Mr. Hobhouse), himself a man of great ability—was, that it is by no means desirable that men of splendid talents should be members of this house,—that in a reformed parliament, solid sense and integrity will be more highly valued. Now, I on the other hand, maintain that nothing tends more to foster the public respect for this house than its being the great arena of talent and eloquence, and that nothing would lower it more in public estimation than that it should be below the average ability of educated gentlemen. But, says the hon. member for Calne, 'Yes, let us have men of ability by all means, but let us select other means for their obtaining seats than close boroughs; give us a purer and more extensive franchise, and they will get at least as much as they do at present. But what' said he 'is your test of ability? Take every hundred men you meet in the street, and one of them will be a man of ability—take one hundred names in the Red Book, and one may be a man of ability—and so of one hundred men of tawny complexion; but are these men to get in by the accident of close boroughs?' And

then the hon. member asked 'was it fair to judge by the
accident instead of the general tendency of a system?'
Now I am content to judge by the tendency and not by the
accident of the close borough system, and I maintain that
that tendency is essentially favourable to the entrance of men
of ability into this house.   I have this morning turned over
a list of from twenty to twenty-five of the most distinguished
men that have graced this house for the last thirty or forty
years, — men of whom it might be said, in the glowing
language of Lord Plunkett, that they were possessed of that
'buoyancy of genius which would float them down the stream
of posterity;' and I found that, with three exceptions, they
were all returned for boroughs which the noble lord's bill
would wholly disfranchise.   There was Mr. Gunning, Lord
North, Mr. Townshend, Mr. Burke, Mr. Flood, Mr. Pitt, Mr.
Fox, Lord Grenville, the Marquis Wellesley, Mr. Perceval,
Lord Plunkett, Mr. Canning, Mr. Wyndham, Mr. Horne, Mr.
Huskisson, Mr. Brougham, Sir S. Romilly, Lord Castlereagh,
Mr. Tierney, Sir W. Grant, Lord Grey, and the late Lord
Liverpool, all first returned for close boroughs, and but three
of them ever members for counties.   Nor is the mere facility
of admission the only benefit.   The introduction, by affording
them an opportunity—the essential condition of successful
talent—for displaying their legislative ability on a larger
scale, recommended them to a more extended franchise at a
more mature age ; and again, when they, by caprice, or want
of money, or otherwise, were deprived of their larger seats,
those close boroughs, which the noble lord's bill would destroy
altogether, received them and secured their invaluable labours
to their country.   Such was the case when Mr. Sheridan was
defeated at Stafford.   He found shelter at Ilchester.   Mr.
Wyndham, having failed at Norwich, took refuge at Higham
Ferrers ; and Lord Castlereagh, in like manner, having lost
his election in the county of Down, was returned for Oxford.

Mr. Tierney, also, when he lost Southwark, was returned for
Knaresborough ; and Lord Grey for Tavistock, when defeated
in Northumberland. All this proves that the tendency, and
not the mere accident, of the close borough system, is to
facilitate the entrance of men of ability, who otherwise could
not obtain a seat in this house. And is this system, thus
working so advantageously for the general weal,—so fostering
of talent and statesmanlike ability,—to be destroyed, in
obedience to the noble lord's plan ? During 150 years the
constitution, in its present form, has been in force ; and I
would ask any man who hears me to declare whether the
experience of history has produced any form of government
so calculated to promote the happiness and secure the rights
and liberties of a free and enlightened people ? Many other
experiments have been tried to engraft democratical on
monarchical institutions, but how have they succeeded ? In
France, in Spain, in Portugal, in the Netherlands, in every
country on the face of the earth, with the exception of the
United States, has the experiment of forming a popular
government, and of uniting it with monarchy, been tried ; and
how, I will again ask, has it succeeded ? In America, the
house has been told that the most beneficent effects of a
representative form of government are plainly visible. But
I beg to remind the house that there is a wide difference
indeed between the circumstances of this country and of
America. In the United States the constitution has not
been in existence more than forty years. It was not till the
year 1779 that the representative part of the American
system of government was established, and since that time
many important changes, as every body knows, have been
made, respecting the mode of electing their president. As
yet, everything is in uncertainty, for ever since the first
establishment of the government of the United States it has
been undergoing a change. I will not say it has been

deteriorating, for I wish to avoid all invidious phrases, but it
has been rapidly undergoing a change from a republic to a
mere democracy. The influence of the executive,—the influence of the government has been daily becoming less, and
more power has, consequently, been vested in the hands of
the people. And yet, in that country, there is land uncul-
tivated to an extent almost incalculable,—there is no established church—no privileged orders,—property exists on a
very different tenure from that on which it is held in this
country; therefore, let not the people of England be deceived,
let them not imagine, from the example of the United States,
that because democracy has succeeded and triumphed there,
it will also succeed and triumph here."

He next pointed out the failure of democracy in the
States of South America, and maintained that the question
of Reform always flourished when there was either the pressure of some great difficulty in the country, or a revolution
on the continent. In support of this assertion, he instanced
its being brought forward in 1745, during the American war;
in 1817, 1819, and 1822, in a word, in every period, when
there was great commercial and agricultural distress in this
country. And again, in 1780, on the establishment of
American independence; in 1790, at the commencement of
the great French revolution; and now again, when a new revolution had occurred in France. He concluded as follows :—

"I lament exceedingly that government should have
determined to agitate such a question as that of Reform, at
this particular crisis; it would have been wiser, in my opinion,
to have avoided these new causes of excitement, for depend
upon it, that by this process throughout the land, the first
seeds of discontent and disunion are sown. In every town
there will be a conflict—a moral conflict, I mean, between
the possessors of existing privileges and those to whom the
existing authority and existing privileges are to be transferred.

CHAP. II.   Oh, sir, I lament beyond measure, that government had
  1831.   not the prudence to adhere to that temperate course of
          policy that they had pursued elsewhere.   I lament that, if
          they did think it necessary to propose a plan of Reform, in
          this excited state of the public mind, they did not confine it
          within those narrow limits which are consistent with the
          safety of the country and the dignity of their own characters.
          They have thought proper, however, to adopt another course ;
          they have sent through the land the firebrand of agitation,
          and it is easy so far to imitate the giant enemy of the Philis-
          tines, as to send three hundred firebrands through the
          country, carrying danger and dismay in all quarters ; but it
          is not easy, when the mischief is done, to find a remedy for
          it.   In the present difficulties of your situation, you should
          have the power of summoning all the energies of life, and
          should take care that you do not signalise your own destruc-
          tion by bowing down the pillars of the edifice of your liberty,
          which, with all its imperfections, still contains the noblest
          society of freemen known to the habitable world."

Mr. Stan-   This speech was answered by Mr. Stanley,* the brilliant
ley.   and fiery scion of the house of Derby.   Referring to the
          passage in which Sir Robert Peel said that he would take the
          bill in his hand, and go with it to his constituents, and appeal
          to them on the ground of his opposition to it, Mr. Stanley
          observed :—

          " I suppose that every gentleman opposed to this measure
          will make his appeal where he has constituents ; and those
          who are so fortunate as not to have any constituents—I mean
          individuals who are returned by patrons of boroughs—will
          doubtless make the same representation in the proper quarter.
          It is therefore evident, that those gentlemen look more to the
          private interests, passions, and feelings of a large portion of

          * Now Lord Derby.

the people, than to the welfare of the country at large. But
the right hon. baronet said, 'If any danger arises from this
measure, impute it not to those who oppose it. I throw the
responsibility on your own shoulders.' I however will contend, that the responsibility must rest with those gentlemen
on the other side of the house, who could not go on with the
government, because they were prepared to resist all reform,
and went out when they could not prevent it from being
carried, though it was loudly called for by the people. If they
afterwards endeavour to baffle the efforts of those who have
succeeded them, they must take upon themselves the responsibility that will attach to the loss and defeat of that great
measure.

"I was in hopes that a gradual Reform would have been
effected in parliament, by selecting, one after another, the most
notorious cases of delinquency. If a determined desire to
reform by degrees the abuses of the present system had been
manifested, then the public would have been satisfied with a
less sudden change than that which is now contemplated. But
let the house look back for the last few years, and mark the
time, the money, and the talents, which have been wasted in
discussing useless questions respecting boroughs charged with
malpractices; inquiring for instance, whether one voter received one guinea and another five, when it is as notorious as
the sun at noonday, that boroughs are commonly bought and
sold in the market by the proprietors. And, after all this
labour, after all this investigation, after all this minute inquiry,
what has been gained for the cause of Reform? Not one
great town—not one great district—has been added to those
represented in this house. Not one corrupt borough has been
deprived of the means of corruption.

"My honourable friend (Sir R. Peel) talked of the advantages to be derived from nomination—he contended that it
afforded an opportunity of admitting very clever men into

the house, who might not be able to find a seat in any other way. Whatever advantage might be derived from this mode of admission, would be more than balanced by this disadvantage—that the class of persons thus introduced would, whatever may be their talents and acquirements, not be looked upon by the people as representatives.

"We were told, last night, that this measure would admit 500,000 persons to the councils of the nation. In my opinion it will do no such thing. It will admit them to the possession of rights which belong to them from their wealth and intelligence, and consequent importance in the political scale. By this means we shall attach them to the institutions of the country, and gain more from their affection than we could by keeping them unconnected with, and at a distance from, the benefits of the constitution. But then it is said that the measure is revolutionary. To this it is scarcely necessary that I should urge more in reply than a mere denial of any such object on the part of those who introduced it. Is my noble friend who introduced the measure into this house a man without any stake in the country? Is not the name he bears in itself a guarantee against any such intention? Is my noble friend at the head of the government, who is said to be strenuously attached to the privileges of his order,—who has on more than one occasion been made the subject of attack on that ground,—likely to advocate a measure which is to involve those privileges and the monarchy in one common ruin? Look round at the other members of His Majesty's government, and at those who come forward to support them on this occasion,—are they men of no fortune, mere adventurers, who would have everything to gain, and nothing to lose, by a revolution? Are they not men who have large stakes in the country, and whose individual interests are bound up with the permanent peace and security of the state? What, then, could they

gain by a revolution ? They conceive that they cannot more
effectually secure the true interests of the country, and render
its institutions permanent, than by basing them on the affections of the people. For my own part, I feel no alarm of the
kind for the results of the bill. By that bill the influence of
of the aristocracy will be upheld—I mean the influence which
they ought to possess, not the influence of bribery and corruption, not the influence of direct or indirect nomination.

"Ministers came into office pledged to economy, reduction,
and Reform. These pledges they have redeemed. They
have cut off from themselves and their successors, for ever,
that corrupt patronage on which, heretofore, so much of the
influence of government depended. With these views of the
measure before the house, I earnestly implore honourable
members, by their sense of justice to the country,—by their
respect of what is due to the people,—by their regard for that
glorious constitution which has been handed down to them
from their ancestors, (great cheering from the opposition,)—
I repeat," said the hon. member, raising his voice, and looking his opponents full in the face, "I repeat, that constitution
which ministers are now endeavouring not to violate, but to
amend,—by their regard for the permanency of our institutions, and the peace and security of the state,—I call on
them, by all these considerations,—by their respect for the
petitions of the people for what may be lawfully asked, and
cannot be constitutionally refused,—to support His Majesty's
ministers in their endeavour to uphold and cement the legiti-
mate rights of the crown, the aristocracy, and the people,—
and by so doing, to fix the whole, as well as their own fame,
on the imperishable basis of the affections of the people."

The speech of Mr. C. W. Wynn must not be passed over,
because, though a member of the government, and cordially
approving certain portions of the bill, he expressed his disapprobation of it as a whole. He stated that he did not

concur in many of the objections which had been urged against
it. Not having a seat in the cabinet, he had had no share
in the preparation of the measure, and was not aware of its
provisions until about a week before it was introduced into
the house. After specifying the parts which he approved,
and those from which he dissented, he concluded by saying—

"It is with pain I state that, unless the proposition
brought forward by the noble lord undergoes a modification
greater than I have reason to expect, I cannot give it my support. Much has been said of the present state of the country,
but I have seen times much more perilous, which have been
safely passed through by the firmness and energy of parliament; and I have known instances when members returned
for those boroughs which it is now proposed to annihilate,
formed the safeguard of the constitution. It is on these
accounts that I am not prepared at once to support such a
sweeping measure of Reform. I am aware that it may be
said that the proposed measure, if agreed to, would preclude
any future change; but that if the measure should be rejected, demands for greater change would be made by the
people. I do not believe that to be the case; but even if it
were, and if I felt certain that in ten years time the whole of
the proposed measure would be adopted, I would still rather
at the present moment adopt only a small part of it; and if
I found that that part had succeeded in practice, then I would
adopt the whole. It has been well observed by a noble friend
of mine, that every man who wishes for Reform should
seriously reflect before he adopts an untried plan. I
would proceed cautiously, and as strong and marked cases of
corruption occurred, I would disfranchise the delinquent
boroughs, and transfer the right of election to the great
trading towns; and as I found that plan succeed, I would
persevere in it, or not. I see the necessity of something being
done. I always thought that these great towns ought

to have representatives, and believed that their possessing CHAP.II.
the franchise would be beneficial to the peace of the country. 1831.
I feel regret in being obliged to differ from many of those
whom I respect, and from a large body of my own constituents, who are strongly in favour of a measure of Reform,
on principles like those on which the present measure is
founded. But there are occasions when a man would be contemptible if he did not act on his own opinions, be the consequences what they might ; and it was my duty, when I
accepted the charge of being the representative of a respectable county, to state my sentiments in the best manner I
could. I have done so honestly. It has been my lot, on former
questions, to differ from my hon. friends near me; and they
have uniformly extended to me their confidence, that the
opinions I expressed were those which I honestly entertained,
and I trust they will still extend the same confidence to me."

On Tuesday, March 8th, Mr. O'Connell resumed the Mr.
adjourned debate. We have already seen the effect produced O'Connell.
by his eloquence on the Irish peasantry, it proved to be hardly
less successful in the House of Commons. He played on the
passions of that highly cultivated assembly, with the same
ease and success as on those of his ignorant countrymen, now
convulsing them with laughter, now almost melting them to
tears, now firing them with indignation. On this occasion he
gave the bill his most decided and anxious support, as a large,
liberal, wise, and even generous measure. " There are, however," he added, " objections to the measure. I am, upon
conviction, a Radical reformer, and this is not a measure of
radical Reform. I am of opinion, that in every practical
mode, universal suffrage should be adopted as a matter of
right; that the duration of parliaments should be shortened
to the time stipulated in the glorious revolution of 1688; and,
above all, that votes should be taken by ballot. As a Radical
reformer, I accept this measure heartily. But there is

another point of view in which I have a right to object to it. It will not carry its own principle into effect in Ireland. I think Ireland has been badly treated by it. The measure is, however, too advantageous to be cavilled at, and this consideration makes me waive all paltry objections to a measure which I believe will be highly advantageous to the people of England."

After dealing in detail and at great length with various objections which had been urged against the bill, the hon. member proceeded as follows :—

"The charge of inconsistency and of creating anomalies, comes with a very bad grace from honourable gentlemen who contended for the beauty of that system which gave Gatton as many members as Westminster. The truth is that the ancient system has been dilapidated and disfigured by those who now pretend to venerate it, and the government is endeavouring to build up again the old and simple fabric of the constitution. The gentlemen on the other side have, in some cases, destroyed the very foundations of that fabric, and have left no basis whereon a structure could be raised; but, wherever they have left even the ruins of the ancient edifice, the government has endeavoured to build up again on such remnants, scanty as they are, which have escaped the lawless hands of the spoliators. We have next been told that this bill is a corporation robbery, and we have had that assertion sounded in every tone, except a low tone, and every key, except a minor key. But, being a lawyer, and having a little of the curiosity which belongs to my profession, I have gone through the boroughs, with the view of ascertaining how many of them are corporations; and I have found that only sixteen out of sixty are so. Then again, we have been told that this bill is a seizure of franchises and of the rights of the people. Now I should be glad to know if the gentlemen who hold this language, mean to assist me in my endeavours

to carry the repeal of the Union. For, if they think that
the legislature has no right to take away franchises, what do
they think of two hundred boroughs being disfranchised by
one single Act of Parliament? Yet this was done by the
Union. And were the voters tried and convicted? Oh no;
so far from it, that forty of them were so innocent, that it
was thought right to give £13,000 a piece, of the public
money, to each of the forty. It was acknowledged that the
people so disfranchised were innocent and guiltless; and I
would ask the honourable member for Tamworth, who has
called the present bill atrocious, and the noble lord who has
called it iniquitous, whether they mean to join with me in
repairing those acts of greater iniquity and greater atrocity
which were committed at the time of the Union."

After dwelling at some length on the advantages which
the bill would confer on Scotland, the speaker thus continued :—

"Let me be believed, when I say that I entertain no
ungenerous jealousy at advantages that are conferred on
England and upon Scotland. All I seek is, that Ireland
should not be excluded from a share of those advantages. I
have always seen in this house and in this country the most
unbounded benevolence, and the most splendid munificence,
towards the distresses of Ireland; and while I make this just
admission, I hope I shall be pardoned when I say—believing
that I say it with truth—that when the political rights of
Ireland are concerned, I have not observed the same liberality
of spirit here.

"The population of Dublin amounts to considerably more
than the fourth of the population of London, and on that
ground I am of opinion that Dublin is fairly entitled to a double
representation. It appears, from statistical tables in my possession, that out of twenty-eight counties in England, to which
it is proposed to give two additional members each, fifteen

CHAP. II. possess a population less than that of the county of Antrim,
1831. nineteen of them less than that of Down, twenty-two of them
less than that of Tipperary ; and there is not one of them,
with the exception of Lancashire and Yorkshire, that has
anything like the population of the county of Cork. But I
may be told that the county of Cork has boroughs in it which
send representatives to this house. Now, I am content to
give up all those boroughs, with all their population, and still
I would find in Cork a population to the extent of 100,000
greater than that of any of those counties in England, with
the exception, which I have already mentioned, of Lancashire
and Yorkshire. I submit that these facts should be well
weighed before this bill passes into a law. I think that additional members should be given to the counties of Antrim,
Down, Cork, Galway, Kerry, Mayo, Tipperary, and Tyrone.
I would draw a line, with regard to the population, at 200,000.
There are seven or eight counties in Ireland with a population less than that amount. But I contend that those counties which have more than 200,000 have a right to additional
members. You propose, by the present bill, to get rid of
sixty-two members; you have, therefore, so many members
in bank,—they are a fund that you c̆an draw upon,—and it
would be but just and reasonable to give those additional
members to the Irish counties I have named. There is
another objection that I have to the details of this bill as
regards Ireland. You propose to give an additional member
each to Limerick and Waterford ; the proposition is a most
proper one, though the interests of those towns are, at present, very well taken care of in this house. But there is
Galway, with its vicinage, which has a larger population than
one of those towns ; and Kilkenny, with its vicinage, which
has a larger population than either of them, and which, let me
inform the house, before the Union, returned four members to
parliament. Now, it appears to me that you should give

additional members to Galway and Kilkenny. In making
these observations—in urging these objections—I do not wish
to be at all considered as arguing against the bill. I am determined to vote for the bill, even in its present shape. I do
not wish to make any bargain or contract, as the condition
on which I should give my support to this excellent measure.
I am ready to give my cordial support to it, even though my
suggestions should not be attended to. But I offer them to
His Majesty's government in the spirit of candour and fairness, as suggestions which are worthy of their consideration.
I would appeal to their common sense on the subject. I am
stated to possess an irregular power or influence in Ireland.
If His Majesty's ministers wish to take that power out of my
hands, I will tell them that the best way of doing so consists
in giving Ireland the full and entire benefit of the principles
of this measure. What are the facts which I have to urge on
your attention? I find, on the list of the counties in my hand,
Antrim with a population, taking it in round numbers, of
260,000 inhabitants. In that county I find that there are
disfranchised at one blow, by many of those who talked of the
iniquity of this measure, 6,246 freeholders, almost all of them
Protestant freeholders, who had not been even accused of any
crime which could justify such a measure against them. And
thus the constituency of that county is reduced to seven
hundred. They disfranchised the forty shilling freeholders in
Galway to the amount of 32,000. In Cavan they disfranchised
5,000; in Dublin, 10,000; in Kerry, 3,776; and in Tyrone,
6,600. They reduced the constituency of Tyrone to 364, and
that of Carlow to 140, and by similar reductions in the other
Irish counties they reduced the constituency of Ireland by
this bill almost to the narrow limits of the constituency of
Scotland. That being the case, I think there are fair and
just grounds now to call for an enlargement of the representation in Ireland. There is another objection that I have to

CHAP. II. this bill, as far as it applies to Ireland. Where there are
1831.   boroughs, this bill will not allow the freeholder in a borough
to vote at the election of a member for a county in which the
borough is situated. The effect of that part of the bill in
Ireland will be this—it will take the right of voting from
the most numerous and better class of voters—the shopkeepers
residing in the towns, who have grown rich on the fruits of
their industry, and who will not be subservient to the lordly
dominion of the county aristocrats and landlords. This is a
part of the bill which, it appears to me, requires to be modified. Again, the present measure proposes to give the right
of voting to the copyholders and the termers for years in
England, and to the termers for years in Scotland. Why not
also throw it open to the termers for years in Ireland, where
one third part of the land could only be let to termers, being
land belonging to the church? I need not say that I do not
want to increase the influence of the church, but I want to
give to the termers in Ireland that right to which they are
justly entitled. You may tell me that you will not restore
the forty shilling freeholders. I think that you ought, but
at all events that you ought not to stop at £10 as the qualification for voters there. In my judgment the qualification
should be only £5; but suppose we should say £6. It will
be absurd to talk of legislative Union unless you do that. At
the same time I admit that the bill, even in its present shape,
would be of considerable advantage to Ireland, as well as to
every other part of the empire. It would open seventeen or
nineteen of the rotten corrupt boroughs there.   .   .   .
It is said that the system has worked well. I would ask you
to inquire from your agricultural population whether such is
the case—whether such a fact is reflected from the fires
which lately blazed through the counties—and whether such
would be the statement we should receive if we inquired
from the unfortunate men who fill our gaols, on account of

the late disturbances in the country. Does the wilful trespass Act, which gives the magistrates such dominion over the
poor, evidence the well-working of the system ? Are the game
laws a proof of such a fact ? Has the house listened to the
complaints of the people? I will give specimens to show how
the boroughmongering representatives have voted upon questions of retrenchment, as an exemplification of the working
of the close borough system. From returns which have been
made, with regard to divisions on questions of retrenchment
in 1822, it appears that of nineteen representatives for
boroughs, with a population under five hundred, all voted
against retrenchment ; that of the representatives of boroughs
with a population above five hundred, and not exceeding one
thousand, twelve voted for retrenchment, and thirty-three
against it ; that of the representatives of boroughs with four
thousand inhabitants, seventeen were for retrenchment, and
forty-four against it ; and that of the representatives of
boroughs with a population beyond five thousand, sixty-six
voted for retrenchment, and sixty-seven against it. It was
the boroughmongering parliament which saddled the country
with a debt of £800,000,000, or £900,000,000. It is said that
the country has enjoyed prosperity under this system. True,
it has, but why has it been prosperous ? On account of its
great resources, and in spite of the evil effects of the boroughmongering system. Is there a heart in a true British bosom
that does not wish success to the brave and generous Poles ?
But if the despot of Russia should trample them in the dust,
could this country interfere ? No, for the debt at once
prevents her from doing so. The aristocracy and their
dependents have fattened upon the public plunder, and the
consequence is, that the country is bound up in the manner
I have described, and the only way for extricating it consists
in calling the universal people of England around us.
When I hear such triumphant assertions made as to the

working well of the system, I would refer you to Ireland for the illustration. We have had a complete trial of it for thirty years at least, and yet Ireland is one of the most miserable countries on the earth, with wretchedness and starvation spreading desolation through the land. I call upon you in the name of that God of charity, whose spirit inhabits your bosoms, to do this great act of justice to Ireland, in the spirit in which it is intended, for the benefit of the people of England and of the people of Scotland; and by so doing to secure us against a revolution, the consequences of which no man can foretell."

Mr. D. W. Harvey. Mr. D. W. Harvey, though one of the ablest and most pleasing speakers in the house, was regarded as an adventurer, and did not command that respect and attention to which his talents entitled him. Nevertheless, he was a man who had considerable weight with the Radical party outside, and was one who might be regarded as speaking the sentiments of a section of that party, which had no other representative. He began by promising not to detain the house long, and after some preliminary observations, he proceeded thus to point out what in his eyes was a defect, but what would by some be regarded as a recommendation of the measure. " On looking over the returns made of the number of householders rated at £10, who, if I understand the bill of the noble lord correctly, will, in the course of time, be the only persons qualified to vote ; it appears that in only one of the forty-seven places which are to have one member each, will the number of voters exceed two hundred and six. But many of them will have as small and select a number of voters as most of the honourable members opposite could desire; for example, in Bewdley, there will be only twenty-one; in Downton, nine; Liskeard will have ninety-five; Lyme Regis, one hundred and thirty-five; Marlow, one hundred and eighty; Sudbury, one hundred and eight;

Shaftesbury, seventy-eight; and Westbury, that pattern of Chap. II.
pure and uncorrupt boroughs, only fourteen. These will, no   1831.
doubt, tend to keep up the principle of aristocratic influence,
for which so many honourable members opposite contend."

Thus during seven nights did this debate drag on its weary Termina-
length to a late hour of the 9th, or rather an early hour of tion of the debate.
the 10th of March, when Lord J. Russell at length rose to
reply. The number of those who had addressed the house in
the course of this debate was seventy-one. Of these, thirty-
four spoke in favour of the measure, and thirty-seven against
it. Of the former, three sat for boroughs which the bill proposed to disfranchise, and two for boroughs which it deprived
of one member. Of the thirty-seven adverse speakers, thirteen
were members for boroughs which were to be disfranchised,
and seven for boroughs which were to be reduced to one
representative. Lord J. Russell, in his reply, briefly and tem-
perately answered some of the chief objections which had
been urged against the measure. The Speaker then put the
question, "That leave be given to bring in a bill to amend the
representation of the people in England and Wales." This
motion, in accordance with an understanding between the
leaders on both sides of the house, was agreed to without a
division. The ayes were shouted with a vehemence that
made the old walls of St. Stephen's ring, while the noes proceeded from only three members, one of them was uttered in
a loud and defiant tone, the other two in a weak and
dispirited manner, like faint echoes of the first. Leave was
subsequently granted, after some discussion, to introduce
Reform Bills for Scotland and Ireland. The bill was read a
first time on the 14th, without opposition.

The plan thus brought forward, was received by the Reception
Radical party with delight, by the Whigs with doubt, by the of the plan by the
Tories with terror. It surprised all, for though it did not country.
come up to the wishes of the Radicals—who desired the ballot,

CHAP. II. more frequent parliaments, and universal suffrage—it sur-
1831.   passed the expectations of all parties. By the great body
of the people it was hailed with enthusiasm. From the
moment of its first announcement they seemed to forget all
the other measures which had been prayed for in their
petitions, and adopted the cry of "the bill, the whole bill,
and nothing but the bill," which they sustained under all
the changes and vicissitudes it underwent, till it finally
became the law of the land. On the other hand, the
higher and better educated classes generally regarded the
measure with great alarm, as the commencement of the
overthrow of all the established institutions of the country.
They had not forgotten that, under the first French revolution, the landed proprietors had been stripped of their
property and driven into exile, or put to death, and they
dreaded that what they regarded as similar beginnings would
lead to similar results. The clergy, especially, remembering
the fate of the French priesthood and the spoliation of the
French church, were almost unanimous in their hatred of the
proposed innovation. Already highly unpopular, partly on
account of the determined opposition which as a body they
had offered to every proposal for the extension of civil and
religious liberty, and partly on account of the vexations and
disputes attendant on the collection of tithes, they rendered
themselves still more odious by their undisguised detestation
of the new measure. Their growing unpopularity increased
their fears, and presented yet another feature of resemblance
in the parallel they drew between the England of 1831 and
the France of 1793. And it must be admitted, that the
danger was not wholly imaginary. There can be no doubt
that if during the Reform struggle, or immediately after its
conclusion, the government had introduced a measure for the
secularization of church property, the proposal would have
been welcomed by the nation with an enthusiasm which

would have borne down all resistance. But the danger which
they had so much reason to apprehend was of their own
creation. They allowed themselves to be frightened by the
declamations of a few violent demagogues, who themselves
probably would not, in their cooler moments, have supported
the measures which they advocated in a season of national
exultation and excitement, whose followers would not have
gone along with them, and who would have been controlled
by the good sense and moderation of the overwhelming
majority. Under the influence of terrors thus excited, the
clergy set themselves to oppose that which the nation fondly
and almost unanimously desired. Had they yielded to the
movement, or even preserved as a body an honest neutrality,
they might have rendered the change less violent, and have
retained the affection and respect of their flocks. The consequence of their grievous but very intelligible error was,
that for many long years after the termination of the struggle,
the church was endangered in her stability, crippled in her
usefulness, and greatly diminished in the number of her
children, while the government which was sincerely anxious
to aid her in her difficulties, and which being the only strong
government that had existed for many years, was able
effectually to befriend her, were alienated by the impolitic
opposition of the clergy, and hindered by the hostility it
excited in their supporters. The moneyed interest too, as a
whole, and of course the proprietors of the nomination
boroughs, and the holders of places and pensions, were, with
few exceptions, arrayed against the bill. The mercantile
interest was also, though not so unanimously, hostile to it.
On the other hand, a class rapidly rising in importance, the
manufacturers of Lancashire and Yorkshire, was as a whole
strongly in favour of the measure. They felt that they did
not enjoy the influence in the legislation of the country,
which their rapidly increasing wealth and intelligence fairly

entitled them to claim; and that their trading operations were shackled and fettered, owing to the want of representation in the House of Commons. But the chief strength of the ministry lay in the shopkeepers and in the labouring class, whatever the nature of their employment, who, though as a class they were not admitted to the franchise by the bill, and were apparently not gainers by it, felt, and rightly felt, that it would benefit them indirectly by giving legislative influence to classes whose interests were in many respects identical with their own, and who were much more likely to attend to their representations than the present monopolists of political power. Thus was the country divided into two hostile camps, regarding each other with feelings of increasing exasperation. On the one hand, the anti-reformers, though comparatively few, were immensely strong in position and prestige. They had the court, the House of Lords, the clergy, the army, the navy, the magistracy, the gentry, the old functionaries in all the public departments, the universities, the inns of court, and the influence belonging to the collection of the greater part of the revenue. On the other hand, the reformers could count upon the support of the great mass of the people. Thus on the one side were the wealthy and educated portion of the community, with those whom they were able to command; on the other, the distressed and the suffering classes, but with them the vigorous, robust, and progressive, though generally untrained, thought of the country. On the one side, they who lived in the past; on the other, they who lived in the future. On the one side, they who recoiled under the influence of fear; on the other, they who marched onward under the inspiration of hope. On the one side, the old and middle aged; on the other, the young. All took their part, none could stand aloof. The very children were carried away by the pervading party feeling, and often outdid their

parents in enthusiasm for or against "*The Bill*," as it was Chap. II.
now emphatically denominated.   1831.

It may seem strange that a change, which all men now Explana-
admit to have been a great and necessary improvement, division of
should have been resisted by the wealthy and educated few, parties.
and carried mainly through the exertions of the poor and
uneducated many ; but there is really nothing very surprising
in this circumstance.   The same may be said with regard to
almost every great improvement that has been effected in
this or in any other country.   The leaders of the movement
have usually been men of rank and intelligence, and there
have been found amongst their followers many men of liberal
and highly cultivated minds, nay sometimes whole classes of
such persons on whom the existing abuses have pressed with
unfair severity, may have joined them ; but as a general rule,
the rank and file of the army of progress has been composed of the classes which constituted the chief strength
of the Reform party.   But, perhaps, this truth was never
more strikingly exemplified than in the instance now before
us, for if we would put our hands on the men who brought
the Reform struggle to its triumphant conclusion, we must
not seek them in the ministry ; in "the leading bankers,
manufacturers, and tradesmen," who in various parts of the
kingdom petitioned for Reform, but in the London mob,
in the two or three hundred thousand members of the
Birmingham political union, in the determination of the
great mass of the people in all parts of the kingdom to march
on London at the first signal given by their leaders ; and
if, on the other hand, we are asked to put our hands on the
quarters from which the most formidable and pertinacious
resistance to the bill proceeded, we must fix on the court, the
two universities, the inns of court, and the other ancient seats
of learning.   The true explanation of this seeming paradox
is, that in political questions the belly is generally much more

logical than the head.   They who are well off deprecate
change, because, if it does not bring with it peril to their fortune and position, it, at least, renders necessary some exertion
for the preservation of the one or the other, and that often of
a character to which they are unaccustomed, and which,
therefore, they do not like.   But truth and right must ultimately prevail, and the resistance thus offered may, indeed,
defer the dreaded change, but cannot prevent its advent, and
is certain to render it more violent the longer it is protracted.
On the other hand, the very poor are the first to feel the
evils which result from a vicious state of things, and they
feel them strongly and acutely, and their demand for the
remedy is sure to cause its production, which they, guided by
a blind, but sure, instinct, readily recognize and earnestly
demand.   And this is, perhaps, the true explanation of the
old maxim, *vox populi vox dei*, a maxim which certainly
rests on a foundation of facts very far from contemptible.   It
is not, of course, meant to be asserted that everything the
people clamour for ought to be granted ; but it is a matter of
fact, confirmed in each case by the verdict of posterity, that
they have almost invariably been right in their demands
when they have generally and persistently supported any
measure of alleged improvement.   The opinion of the rabble,
as they are sometimes called, is by no means to be despised,
for it has often proved to be more correct than the judgment
of men who have enjoyed a high reputation for statesmanship.
Unquestionably, in the Reform struggle the mob were right,
and their learned, wealthy, and aristocratic opponents clearly
and decidedly wrong.

The
government
gains con-
fidence.
The government, encouraged by the feeling in favour of
the bill, manifested by an overwhelming and rapidly increasing majority of the people, gradually assumed a bolder
attitude, and openly declared their intention not to consent
to any serious modification of its provisions.   In fact, there

was now no drawing back. The people were determined to be
satisfied with nothing short of it, and if the government had
faltered in their adhesion to it, men, prepared to go further
still, would speedily have occupied their places. Had the
opposition succeeded in their efforts to defeat it, they would
have produced at once that revolution which they dreaded
and predicted as the ultimate result of the proposed change.
In the temper of the English people at that time, no ministry
of a less decidedly liberal character could have stood its
ground. From the moment that the Reform Bill was proposed by the government, there could be no safety for the
country until it was carried. And the wisest course would
have been to have allowed it to pass as speedily as possible
without exasperating the popular passions by protracted
resistance. Many of those who thought the proposed change
far too sudden and violent supported it, nevertheless, justly
deeming that the dangers of delay or rejection were far
greater than any which could arise from the adoption of the
measure. Others did not see this—indeed, from their position
and habits of thought, could not possibly see it, and so they
continued to obstruct and delay the passage of the bill until
it had become too evident to almost all men, that the country
was on the verge of revolution, and that concession was indispensable and inevitable.

Among the measures to which reformers at this time had
recourse, to ensure the success of the bill, was the formation
or extension of societies called political unions. These societies, which were now established in all the chief towns of
the empire, had a kind of military organisation, with the
avowed design of "defending the king and his ministers
against the boroughmongers;" a name which now began to
be applied not only to those who trafficked in seats, but
indiscriminately to all the opponents of the bill. The chairman of that at Birmingham publicly boasted that his union

CHAP. II.
1831.

would supply two armies, each of them as numerous and brave as that which had conquered at Waterloo, if the king and his ministers required them in their contest with the boroughmongers. Colonel Evans, at a Reform meeting held in London, stated that he had just arrived from the county of Sussex, where two Reform meetings had been held, and he knew that ten thousand men were ready to march from Reigate if the measure before the house should be defeated. Almost every town was paraded by large bodies of men, marching in procession with banners and bands of music, and in a sort of military array, evidently for the purpose of intimidating the opponents of the bill by a display of their physical force. They were still tolerably good humoured, for they were confident of speedy success. Though the whole country was at the mercy of these Reform volunteers, no breach of the peace was committed, but threats were openly uttered, and it was evident that if the measure could not be carried by regular constitutional means force would be employed to secure its adoption. As for the poor anti-reformers, it was clear enough that they were not likely to take arms, and that the king and his ministers could not require the irregular assistance of these unions in order to resist them. The true object of these demonstrations was to strike terror into the hearts of the opponents of the bill, and to prevent the government, and especially the king, from faltering in their adherence to it. The latter accordingly regarded these movements, and especially the political unions, with great uneasiness, frequently urged his ministers to take measures for their suppression, and there can be no doubt that the terror which these organisations inspired caused him to waver in his support of the measure, and induced him to yield at several important crises of the struggle.

The press.   The press, as a whole, headed by the *Times*, rendered great assistance to the Reform cause, by keeping alive the

enthusiasm for the bill, by directing public opinion against
its foremost opponents both in and out of parliament, and
terrifying the more timid of them into silence. Many
newspapers which had hitherto supported the Tories now
yielded to the torrent, and joined their opponents, whilst others
ceased to appear. Many new journals and penny sheets came
into existence at this period, and largely contributed to swell
the demand for Reform, to which they owed their existence.
The anti-reformers, on the other hand, started a few papers,
and purchased others. Many of these were edited with
great ability, but their circulation was almost confined to
the small minority whose opinions they represented, and
they had little or no success in their endeavours to stem the
tide of popular feeling which was running so strongly in
favour of the bill.

We have already mentioned the large number of public
meetings that were held, and petitions sent up in favour of
Parliamentary Reform, while the character of the ministerial
measure was yet a secret. These demonstrations became far
more numerous after the provisions of the bill had been
announced, and they now, almost without exception, urged
on the legislature to adopt the measure as it stood as speedily
as possible. On the other hand, meetings of a more private
character, less numerous and less numerously attended, and
petitions with fewer signatures, were diligently got up by the
anti-reformers to counteract, in some degree, the impression
made by those in favour of the bill, and to encourage its parliamentary opponents in their resistance. These proceedings,
however, only served to render yet more strikingly manifest
the generality of the feeling in favour of Reform, and the
numerical weakness of the party by whom they were promoted.
The grounds on which this opposition was based, and the
manner in which the bill was regarded at this time by some
of its ablest and most reasonable opponents, are well stated in

Chap. II. a declaration drawn up soon after its first introduction, and
1831.   signed by several hundred merchants, bankers, and other
influential citizens of London.

" While we should have been far from opposing ourselves
to the adoption of any proposition so recommended of a temperate character, gradual in its operations, consistent with
justice and the ancient usages of this realm, and having for
its object the correction of acknowledged abuses, or any
amelioration in the administration of public affairs, which
might seem to be called for by the changes or necessities
of the times, we feel it impossible to regard in that light
a measure which, by its unprecedented and unnecessary
infringements on the rights and privileges of large and
wealthy bodies of the people, would go far to shake the
foundations of that constitution under which our sovereign
holds his title to the throne, his nobles to their estates, and
ourselves and the rest of our fellow-subjects to the various
possessions and immunities which we enjoy by law; a measure
which, while it professes to enlarge the representation of the
kingdom on the broad basis of property, would in its practical
operation have the effect of closing the principal avenues
through which the moneyed, the funded, the commercial, the
shipping, and the colonial interests, together with all their
connected and dependent interests throughout the country,
or dispersed throughout our vast empire abroad, have hitherto
been represented in the legislature, and would thus, in reality,
exclude the possessors of a very large portion of the national
wealth from all effectual voice and influence in the regulation
of the national affairs."

Public
feeling.

Never, probably, in the whole previous history of this
country, had the public feeling been so strongly and rapidly
excited, as at the moment when the bill was brought before
the House of Commons for a second reading. In every town
of the empire thousands each day were waiting with eagerness

the arrival of the coach which brought down from London
the reports of the parliamentary debates. They were read
with the utmost avidity, every argument was warmly discussed in the streets, and in every public place to which
newspapers came. Men who are accustomed to the calm and
almost careless manner in which the proceedings of parliament are read in the present day, can hardly realize the fiery
excitement with which they were expected and discussed
during the debates on the Reform Bill. And this excitement
became more and more intense as the time approached when
the great trial of strength was to take place between the
supporters and opponents of the bill, on the division at the
second reading, by which the general principle of the bill
would be affirmed or rejected.

On the evening of the 21st of March, the day appointed
for the second reading of the bill, the house was occupied for
a considerable time with the consideration of a complaint
made by Sir R. H. Inglis, against the following paragraph
which had appeared in the *Times* newspaper, and which illustrates the feeling that prevailed on both sides, and the mode
in which the warfare was carried on.

"When, night after night, borough nominees rise to infest
the proceedings of the House of Commons with arguments
to justify their own intrusion into it, and their continuance
there, thus maintaining what lawyers call an adverse possession, in spite of judgment against them, we really feel inclined
to ask why the rightful owners of the house should be longer
insulted by the presence of such unwelcome inmates. It is
beyond question a piece of the broadest and coolest effrontery
in the world, for these hired lackeys of public delinquents,
to stand up as advocates of the disgraceful service they
have embarked in."

After the reading of this paragraph, Sir Robert moved—
"That the paragraph now read by the clerk at the table

is a false and scandalous libel on this house, directly tending to deter members of this house from the discharge of their duty, and calculated to alienate from them the respect and confidence of their fellow subjects."

A long debate ensued, in which the mover and other members complained bitterly of the intimidation to which the opponents of the bill were subjected, especially by the ministerial press. The government admitted that such statements as had just been read were unjustifiable, but argued that in the present state of the public mind, it was not desirable to engage in a contest with the press; they therefore moved the previous question, which was eventually carried.

Second reading.
This matter being thus disposed of, and a short discussion having taken place on the presentation of petitions, Lord J. Russell, without any preliminary observations, moved the second reading of the bill. He was followed by Sir R. Vyvyan, member for the county of Cornwall, who moved that it should be read a second time that day six months, promising at the same time that if his motion should be adopted, he would follow it up by another, which should pledge the house to a bill of a more moderate character. His speech, like many others delivered on the same side of the house throughout the discussions on the bill, related much more to the first French Revolution than to the question of English Parliamentary Reform. One remark, however, which fell from him is worthy of attention, for it bore on a subject respecting which he was a very competent witness. He attributed the cry for.Reform mainly to the denial of the distress under which the country was suffering by the late House of Commons. This amendment was seconded by Mr. Cartwright, and a debate ensued, which was adjourned to the following evening. Both parties were thoroughly wearied with the preliminary skirmishing in which they had been so long engaged, and both were anxious to test their respective strength by a

division. Accordingly, at the conclusion of the second night CHAP. II.
of the debate, the house divided, when the numbers were :— 1831.
March 22.

          For the amendment   301
          For the second reading   302

          Majority in favour of the second reading   1*
     The announcement of these numbers was received with a
perfect storm of cheers from both sides of the house. Nomi-
nally the victory was with the government, and their partisans
felt that they must make the most of their triumph. But
the opposition felt, and justly felt, that the real advantage
was on their side, and that if the principle of the bill was only
affirmed by the balance of one single vote, they would be able
to do what they pleased with it in the committee, and might
very possibly so mutilate it as to compel the ministry to
abandon it altogether. It was true that the government
might resort to a dissolution, but it was known that the king
was averse to this step, and as the parliament had so recently
been elected, it was thought that the ministry would not be
able to overcome an objection which rested on very plausible grounds. At all events, the state of public business,
and especially of the estimates, seemed to render it absolutely
necessary that the sitting should be continued for some time
longer, so that in any case the opposition thought themselves
secure of a considerable interval, and they hoped that before
a dissolution could be effected, the popular excitement in
favour of the measure would abate, and that those portions
of it which they deemed most objectionable, might be

* This result was gained by the defection from the opposition of the Right
Hon. John Calcraft, who had been Paymaster of the Forces in the Wellington administration. In consequence of this one vote he was elected member
for the county of Dorset, instead of for Wareham, which he represented in
this parliament; but he lost the confidence of his former friends without
gaining that of his opponents, sank into a profound melancholy, and committed suicide September 11th of the same year.

removed from it, or that another bill of a less extensive character might be substituted for it. As the Easter vacation was now approaching, the bill was committed for Thursday the 14th of April.

April 12.
Lord J.
Russell's
statement
of pro-
posed
modifica-
tions.
On the 12th of April the house re-assembled, and on the same evening, Lord J. Russell, in reply to a question from Lord Encombe, made the following statement of the modifications which ministers proposed to introduce into their measure.

"I shall be most happy to give my noble friend every information in my power with reference to the returns, and the basis on which they are founded.

"Ministers have endeavoured to procure as correct a return as possible of the population of each city and borough which sends members to parliament. That return was made out at the home office, and as soon as it was obtained, a letter was addressed from the home office to the returning officer of each borough, for the purpose of ascertaining whether the limits of the borough continued the same as they were in taking the population returns in 1821. The sum of the information thus received, which was not altogether very accurate, was laid before the house in a separate paper. The papers to which the noble lord alluded are corrections of the population returns of 1821, so far as had been required, stating merely in the first and second line, the population, sometimes of the borough, and sometimes of the parish. All that was to be found in that book of the population has been made use of. Ministers have selected from the population return everything that regards each particular borough, the more especially, in consequence of the notice which has been taken of the borough of Calne, in order as far as it is possible to come to a just and proper determination, and to place each particular borough on its due footing. Any memorial coming from any particular place, and complaining of inaccuracy

in the existing population returns, will be anxiously attended
to by His Majesty's ministers. There are then, four data on
which we mean to proceed in ascertaining the number of
inhabitants in different boroughs :—1st, the original population returns ; 2nd, the corrected population returns; 3rd,
memorials laid before the Secretary of State, by persons well
known, complaining of inaccuracy in the county returns ; and
4th, the petitions presented to this house on this subject.
Carefully looking to all these documents, we hope that we
shall be able to make an efficient correction with reference to
the places contained in Schedules A and B; so that a fair
and equal course shall be adopted with respect to the different
boroughs concerned. I now beg leave to mention an instance
or two, to show the way in which this will be done, and how
information, which is at present deficient, may be enlarged,
and finally acted on. There is now before the house a petition from the burgesses of Buckingham, showing very clearly
that certain parts of the town of Buckingham are not contained, as they ought to have been, in the population return,
and which, if added to the existing return, would, they believed,
raise the population to 3,000. The whole of this statement
is so particular and so clear, that it contains, in my opinion,
sufficient reason for taking the borough of Buckingham out
of Schedule A. Again, with respect to the borough of Truro,
a memorial has also been presented to the Secretary of State,
which will also be laid before the house, showing in like
manner, that the whole population of the town of Truro is
not fairly represented in the returns of 1821. On the other
side, a memorial has been presented from the town of Guildford, stating that it contains a greater number of inhabitants
than is set forth in the returns ; but, as the inhabitants did
not state what portion of the town had been omitted, unless
some other petition is presented it will be quite impossible to
omit Guildford from Schedule B. I mention this to show to

CHAP. II.   the house on what grounds I mean on Monday next to remove

1831.   from the Schedule any borough which can make out a clear
case.   I thus give notice to such boroughs as can make out a
clear case that their population has been underrated, and that
they contained more than 2,000, or more than 4,000 inhabitants in 1821, in order that they may apply, in proper form, to
the house.   With respect to taking the population in relation
to the borough or parish, ministers think it right to adopt the
same rule with regard to all boroughs, because in many places
it is impossible to distinguish the borough from the parish,
especially where the parish bears the same name as the
borough.

"The whole bill has, during the recess, been maturely
considered by His Majesty's ministers.   Considerable alterations have been made in the wording of the bill, but nothing
has been done to alter the principle of the measure as originally laid down.   With regard to the number of which this
house shall consist, I cannot deny that many persons who
represent themselves as favourable to the bill, object to
having the number of members reduced.   The government,
however, looking to the whole subject with reference to the
advantage of the public interest, and to the prompt and
speedy execution of the public business in this house, are
persuaded that a reduction of members will considerably
assist in attaining those desirable objects.   But, at the same
time, we are not prepared to say that this is a question of
such essential and vital importance, that if the feeling of the
house should be strongly shown in a desire to keep up the
present number, we might not be induced to relax our determination on that point."

April 18   The bill was at length brought into committee on the 18th
of April, when Lord J. Russell stated the alterations which
the government proposed to make in the provisions of the
bill.

1. Five boroughs, viz. Aldborough, Buckingham, Oke- hampton, Malmesbury, and Reigate, to be taken out of Schedule A and added to Schedule B.

2. Eight to be taken out of Schedule B, viz. Chippenham, Leominster, Northallerton, Tamworth, Truro, Morpeth, Westbury, and Wycombe.

These boroughs had established their right to exemption in accordance with the principles laid down in the speech of Lord J. Russell, delivered on the 12th of April.

Eight members to be added to the following counties, having a population of from 100,000 to 150,000 inhabitants:— Bucks, Berks, Cambridge, Dorset, Hereford, Hertford, Oxford, Glamorgan.

Seven members to be added to the following large towns: — Oldham, Bury, Rochdale, Whitby, Wakefield, Salford, Stoke-on-Trent.

The borough of Halifax, which is situated in the parish of the same name, which is of enormous extent, to be restricted to the township, and to return only one member.

The bill provided that the rights of persons who already enjoyed the franchise, should be preserved in places which possessed the right of sending members to parliament. It was now announced, that the same privilege would be extended to their sons on coming of age, provided they were born before the introduction of the bill; and apprentices, having entered into indentures before that time, were to retain their right of voting on taking out their freedom, provided they were resident and were registered under the provisions of the bill.

These changes in the government measure having been General announced to the house by Lord J. Russell, General Gascoyne Gascoyne's rose, and moved that the following instruction should be motion. given to the committee:—"That it is the opinion of this house that the total number of knights, citizens, and

CHAP. II. burgesses returned to parliament for that part of the united
1831.   kingdom called England and Wales, ought not to be dimin-
April 18. ished."

As this motion, though not very important in itself, was
the occasion of a great party struggle, as well as the osten-
sible and immediate cause of the dissolution that followed,
some account of the debate that arose on it seems requisite.
It may be remarked as a significant fact, showing that the
breach between Sir R. Peel and his old friends, produced by
the Catholic Relief Bill, had not even yet been entirely healed,
that the proposer and seconder of this motion were both men
who had strongly opposed that measure.   Events, as we shall
see, afterwards inclined the Tories to restore their allegiance
to their old leader, though a leaven of discontent and suspicion always remained.

General   General Gascoyne, after urging Lord J. Russell to with-
Gascoyne's   draw the bill for the present, said :—" My motion is directed
speech.
against the proposed reduction of the members of this house,
and is not founded on any superstitious attachment to a
particular number, but on an anxiety to prevent the aggran-
disement of the Irish and Scotch at the expense of the English
representation.   The proposed spoliation of the English
representation is indefensible on any ground of justice or
expediency.   It cannot be defended on the ground of the
population of Ireland having increased so much as to warrant
an increase in the relative number of its representatives in
this house.   At the time of the legislative union, the population of Ireland amounted to 4,200,000 persons, and the
taxation to £4,600,000; while the population of England was
10,700,000, and the taxation £27,700,000. At present, Ireland
does not contribute more than one-tenth of the taxes in proportion to its population, as compared with this country : so
that if the population is to be taken as the ground for adding
to the representatives of the country; it ought also to be

made the basis of a more equal taxation. Ireland may obtain
her five additional members, and Scotland hers ; but let it
not be at the expense of the people of England. What would
be the feelings of those countries, if the bill proposed to add to
the English representation at the expense of the representation of Ireland and Scotland ? Are you blind to the unanimity with which the representatives of Ireland and Scotland
resist every plan, emanate from what quarter it may, which
tends to equalize the burdens of the state in all parts of the
united kingdom? In the division on the property tax, on the
assessed taxes, on the spirit duties—in fact on every new
impost whatever—the Irish and Scotch members always vote
in such a way as to throw the weight of the taxes off their
own shoulders on to the people of England; and yet the noble
lord comes forward with a proposition which takes from the
English representation, and adds to that of Scotland and
Ireland. Do you forget that ministers were compelled to
exempt Scotland and Ireland from the operation of the
metallic currency bill, in consequence of the opposition of the
members of those countries? That 83 out of 100 Irish members came to the resolution to oppose ministers altogether if
they persisted in depriving Ireland of her small note currency,
and that they succeeded in their object ? Look how the Irish
members contrive to throw the burden of supporting their
own poor on this country, as indeed they will every other
burden, if the relative superiority of the representation of
this country is destroyed as the bill intends. On the other
hand, consider the dangerous influence which the Irish representation places in the hands of any minister who chooses to
court it at the expense of this country. By conciliating it he
might carry any measure he pleased, no matter how it might
affect the interests of the people of England. If the bill is
altered, so as to transfer the franchise of the boroughs in
Schedule A to places in England, I shall not object to it, but

CHAP. II. if it is retained in its present form, I will offer it every oppo-
1831.   sition in my power."
April 18.
Mr Sadler.   Mr. Sadler, who spoke at great length in seconding the
motion, did not use a single argument bearing directly on the
proposition which he supported. The whole of his speech was
made up of declamation against the bill, and might more
properly have been delivered on the question of the introduction of the bill, or of its second reading.

Lord   Lord Althorp said: "This motion is the first of a series of
Althorp.   motions, by which it is intended to interfere with the progress
of the committee, and which, if agreed to, will be fatal to the
bill, at least so detrimental to it, as to render it impossible
that it should be proceeded with. We have heard a good
deal about the injustice of spoliating England for the sake of
Scotland and Ireland; but the honourable member who introduced that topic might as well have talked of the injustice of
spoliating Cornwall for the sake of the united kingdom. The
honourable member next made an appeal to the feelings of
the English representatives, and endeavoured to persuade
them that their interests and the interest of their constituents
would be endangered by the proposed arrangement. But what
was the fact? Why, the members for Great Britain would be
as five to one, to the members for Ireland, and yet this is
the proportion which the honourable member pretends will
endanger Great Britain. I beg all those who are friendly
to the measure, not to be deceived as to the consequences
of the proposition now submitted to the house. If it is
carried it will effect such damage to the bill, it will be
such a blow to it, that it must be fatal to the success of
the measure. I appeal, therefore, to all who are friendly to
the bill to join in opposing the proposition of the honourable
member.

Mr   Mr. Stanley, referring to the speech of Lord Stormont, in
Stanley.   which it had been argued that the bill in its present shape

would give too great a preponderance to Catholic Ireland,
and contending that the proportion laid down at the Union
should be preserved, spoke as follows :—

"That proportion was not then determined as a matter
that should not be interfered with, and, in fact, the amendment moved by the gallant member for Liverpool does not
go to preserve that relative proportion between the three
countries, for proposing to disturb which some supporters of
this motion have attacked His Majesty's government. For
my part, I am not inclined to attach any great importance to
the strict maintenance of the present relative proportion
between the three countries, and as long as I find large,
wealthy, and populous places unrepresented in any of those
three countries, I care little whether those places are to be
found in England, Scotland, or Ireland. I thank God that this
is now an united empire, and I am for meting out the same
measure with strict impartiality to all. I caution honourable
members who stickle so pertinaciously for the maintenance of
the proportion of members between the three countries, and
who grudge to Ireland any increase of representatives beyond
the number given to her at the period of the Union, to consider well the arguments which they are thus putting into
the hands of those who are contending for a measure which
I conceive would be most mischievous both to England and
Ireland—I mean the repeal of the Union—and who put forward the doctrine that Ireland is not adequately represented
in this house, and is therefore entitled to have a domestic
legislature of her own. Where, I would ask, is the danger of
giving the proposed additional members to Ireland ? Surely
they are not afraid that the half-stifled ashes of religious
dissension will break forth again ? Surely, they are not
afraid that religious feelings and religious prejudices will
be brought into play? Or, if they do entertain such unfounded apprehensions, if they do fear to give any more

members to 'Catholic Ireland,' as it is called, why did they pass the Relief Bill? Why did they grant Catholic Emancipation?"

Referring to the argument, that in proportion as the business of the country augmented, an augmentation was necessary in the number of the representatives in the House of Commons,

"The utter and complete fallacy of such an argument as that," he exclaimed, "is proved by the experience of committees upstairs, where it is found, invariably found, that in proportion to the smallness of their numbers the business they have to do is more expeditiously performed. I maintain that the business of this house would be better done by a smaller number of representatives, who really represented constituents here, than it would be by a larger number of representatives, a great number of whom have no constituents at all. I will appeal to the experience of honourable members whether it is the members for the nomination boroughs who perform the business of the country in this house? With the exception of the great leading questions on which the members of nomination boroughs are made to come down to the house, is it not done by the county members alone?

"It is said that we propose to diminish far too much the proportion, as it already exists, in favour of England. Now, the boroughs which it is proposed to disfranchise, do not in fact form a portion of the real representation of England, they are the property of the first man who chooses to buy them; and the members who are sent to this house from them are subject either to the man who has bought the borough, or of the patron of the borough. It is expected that the disfranchisement of such boroughs will take from England its just proportion of representatives. But what is the fact? That in many instances the boroughs are represented by Scotchmen and Irishmen. The boroughs, therefore, at present can be

employed to incline the balance in favour of Scotland and
Ireland, and if we are to have an united parliament we ought
not to adhere too strictly to the existing scale of proportion
between the representatives of the three kingdoms."

Our account of this debate would be very imperfect if it
did not include some portion of the speech of Mr. O'Connell,
the member for Ireland, as he was sometimes called, and
whose speech, on a question which so greatly affected the
country of which he was regarded as the representative, was
naturally looked for with no ordinary expectation.

"One great objection to the Union is the gross partiality
of the arrangement by which Ireland has only 100 members
to watch over her interests, whilst England, with only twice
its population, has five times the number of representatives.
England, Scotland, and Wales are combined in an attempt to
prevent an addition of members in Ireland. The honourable
member for Liverpool, in calling on the house to retain all the
English members in the house, told them that Irishmen could
get seats for places in England and Scotland. Do those who
say this believe it themselves? There is not an individual in
Ireland who will believe it. I will remind the house of
another thing. No person has pointed out a place in England
fit to have representatives, which place is not in consequence
found on the ministerial list; but, has any one place in Ireland
been so treated? It is always so carried against Ireland. The
Scotch members have, with few exceptions, joined the gallant
general, and not even an Irish member, before I rose, has
advocated Ireland. The Union is a measure, the professed
object of which was to give good government to Ireland. Has
it done so? Is there a country worse governed? It is not
political feeling which has produced its present disorders, but
distress and misery. I want adequate protection for Ireland.
I call on the house to give me that adequate protection which
is to be found in a domestic legislature; and while my tongue

CHAP. II. can utter and my heart throb, I will look for that domestic
1831.   legislation. The gallant general has called reduction of the
April 19. representation a monstrous thing; but look at Ireland, look
at her 300 members reduced to 100. The honourable member said that 'there might be a combination of Irish members
against the interests of England,' and he referred to a recent
instance, but he gave a credit to Irishmen which they did not
deserve. I proposed it, but it was declined. The next charge
of the honourable member was, that Irish members would
resist anything for the improvement of England. What
improvement have they opposed? It is said that Ireland does
not pay the same proportion of taxation as England, but Ireland does pay the same proportion. (A laugh.) I thank you
for that laugh. It shows how ignorant you are of Ireland.
Do those gentlemen who laughed know that the taxes of the
customs are never brought into the Irish treasury? that half
a million for teas is all paid in London? that the duties on
rum and wine are paid in England, and not one farthing from
those taxes finds its way into the Irish treasury. But what
do you say to the sums taken by absentees? Take a single
estate, that of the Marquis of Hertford; he takes £42,000 a
year from Ireland. Is not that taxation? It is said that
taxation is like the moisture absorbed by the solar ray, which
falls in refreshing dews; but, in Ireland there is a scorching
sun but no dew descends again. In Ireland there are thirty-
two counties, and if there was a real union between England
and Ireland, there would be an increase of thirty-two members for Ireland. Only two of the counties have less than
100,000 inhabitants; twenty counties have above 150,000;
twelve have above 200,000; four above 300,000; and one
about 600,000. Why should not Tyrone, with 200,000 inhabitants, be equally represented with Glamorgan? and Down
with 313,000, with Oxford, having only 100,000? Talk not
then of agitation. The honourable members for Liverpool

and Drogheda are the agitators. The first object in this proposition is to raise English prejudices; the next to excite
Irish prejudices. But it is a base calumny to say that the
Catholics of Ireland would prefer a Catholic to a Protestant,
if their merits were equal. Show me any instance of it. I
call on the honourable member for Drogheda, who is the chief
calumniator of Ireland." These words, spoken in a most
excited and passionate manner, naturally produced a loud
cry of order, and the Speaker called upon Mr. O'Connell to
abstain from such observations, remarking at the same time,
that his manner was as objectionable as his language.

Mr. O'Connell continued : " I have not stated half the case
of Ireland, I have not referred to the towns. There are
fourteen towns in Ireland which, if they had been in England,
would have had representatives. I believe, however, that the
bill is for the benefit of England, and no mean rivalry shall
prevent me from supporting it. I call upon the gallant
gentleman to give his motion to the winds, that Ireland may
have some benefit from the measure." This apostrophe called
forth a loud shout of derisive laughter, whereupon Mr.
O'Connell at once resumed his seat, exclaiming in a tone of
great bitterness, " Oh, I am laughed at, I have my answer."

The rest of the speeches were made up of criminations
and recriminations, and of arguments applicable rather to the
general question of Reform than to the particular motion
before the house. It was evidently regarded on both sides
as a party struggle. It was past four o'clock in the morning
when the house divided, when there were—

For General Gascoyne's motion . .   299

Against   291

———

Majority against ministers . . .   8

The effect of this victory of the opposition was to keep
the House of Commons at its existing number, and thus to

CHAP. II. place at the disposal of ministers a larger number of seats for
1831. enfranchisement than they had asked for, and as ministers
according to the principles of the bill would unquestionably
propose to give the additional seats thus gained to populous
towns and counties, the result would be that the popular, or,
as the opposition termed it, the democratic element, would
receive a further reinforcement. To use the language of the
Times, in its remarks on the decision, it gave the reformers
more of a good thing than they wanted. But this circumstance only showed more clearly the determination of the
anti-reformers to offer a thoroughly vexatious opposition to
the progress of the bill, and to avail themselves of every
opportunity for mutilating the measure and defeating its
authors. It was quite evident that the motive which actuated the great majority of them was not a desire to strengthen
the popular element in the house, but a wish to embarrass
the ministry. Therefore, to prolong the struggle would have
been a manifest waste of time and energy, and would only
have served to help the opposition in the game of delay which
they were playing. The ministers had already hinted that an
adverse decision on this question would in all probability lead
to an appeal to the people. It was now resolved that the
appeal should be made as speedily as the state of public
business would allow.

Obstacles   There were, however, two great difficulties to be overcome
to a disso- before this resolution could be carried into effect. In the first
lution. place, the king was adverse to a dissolution, and had distinctly intimated to his ministers, on their accession to office,
that he was not prepared to dissolve the newly-elected parliament, in order to enable them to carry their Reform Bill.
They therefore had no right to claim the consent of the
sovereign to a dissolution, and it was doubtful whether they
could extort his compliance by the threat of a resignation.
In the next place, the supplies had not yet been passed, and

many who were bitterly hostile to the ministerial measure,
though they did not dare to oppose it directly, were willing to
join the avowed opponents of the bill in throwing impediments
in the way of a dissolution. It was probably owing to the
embarrassment produced by these difficulties that ministers,
on the evening which followed their defeat, abstained from
giving any explanation of the course they intended to take.
Nevertheless rumours of an intended dissolution were very rife,
and Mr. Hume, who was generally the chief advocate of retrenchment, and who was, not unnaturally, dissatisfied with
the ministerial financial proposals, declared that he would
withdraw from all opposition to the ordinance estimates that
were then before the house, and would do everything in his
power to facilitate their adoption, in order that a dissolution
might take place without delay.

Meanwhile, great and not altogether groundless complaints
were being made, on account of the language applied by many
of the reforming journals to the queen, the Archbishop of
Canterbury, and many of the opposition peers. At length,
on the 18th of April, the Earl of Limerick brought under the
notice of the House of Lords an article, which had appeared
two days before in the *Times*, and in which, though not mentioned by name, he was evidently alluded to. The writer of
this article spoke of "men or things with human pretensions;
nay, with lofty privileges, who do not blush to treat the mere
proposal of establishing a fund for the relief of the diseased
or helpless Irish with brutal ridicule, or almost impious
scorn. . . . There are members of that house
who surprised nobody by declaring their indifference to
popular odium, especially when they are at such a distance
from Ireland as to ensure the safety of their persons." The
question that the paragraph, from which we have made these
extracts, "is a libel on the house and a breach of its privileges," was put. The Lord Chancellor endeavoured to dissuade

CHAP. II. the house from adopting the motion, urging that such
1831.   courses brought their lordships into painful dilemmas, and
ended in regrets. Notwithstanding this advice the motion
was carried, and Mr. Lawson was ordered to appear at the
April 19. bar of the house on the following day. He did so accordingly,
expressed his regret that the article should have appeared,
explained that, owing to the rapidity with which the
Times was printed, and the multiplicity of articles which
found their way into it, it was almost impossible for him,
using every diligence in his power, to peruse every separate
article that appeared in the paper, and stated that the paragraph complained of had been admitted inadvertently. Being
asked to give the names of the editor and proprietor of the
paper he declined to answer, having been previously informed
by the Chancellor that he was not bound to do so.

When he had withdrawn, Lord Wynford suggested that
a fine of £100 should be imposed on him. This was opposed
by the Lord Chancellor, whose opinion was supported not
only by Lords Grey and Lansdowne, but also by the Duke of
Wellington. Ultimately it was agreed that he should be
committed to the custody of the Usher of the Black Rod, and
should be brought before their lordships on the following
morning.

April 20.   Next day a petition was presented by Lord King, from
Mr. Lawson, in which he expressed his regret at having given
offence to the house, and especially to the Earl of Limerick,
and craved pardon for the same, humbly begging that in consequence of his acknowledgment of his error, and his expression of regret for it, he might be set at liberty. A long
discussion having arisen on the question of the right of the
house to inflict a fine, he was not brought up till the following
day, when, by the direction of the house, he was reprimanded,
and discharged on the payment of the fees.

While this matter was being debated, another question,

of far greater interest to all men in and out of parliament, was Chap. II.
being agitated. Will there be a dissolution ? This was the   1831.
event which, of all others, reformers desired and anti-reformers Question
dreaded and deprecated. The leaders of the opposition knew lution.
that on this question the king was with them, and they hoped
that, if properly backed, he would be firm. If so, either the
ministry and their bill would be got rid of altogether, or a
compromise would be effected which would render the obnoxious measure comparatively harmless. In this hope, the
question of the dissolution was brought before both Houses of
Parliament on the 21st of April.   April 21.

In the upper house, after the presentation of petitions
and discussion on them had ended, the following conversation
took place :—

Lord Wharncliffe : " As allusion has been made by the
noble lord (Farnham) to certain reports that are in circulation on the subject of the dissolution of parliament, I wish to
ask His Majesty's ministers whether there is any truth in the
statement, that they have advised His Majesty to dissolve
Parliament, and that it has been resolved to adopt that
course ? I ask this question, because, if I should receive an
answer in the affirmative, it is my intention speedily to adopt
some measure on the subject."

Lord Grey : " I believe the noble lord's question will be
admitted to be one of a very unusual nature, and I can hardly
bring myself to believe that when he put it he expected an
answer. But, whatever the noble lord's expectation may
have been, I have only to say I must decline answering his
question. As to any measure which he may think it necessary to propose, he will consult his own discretion, and take
whatever course he sees fit. I can offer him no advice
whatever."

Lord Wharncliffe : " My lords, I now give notice that I
shall, to-morrow, move your lordships that an humble address

CHAP. II.   be presented to His Majesty, praying that His Majesty will
1831.   be graciously pleased not to exercise his undoubted preroga-
April 21.   tive of dissolving parliament."

In the lower house, Sir R. Vyvyan asked Lord Althorp,
"whether it is the intention of ministers to proceed with the
Reform Bill, or whether they will advise His Majesty to
dissolve parliament because the House of Commons will not
consent to reduce the number of the English members?"
In the observations with which Sir Richard prefaced this
question, he appealed to the Protestant feeling of the house
and the country, representing the issue on which the appeal
was to be made to the country as being virtually a question
between Popery and Protestantism.

The Chancellor of the Exchequer made the following
reply: "I have no hesitation in saying that ministers, having
considered the necessary consequence of the division of the
house the other evening on the bill, it is not their intention
to proceed further with it. It would not be consistent with
my duty to answer the honourable baronet's second question."

This reply was regarded by the house as an intimation
that a dissolution had been resolved on, and a long and
irregular debate followed, in which the policy and propriety
of that measure were very freely discussed. An adjournment
of the house was moved by Mr. Bankes, on the ground that
several other gentlemen wished to express their opinions on
the subject, but for the real purpose of preventing the consideration of the supplies, and, as it was hoped, an immediate
dissolution. Lord Althorp earnestly resisted the motion,
urging that, if adopted, it would hinder the house from proceeding with the report of the committee of supply on the
ordnance estimates, which had been ordered to be brought
up this evening. This was precisely what the opposition
desired. They thought that if they succeeded they should
at least delay the prorogation of parliament over the following

afternoon, when Lord Wharncliffe's address to the king, praying him to refuse his consent to a dissolution, would be brought forward in the upper house and no doubt carried. It was hoped that the king, thus encouraged, would accept the resignation of ministers rather than allow them to dissolve, or at all events would urge them to avoid the necessity for a dissolution by making such concessions with regard to the Reform Bill as the opposition desired to extort from the government. Moved by these considerations, Mr. Bankes and his friends pressed their motion to a division, and carried it by a majority of twenty-two.

The position of the ministers was now highly critical. The king was hostile, the lords were hostile, the commons were hostile. The old Tory party had by this time discovered the mistake they had committed in assisting to overthrow the Wellington administration, and were ready to give a steady support to their old leaders. The parliament had still six years to run before the legal term of its existence expired, and during that time it was hoped that the duke might rally the Tories, pass a bill giving the representation to a few large towns, and the Whigs and their projects might be got rid of for another twenty years.

Under these circumstances, ministers acted with promptitude and decision. Their defeat had occurred on the morning of the 22nd of April; on the same day summonses were issued, calling a cabinet council at St. James's Palace. So short was the notice, that the ministers were unable to attend, as was customary on such occasions, in their court dresses. At this council it was unanimously resolved that the parliament should be prorogued the same day, with a view to its speedy dissolution, and the royal speech, which had been prepared for the occasion, was considered and adopted. All necessary arrangements having been made, in order to take away from the king all pretext for delay, Earl

(margin notes) Chap. II. 1831. April 21.

Interview of Lords Grey and Brougham with the king.

CHAP. II. Grey and Lord Brougham were deputed to wait on the king,
1831. and communicate to him the advice of the cabinet. From
April 22. what has been already said, the reader will be prepared to
anticipate that this advice was far from palatable. The
unusual haste with which it was proposed to carry out that
measure, naturally increased the king's known objections
to the proposed step, and furnished him with a good excuse
for refusing his assent to it. Earl Grey, the pink and
pattern of loyalty and chivalrous courtesy, shrunk from the
disagreeable errand, and requested his bolder and less courtly
colleague to introduce the subject, begging him at the same
time to manage the susceptibility of the king as much as
possible.

The Chancellor accordingly approached the subject very
carefully, prefacing the disagreeable message with which he
was charged, with a compliment on the king's desire to
promote the welfare of his people. He then proceeded to
communicate the advice of the cabinet, adding, that they
were unanimous in offering it.

"What!" exclaimed the king, "would you have me dis-
miss in this summary manner a parliament which has granted
me so splendid a civil list, and given my queen so liberal an
annuity in case she survives me?"

"No doubt, sire," Lord Brougham replied, "in these
respects they have acted wisely and honourably, but your
Majesty's advisers are all of opinion, that in the present state
of affairs, every hour that this parliament continues to sit is
pregnant with danger to the peace and security of your kingdom, and they humbly beseech your Majesty to go down this
very day and prorogue it. If you do not, they cannot be
answerable for the consequences."

The king was greatly embarrassed, he evidently entertained the strongest objection to the proposed measure, but
he also felt the danger which would result from the resignation

of his ministers at the present crisis. He therefore shifted
his ground, and asked—" Who is to carry the sword of state
and the cap of maintenance ?"

" Sire, knowing the urgency of the crisis and the imminent
peril in which the country at this moment stands, we have
ventured to tell those whose duty it is to perform these and
other similar offices, to hold themselves in readiness."

" But the troops, the life guards, I have given no orders
for them to be called out, and now it is too late."

This was indeed a serious objection, for to call out the
guards was the special prerogative of the monarch himself,
and no minister had any right to order their attendance
without his express command.

" Sire," replied the Chancellor, with some hesitation, " we
must throw ourselves on your indulgence. Deeply feeling
the gravity of the crisis, and knowing your love for your
people, we have taken a liberty which nothing but the most
imperious necessity could warrant ; we have ordered out the
troops, and we humbly throw ourselves on your Majesty's
indulgence."

The king's eye flashed and his cheek became crimson.
He was evidently on the point of dismissing the ministry in
an explosion of anger. " Why, my lords," he exclaimed,
" this is treason ! *high* treason, and you, my Lord Chancellor,
ought to know that it is."

" Yes, sire, I do know it, and nothing but the strongest
conviction that your Majesty's crown and the interests of the
nation are at stake, could have induced us to take such a step,
or to tender the advice we are now giving."

This submissive reply had the desired effect, the king
cooled, his prudence and better genius prevailed, and having
once made up his mind to yield, he yielded with a good grace.
He accepted, without any objection, the speech which had
been prepared for him, and which the two ministers had

brought with them, he gave orders respecting the details of the approaching ceremonial, and having completely recovered his habitual serenity and good humour, he dismissed the two lords with a jocose threat of impeachment.

At half-past two o'clock the king entered his state carriage. It was remarked that the guards on this occasion rode wide of it, as if they attended as a matter of state and ceremony, and not as being needed for the king's protection. Persons wishing to make a more open demonstration of their feelings, were allowed to pass between the soldiers and approach the royal carriage. One of these, a rough sailorlike person, pulled off his hat, and waving it round his head, shouted lustily, "turn out the rogues, your Majesty." Notwithstanding the suddenness with which the resolution to dissolve had been taken, the news had already spread through the metropolis, an immense crowd was assembled, and the king was greeted throughout his whole progress with the most enthusiastic shouts. He was exceedingly fond of popularity, and these acclamations helped to reconcile him to the step he had been compelled to take, and to efface the unpleasant impression which the scene which had so recently occurred could not fail to leave behind it.

Scene in the House of Lords.
Meanwhile, another scene of a far more violent kind was taking place in the House of Lords. The Chancellor on leaving the king went down to the house to hear appeals. Having gone through the cause list he retired, in the hope that he should thereby prevent Lord Wharncliffe from bringing forward his motion. But the opposition lords had mustered in great force, and the house was full in all parts. It is usual on the occasion of a prorogation by the sovereign, for the peers to appear in their robes, and most of those present wore theirs, but owing to the precipitation with which the dissolution had been decided on, several peers, especially on the opposition side of the house, were without them. A large

number of peeresses in full dress, and of members of
the House of Commons were also present. And now a
struggle commenced between the two parties into which the
house was divided. The object of the opposition was to press
Lord Wharncliffe's motion before the king's arrival; the supporters of the ministry wished to prevent it from being
passed. The firing of the park guns announced that the
king was already on his way down to the house, and told the
opposition they had no time to lose. On the motion of Lord
Mansfield, the Earl of Shaftesbury presided, in the absence of
the Lord Chancellor.

The Duke of Richmond, in order to baffle the opposition,
moved that the standing order which required their lordships
to take their places should be enforced. The opposition saw
at once that this motion was made for the sake of delay, and
angrily protested against it; whereupon the duke threatened
to call for the enforcement of two other standing orders which
prohibited the use of intemperate and threatening language
in the house. Lord Londonderry, furious with indignation,
broke out into a vehement tirade against the conduct of the
ministry, and thus effectually played the game of his opponents. So violent was the excitement which prevailed at this
time in the house, that the ladies present were terrified,
thinking that the peers would actually come to blows. At
length Lord Londonderry was persuaded to sit down, and Lord
Wharncliffe obtained a hearing. But it was too late to press
his motion, and he contented himself with reading it, in order
that it might be entered on the journals of the house.

At this conjuncture, the Lord Chancellor returned, and
the moment the reading of the address was concluded, he
exclaimed in a vehement and emphatic tone—

" My lords, I have never yet heard it doubted that the
king possessed the prerogative of dissolving parliament at
pleasure, still less have I ever known a doubt to exist on the

subject at a moment when the lower house have thought fit
to refuse the supplies." Scarcely had he uttered these words
when he was summoned to meet the king, who had just
arrived and was in the robing room; he at once quitted the
house, which resounded on all sides with cries of " hear " and
" the king."

This tumult having in some degree subsided, Lord Mansfield addressed the house, regretting the scene which had just
occurred, and condemning the dissolution, which he qualified
as an act by which the ministers were making the sovereign
the instrument of his own destruction.

The king's
speech.
He was interrupted by another storm of violence and
confusion, which was at length appeased by the announcement that the king was at hand. When he entered, the
assembly had recovered its usual calm and decorous tranquillity. The members of the House of Commons having
been summoned to the bar, the king, in a loud and firm
voice, pronounced his speech, which commenced with the
following words :—

" My lords and gentlemen,

" I have come to meet you for the purpose of proroguing
this parliament, with a view to its immediate dissolution.

" I have been induced to resort to this measure for the
purpose of ascertaining the sense of my people, in the way in
which it can be most constitutionally and authentically expressed, on the expediency of making such changes in the
representation as circumstances may appear to require, and
which, founded on the acknowledged principles of the constitution, may tend at once to uphold the just rights and prerogatives of the crown, and to give security to the liberties of
the people."

Scene in
the House
of Com-
mons.
While the House of Lords was agitated in the manner we
have just described, a scene of scarcely less violence was
occurring in the House of Commons. As the approaching

dissolution had become pretty generally known, the house CHAP. II.
was crowded with members at half-past two o'clock, when the 1831.
Speaker, attired in his state robes, took the chair. April 22.

Mr. Hodges rose to present a petition from Hythe, in the
county of Kent, in favour of Parliamentary Reform.

On the question being put that the petition be now read,
Sir R. Vyvyan rose and made a long rambling speech, in
which he asserted that the country was on the eve of a revolution, denounced the Reform Bill, the conduct of ministers,
and especially their resolution to dissolve. At length he
exclaimed, " the question before the house is, whether we
shall be dissolved or not, because we have voted that the
number of the English representatives shall not be reduced."

Sir F. Burdett called him to order.

The Speaker : " The question before the house is the reading of a petition, opened by the honourable member for Kent,
on the subject of Parliamentary Reform. The point of dispute
then comes to this—whether, when the honourable baronet
speaks of the dissolution of parliament, he does not touch on
matters applicable to the question of Parliamentary Reform.
I cannot say it is not applicable to the question."

Mr. Tennyson endeavoured, amidst indescribable uproar,
to address the house, in support of Sir F. Burdett's call to
order.

The Speaker again rose and said : " This is not a question
of order, as to whether an honourable member is to confine
himself to the matter contained within the four corners of a
petition, but whether the general scope and tenor of his
speech has or has not reference to the subject matter of the
petition, that subject matter being Parliamentary Reform."

Mr. Tennyson : " I entirely agree with what has fallen
from the Speaker, who has drawn the line very clearly. But
I will contend, that the course taken by the honourable
baronet is disorderly, and, even though the Speaker should

gainsay it, I will maintain that the honourable baronet is out of order." Here the honourable member was interrupted by tremendous shouts of "chair." "It is, I repeat, most disorderly and most unconstitutional for any honourable member of this house, be he who he may, to discuss before the House of Commons the question whether parliament should be dissolved or not." The cries of "chair" were again repeated in the most tumultuous manner as before.

At length Sir R. Vyvyan was enabled to continue his speech, and was still proceeding in a very excited strain, when the report of the first piece of artillery announced the approach of the king. This report was received by the ministerial party with triumphant cheers and loud laughter, and cries of "the king," "the king." Each successive discharge increased the excitement and enthusiasm that prevailed within the house.

Sir F. Burdett and Sir R. Peel rose at the same moment, but the Speaker decided that the latter had possession of the house. Having given his decision, he further observed:—
"When honourable members called upon me to decide on questions of order, and I have endeavoured to give my opinion impartially, it is not perfectly consistent with the respect due to the chair, to proceed further with the matter."

Sir R. Peel then began to address the house, which was now seething and boiling with excitement; he himself too, for the first and perhaps the only time in his parliamentary life, was carried away by violent passion, which strikingly contrasted with his usual self-possessed and impassive demeanour. An eye-witness of the scene told the author that he had never seen a man in such a passion in his life.

"The rules which the Speaker has laid down, he exclaimed, "are the rules under which this house has hitherto acted, although they may not be the rules that will suit a reformed parliament. I, for one however, can never agree to set at

defiance, as has this day been done, that authority to which
the House of Commons has been accustomed to bow. I do
not, I am happy to say, share the desponding feelings of my
honourable friend the member for Cornwall. I do not desire
the people of England to sit quietly, with their hands before
them, patiently expecting the confiscation of the funds and
the destruction of tithes. I have confidence in the power of
the property and the intelligence of this country, that if they
will unite in support of a just and honest cause I do not
despair of a successful and prosperous issue to their joint
exertions. Is it decent, I ask (said the honourable member,
his excitement rising with each manifestation of triumph
made by his opponents), is it decent that I should be interrupted, as I have been, contrary to order, when I am invading
no rule of the house, and have regularly risen to address it ?
If that is the way in which we are to proceed in future, let
the people of England beware of the consequences. If your
reformed parliament is to be elected, if the bill and the whole
bill is to be passed,—it does appear to me that there will be
established one of the worst despotisms that ever existed.
We shall have a parliament of mob demagogues—not a parliament of wise and prudent men. Such a parliament, and
'the spirit of journalism,' to use a foreign phrase, has brought
happy countries to the brink of destruction. At this moment
society is wholly disorganised in the west of Ireland ; and the
disorganisation, I am grieved to say, is rapidly extending elsewhere. Landed proprietors, well affected to the state and
loyal to the king, anxious to enjoy their property in security,
are leaving their homes to take refuge in towns, and abandoning the country parts as no longer affording a safe residence.
At this critical conjuncture, instead of doing their duty and
calling for measures to vindicate, from the visitation of lawless and sanguinary barbarians, the security of life and the
safety of property, His Majesty's ministers, anxious only to

CHAP. II.
1831.
April 22.

protect themselves, and fearful of the loss of power, are demanding a dissolution of parliament. Alas! I already perceive that the power of the crown has ceased. I feel that it has ceased to be an object of fair ambition with any man of equal and consistent mind to enter into the service of the crown. Ministers have come down here and have called on the sovereign to dissolve parliament, in order to protect themselves. But they have first established the character of having shewn, during their short reign of power, more incapacity, more unfitness for office, more ignorance of their duties, than ever was exhibited by any set of men who have, at any time, been called on to rule the proud destinies of this country. After having assured their predecessors, during the last two years, of having done nothing—of having expended much time in useless debates—not one single measure have they themselves perfected. What have they done in the last six months? They have laid on the table certain bills—the Emigration and the Game Bills, for instance— founded on their so much boasted Liberal principles. And what then? Why there they have left them—"

At this moment the Sergeant-at-Arms knocked at the door of the house, and though Sir Robert continued to speak for some minutes longer in the same excited tone as before, the noise and confusion prevented his remarks from being heard. The Sergeant-at-Arms, summoned the Commons to attend the House of Peers to hear the prorogation of parliament. Thereupon the Speaker, followed by a great number of members, proceeded to the House of Lords, and after his return read the King's Speech to the house, which then broke up. A great number of members, from both sides of the house, shook hands warmly with the Speaker. Let us hope that Mr. Tennyson was one of them. On the following day, parliament was dissolved by proclamation.

Dissolu-
tion of par-
liament.

CHAPTER III.

THE dissolution of the parliament was a signal for general rejoicing. It was celebrated by illuminations throughout the country, which took place as soon as the preparations could be conveniently made for them. In London, the Lord Mayor finding that he could not prevent the demonstration, wisely put himself at the head of it, and issued a notice regulating the manner in which it was to be carried out. Some evil-disposed person caused another notice to be printed and posted, purporting to emanate from the chief magistrate, in which it was stated that the protection of the police would not be afforded to those who refused to illuminate. Fortunately, however, little or no mischief resulted from this forgery. Almost every house in the city was lighted up, and in the few exceptions that occurred, little damage was done by the mob. At the West end, however, the houses of several leading anti-reformers, who naturally refused to illuminate, were attacked, and their windows demolished. The chief sufferers on this occasion were the Duke of Wellington and Mr. Baring.

And now the election struggle commenced. The last that took place under the old system, which allowed the poll to be kept open for fourteen days, during the whole or a part of which drunkenness, rioting, bribery, and every kind of excess prevailed. On this occasion, the cry of "the bill, the whole bill, and nothing but the bill," rang from one extremity of the country to the other. The one question put to all candidates was, "will you support or oppose this bill?" The nation was now thoroughly roused, and there could be no doubt in the

CHAP. III.   mind of any impartial person, that nine-tenths of the popu-
1831.   lation were zealously and enthusiastically in favour of the
measure, and firmly resolved to put forth every effort to
secure its success. But the other tenth, composed as we
have seen, of the great majority of the educated and moneyed
classes, and of those under their influence, were determined,
partly through interest, partly through panic fear, to strain
every nerve in order to defeat it. By each party large sums
of money were subscribed to defray the enormous expense of
the contests. Bribery and improper influence were resorted to
on both sides, but chiefly on that which had most to spend
and most to lose by the proposed measure. On the other
side, popular violence and intimidation was too often employed,
and a society—called the Parliamentary Candidate Society—
interfered everywhere, by recommending candidates supposed
to be favourable to the bill, and denouncing others who were
believed to be opposed to it. The boroughs destined to be
disfranchised by the bill, or rather their proprietors, naturally,
with a few honourable exceptions, returned men resolved to
defend their franchises. But in the great towns, and in all
places in which the election really rested with any large portion
of the inhabitants, the public opinion in favour of the bill
made itself felt. General Gascoyne, after having represented
Liverpool for more than thirty years, could hardly muster the
third part of the numbers polled by his reforming opponent.
Michael Saddler, who seconded his motion, was driven from
Newark, in spite of the hitherto irresistible influence of the
Duke of Newcastle, strongly exerted in his favour. Sir R.
Vyvyan was rejected at Cornwall. Sir E. Knatchbull did not
even venture to contest Kent.* Mr. Ward retired from the

---

* It may be mentioned as illustrative of the popular spirit that a large
number of East Kentish reformers had arranged to march to Maidstone,
where the poll for the county was then taken, and to bivouac in a barn on
the road in order to save all expense to their candidate.

representation of London, which sent four reformers. All Sir
R. Wilson's professions of Radicalism, all his promises of a
general support to the bill, could not cover the sin of having
supported General Gascoyne's motion, and Southwark rejected
him in favour of Mr. Brougham, the Chancellor's brother. Sir
W. Heathcote and Mr. Fleming were beaten in Hampshire.
Mr. Duncombe, Sir T. D. Acland, and Mr. Bankes were driven
from Yorkshire, Devonshire, and Dorsetshire; Sir Edward
Sugden was defeated at Weymouth. Newport rejected Mr.
Twiss, and Malton refused Sir J. Scarlett. Sir J. R. Reid,
though backed by all the influence of the Duke of Wellington,
the Warden of the Cinque Ports, was obliged to yield at Dover,
which had hitherto been regarded as the nomination borough
of the Lord Warden. Mr. Sturges Bourne, a personage of no
small account in those days, ceased to represent Milbourne
Port. Viscounts Ingestre and Grimstone lost their seats. In
a word, in England alone upwards of one hundred of those
who voted against ministers on the two great divisions on the
Reform Bill, ceased to sit in the House of Commons, and in
almost every case made way for thorough-going supporters of
"the bill, the whole bill, and nothing but the bill." On the
other hand, the anti-reformers obtained a few triumphs, to
console them in some degree for these numerous defeats. The
University of Cambridge, chiefly through the votes of the
county clergy, substituted Messrs. Goulburn and Yates for
Lord Palmerston and Mr. Cavendish. Harwich, mindful of past
favours, in spite of the influence of the government, again
returned Messrs. Herries and Dawson. Lymington sent Mr.
Mackinnon. But wherever there was a large and popular constituency, the reformer was in almost every case returned. Of
the eighty-two county members for England, all, with the
exception of about half a dozen representatives of some of the
smallest, were pledged to the bill. Devonshire sent Lord J.
Russell and Lord Ebrington; Lancashire, Mr. Stanley;

CHAP. III. Middlesex, Messrs. Hume and Byng; Cumberland, Sir J.
1831.   Graham. In Ireland and Scotland, the elections were in the
counties and open boroughs equally favourable to the cause of
Reform. In the latter country, the Reform cause was disgraced
by the ruffianly violence of some of its partizans. In Lanark,
the Tory candidate was assailed and pelted in a church in
which the election was carried on. At Dumbarton, Lord M.
W. Graham was besieged in the Town Hall, pelted and hunted
by the indignant populace. He escaped into a house, in which
he hid himself from the search of his pursuers under a heap of
bed clothes, and finally made his way with great difficulty, and
not without injury to the Royal Sovereign steamer, which was
lying-to for him in the offing, and in which several of his supporters, who had been exposed to similar treatment, had already
taken refuge. At Ayr, Colonel Blair and several of his leading
supporters were severely wounded, and their lives saved only
by the timely arrival of the military; they too escaped with
great difficulty into the Largs steamer, and were pursued by
the infuriated mob to several places at which she was expected to touch. Had he fallen into their hands there can
be no doubt that his life would have been sacrificed.

Great was the change in the personnel of the house when
the new parliament met. Never, perhaps, had any election
worked so complete a transformation. The reformers were now
an overwhelming majority. The survivors of the great party
which had carried General Gascoyne's motion, came back a
beaten and dispirited minority, but, nevertheless, resolved to
endeavour to modify, if not defeat, a measure which they
expected to overthrow the institutions of the country, and
effect their own political annihilation.

Re-elec-   The first act of the House of Commons was to re-elect
tion of the Mr. Manners Sutton as Speaker; although it was well known
Speaker.   that his opinions were at variance with those of the majority,
especially on the great question which was destined for some

time to come to occupy their attention, as well as that of the
whole country. It was thought desirable that an experienced
president should occupy the chair of a house which contained
so many inexperienced members. He was proposed by Mr.
C. Wynn, who had been his competitor for the office some
fourteen years before, and was seconded by Sir M. W. Ridley,
the gentleman who at that period seconded the nomination of
Mr. Wynn. In the new parliament, Lord J. Russell and Mr.
Stanley appeared as members of the cabinet.

On Tuesday, June 21st, the parliament was solemnly
opened by the king in person. The intervening days had
been spent in swearing in the members and going through
other customary preliminaries. The king went down to the
House of Lords in the usual state. He was received with the
wildest enthusiasm, not only by the populace who attended
in immense numbers along the line of procession to the two
houses, but also within the walls of parliament, by a well
dressed and fashionable crowd which thronged the painted
chambers and the lobbies through which His Majesty passed
on his way to the robing room, and thence to the House of
Lords. The speech which he delivered on this occasion, contained the following reference to the great question which
engrossed the public attention:—"My lords and gentlemen,—
I have availed myself of the earliest opportunity of resorting
to your advice and assistance after the dissolution of parliament. Having had recourse to that measure for the purpose
of ascertaining the sense of my people on the expediency of
a Reform in the representation, I have now to recommend
that question to your earliest and most attentive consideration,
confident that in any measure which you may propose for its
adjustment you will carefully adhere to the acknowledged
principles of the constitution by which the prerogatives of the
crown, the authority of both houses of parliament, and the
rights and liberties of the subject are equally secured."

CHAP. III.   The answer to the address was couched in terms calculated
  1831.   to disarm opposition, and was agreed to in both houses without
any amendment having been proposed, but not without a good
deal of desultory and unimportant discussion, of which the
mischief done at the illuminations and the words which fell
from the Chancellor during the scene in the House of Lords
were the chief topics.

June 24.   On the 24th of July, a second bill for the Reform of
Re-intro-   Parliament was introduced by Lord J. Russell. His bearing
duction of
the Reform and manner on this occasion were very different from what
Bill.   they had been when he introduced the first bill. Then he
evidently felt that he was addressing an assembly filled with
hollow supporters or determined opponents of the measure he
was bringing before it. His tone, therefore, was deprecatory,
almost suppliant. It was equally evident on the present
occasion that he saw that the game was now in his hands,—
that he felt certain not only of the House of Commons,
but—what was more—of the nation. His bearing betokened
the confidence which this feeling inspired, and when he turned
to his opponents he spoke to them in tones of warning and
almost of menace. "I now rise," he said, "for the purpose of
proposing, in the name of the government, a measure of Reform
which, in their opinion, is calculated to maintain unimpaired
the prerogatives of the crown, the authority of both houses of
parliament, and the rights and liberties of the people. In
rising to make this motion, I cannot but ask—recollecting
what took place in the last parliament—that I may have the
benefit of a patient attention while I attempt to explain the
principles of the measure which ministers have thought it
expedient to propose. I trust now gentlemen will favour me
so far as not to repeat those gestures and those convulsions,
and that demeanour, from which it would seem they thought
the measure was not to be seriously entertained for a moment,
but that it was to be scouted out of the house by jeers, and

taunts, and ridicule. Whatever may be the reception of the
measure, hon. gentlemen may be assured that government
will not yield—as those gentlemen most strongly feel that
government has not yielded nor abated—one iota in consequence of the opposition that has been raised against them.
Neither the taunts nor the jeers which marked the first
reception of the measure, nor the misrepresentations and the
libels by which it had been sought to disfigure it, nor the
firm, and able, and manly opposition which men of talent and
honour had thought it their duty to give it, nor those more
dangerous weapons—those unwarrantable and slanderous
imputations that the sovereign had an opinion on it different
from his constitutional advisers;—none of these obstacles
have prevented the sovereign, the ministers, and the people
from steadily pursuing an object which they considered ought
to be dear at once to all those who loved the ancient ways of
the constitution, and to all those who are sincerely attached to
the liberties of the people. Of that sovereign and of those
ministers it does not become me to speak, but I cannot proceed
further in the discharge of the duty which at present devolves
on me without saying how much I admire the conduct of the
people,—how worthy of all praise and glory the conduct of
the people has been, and I say this without any reference to
the merits of the measure, which measure, it is quite certain,
has been sealed with the approbation of the nation. But, I
repeat, I say this without reference to the merits of the
measure; for let the measure be as bad as the most bitter
enemy of it has represented it to be, still I must say that the
sacrifices which have been made, and the devotedness which
has been manifested even by the humbler classes of the people
in pursuance of what they believed to be their duty to their
country—these are facts of which Englishmen will have reason
to be proud to the latest generation. It has been said that the
late elections were governed not by reason but by passion."

At these words, which expressed the sentiments of many of the anti-reformers in the house, a loud assenting cheer was raised by the opposition, and was replied to by a still louder cheer from the ministerial side. "That the electors," continued the noble lord, as soon as the tumult had subsided, and looking the opposition directly in the face, "that the electors have been moved by passion I will not deny." At these words another loud cry went forth from the opposition. "Yes," continued the speaker, "love to one's country is a passion, and by that love the electors have indisputably been moved. This love—this passion—has kindled in them that noble degree of enthusiasm which makes men forget their own petty interests, and nothing but such a passion would induce men who could earn by their industry but a few shillings a week to refuse the bribes that were within their reach—to withstand the temptations that were thrown in their way, and to give up the prospect for themselves and their children of continuing to enjoy a valuable privilege. And for what have men done this? Why, for the sake of a measure which was not for their own personal benefit and advantage, but which I believe will be for the future benefit and advantage of the millions of these kingdoms."

This manly preamble was very favourably received by the house, and was followed by a defence and explanation of the bill delivered in the same firm tone, and loudly cheered throughout its delivery. Coming to some objections which had been urged against the bill in many parts of the country and in various writings, during the interval between the dissolution of the late parliament and the assembling of the present one, he said :—

"The first and most general objection is, that the plan is far too extensive ; the only answer I can make is, that it was on the conviction that it was the only plan which would satisfy the expectations of the people, that His Majesty's

ministers have proposed it. I think it but fair to state that Chap. III.
neither Lord Grey, nor the Lord Chancellor, nor any other 1831.
member of the cabinet, who formerly advocated Reform, June 24.
have ever expressed themselves in favour of a Reform so
extensive as this. And, in proposing what they do, they afford
a proof of the conviction in their minds that it is absolutely
necessary to introduce so extensive a measure, in order to
satisfy the just expectations of the people, and to lay the
foundation of a Reform of this house, which will secure the
permanent stability of the throne, and preserve the authority
of both houses of parliament. I may have said at other
times, that taking a member from each of these boroughs and
giving them to large towns would satisfy the people, but I am
now well convinced, that if a plan less extensive than the
present were proposed, it would not be like the present,
calculated to be permanent and lasting."

After considering some other objections, of less importance, and announcing some modifications, he proposed to
introduce into the details of the measure, particularly the
addition of the boroughs of Downton and St. Germains to
the list of those which were to be disfranchised, he concluded
his speech amidst loud applause from all sides of the house.

After a short conversation, in which Sir R. Peel, as leader
of the opposition, took the principal share, it was agreed that
the second reading of the bill which ministers had proposed
to bring forward on the following Thursday, should be deferred
to Monday week, on the understanding that the bill should
be read a first time without a division, in order to allow time
for the consideration of the Scotch and Irish Reform Bills,
without which Sir R. Peel urged that it was impossible to
discuss the English Reform Bill. The motion for leave to
bring in the bill was adopted without a division, there being
a loud chorus of "ayes" and only one solitary "no."

During the interval which elapsed between the first and

CHAP. III.   second readings of the bill, the attention of reformers—both
1831.   in the house and out of doors—was being directed to a clause
in the new bill which enacted that £10 householders should
have votes only in case they paid their rents half-yearly, so
that those who paid them quarterly would not acquire the
franchise.   On the part of the ministry it was explained that
this provision was introduced to secure a *bonâ fide* yearly
tenancy, and a promise was given that the clause should be
amended in committee in such a way as to remove the objec-
July 4.   tions which were entertained to it.   On the 4th of July the
Second   question of the second reading was brought forward.   Not-
reading.   withstanding the thoroughness with which the whole question
had been discussed, the interest taken in it by the members
of the house, as evidenced by their attendance, had by no
means diminished.   Members had come down to the house
at seven in the morning, while it was being swept, and had
affixed to the seats they wished to secure cards bearing their
own names or those of their friends.   Mr. Hume, coming
down to the house at ten in the morning, the hour to which
it had been adjourned, found some two or three hundred seats
already ticketed, and among the rest that which he usually
occupied.   Thereupon he complained to the Speaker, who could
only recommend "a spirit of general courtesy and accommodation on the part of the members."   This debate, deeply
interesting as it was to the excited hearers and readers of the
time when it occurred, is totally devoid of interest to the
readers of the present day.   Indeed every argument that
could be urged on either side of the great question had
already been advanced.   The debate was carried on through
three nights, until about five o'clock on the morning of
Thursday, the 7th of July, when a division took place, which
strikingly exhibited the change which had taken place in the
composition of the house and the gain to the ministerial
party, for the majority of one was now changed into a majority

of 136; the numbers being for the second reading 367, against Chap. III.
231—thus shewing a ministerial gain of 135. It was 1831. July 7.
remarked that the minority which voted against the measure
equalled in numbers, as nearly as possible, the members
returned by the boroughs which the bill proposed to disfranchise. A correspondent of the *Times*, under the signa-
ture of " Radical," went through the whole list of the minority,
endeavouring to show that, whatever might be the motives
of their opposition to the bill, every one of them had a direct
personal interest to serve in opposing it.

There was small rest that morning for Mr. Attorney- Prosecu-
General; his colleagues were all going homewards to their tion of Cobbett.
comfortable beds on the dawning daylight of that 7th of
July, but he had to make his appearance at an early hour of
the same morning at the Guildhall, in order to prefer an
indictment against the notorious William Cobbett, charging
him with publishing, on the 11th of December last, a libel,
with the intent to raise discontent in the minds of the
labourers in husbandry, and to incite them to acts of violence
and to destroy corn, machinery, and other property.

The present generation have nearly forgotten the name of
this extraordinary man, who in the beginning of this century,
and especially during the period which elapsed between the
battle of Waterloo and the introduction of the Reform Bill,
exercised a most powerful influence over the minds of the
working classes of England, especially, in reference to the
question of Reform, which by his writings and his lectures he
had done more than any other man in England to promote,
though the extreme violence of his language had procured
many enemies both to himself and the cause to which he
devoted himself. Born in a very humble position, and originally an unlettered private in the army, he had made himself,
by his own almost unaided efforts, one of the greatest masters
of the English language that any age has produced. His

pure, vigorous, racy, masculine Saxon, while it delighted
the man of taste, was intelligible to the meanest capacity,
and the violence of his language and the extreme character
of his opinions, of which we shall presently have a specimen,
were highly acceptable to the more uneducated portion of his
admirers. He was, moreover, one of the most prolific writers
that ever lived ; a man of untiring energy, a good lover, but a
better hater ; bold, ardent, and uncompromising ! Yet extraordinary as were his abilities, his egotism was still more
remarkable. Like most men of a very ardent temperament,
he was extremely intolerant, and almost unable to believe in
the sincerity of any man whose views and opinions did not
square exactly with his own. He often loaded those from
whom he differed with the most unsparing abuse, and sometimes persons who had been his political associates and the
objects of his warm eulogiums, for some trifling offence or
difference of opinion, were attacked by him with the greatest
asperity. He was remarkably temperate, and abstained from
intoxicating drinks at a time when such abstinence was
almost unknown. His personal appearance was commanding.
He was tall and erect, and the dress of an old English country
gentleman of his day, which he usually wore, set off his person
to great advantage. His speech, like his writings, was plain,
forcible, and emphatic. Such was the man whom the government determined to prosecute. They were anxious to show
that while they defied the violence of those who would not go
far enough, they would also do their best to repress the violence of those who went too far, and to prove that while resolved
to effect needful reforms, they would do more for the maintenance of public order than the feeble administrations which
had preceded them. These motives would probably not have
induced them to embark in this unpolitic proceeding if they
had not been urged to it by the king, who was much alarmed
at the language and influence of Cobbett.

Cobbett, by means of his weekly "Register," had given
notice of the day of trial, and when he entered the court the
gallery, which is open to the public, was already crowded,
chiefly by his admirers. On his entrance he was greeted by
clapping of hands which was followed by three loud rounds
of cheering. These tokens of sympathy he acknowledged
with evident satisfaction, and, addressing himself to his
supporters, he exclaimed : "If truth prevails we shall beat
them."

The article for which he was indicted was one that had
appeared in his "Political Register." It was preceded by
the following quotation from a paper published by him on
the 20th of October, 1815 :—"At last it will come to be a
question of actual starvation or fighting for food, and when
it comes to that point I know that Englishmen will never lie
down and die by hundreds by the way side."

The first paragraph in this article which was insisted on
as being seditious was the following :—

"In the meanwhile, however, the parsons are reducing
their tithes with a tolerable degree of alacrity! It seems to
come from them like drops of blood from the heart, but it
comes and must all come now, or England will never again
know even the appearance of peace. 'Out of evil comes good.'
We are not, indeed, on that mere maxim, 'to do evil that good
may come from it.' But without entering at present into the
motives of the working people, it is unquestionable that their
acts have produced good, and great good too. They have
been always told, and they are told now, and by the very
parson I have quoted above, that their acts of violence, and
particularly their burnings, can do them no good, but add to
their wants by destroying the food they would have to eat.
Alas! they know better; they know that one thrashing machine
takes wages from ten men ; and they also know that they
should have none of this food, and that potatoes and salt do

not burn ! Therefore, this argument is not worth a straw.
Besides they see and feel that the good comes, and comes
instantly too.　They see that they get some bread in consequence of the destruction of part of the corn ; and while they
see this, you attempt in vain to persuade them that that
which they do is wrong.　And as to one effect :—that of
making the parsons reduce their tithes, it is hailed as a good
by ninety-nine hundredths, even of men of considerable
property ; while there is not a single man in the country
who does not clearly trace the reduction to the acts of the
labourers, and especially to these fires ; for it is the terror of
these, and not the bodily force, which has prevailed.　To
attempt to persuade either farmers or labourers that the
tithes do not do them any harm is to combat plain common
sense.　They must know, and they do know, that whatever
is received by the parson is just so much taken from them,
except that part which he may lay out for the productive
labour of the parish ; and that is a mere trifle compared with
what he gives to the East and West Indies, to the wine
countries, to the footman, and to other unproductive labourers.
In short the tithe takes away from the agricultural parishes
a tenth part of the gross produce, which, in this present state
of the abuse of the institution, they apply to purposes not
only not beneficial, but generally mischievous to the people
of those parishes."

The following was another of the passages on which the
indictment was founded.　Speaking of the possibility that
some of those who were tried under the special commission
might lose their lives, he said :—" No ; this will not be done.
The course of these ill-used men has been so free from
ferocity, so free from anything like bloody mindedness ! They
have not been cruel even to their most savage and insolent
persecutors.　The most violent thing that they have done to
any person has not amounted to an attempt on the life or

limb of the party; and in no case but in self-defence, except Chap. III.
in the cases of the two hired overseers in Sussex, whom they   1831.
merely trundled out of the carts which those hirelings had   July 7.
had constructed for them to draw like cattle. Had they been
bloody, had they been cruel, then it would have been another
matter; had they burnt people in their beds, which they
might securely have done; had they beaten people wantonly,
which has always been in their power; had they done any of
these things, then there would have been some plea for
severity. But they have been guilty of none of these things;
they have done desperate things, but they were driven to
desperation; all men, except the infamous stock-jobbing race,
say, and loudly say, that their object is just; that they ought
to have that they are striving for; and all men, except that
same hellish crew, say that they had no other means of
obtaining it."

The Attorney-General urged that the tendency of these
passages was to excite the suffering people to a repetition of
their crime. He treated Cobbett with much courtesy, speak-
of him as " one of the greatest masters of the English language
who had ever composed in it."

Cobbett, who was his own advocate, was not disarmed by
the moderation or the compliments of his accuser. Not content with defending himself, he hurled wrath and defiance
against his prosecutors, and especially the Attorney-General.
Indeed, his object seemed rather to be to assail the ministry
than to defend himself, and he appeared to revel in the
opportunity afforded him of pouring out the vials of his
indignation upon them.

" Our present Whig government " he exclaimed, " entertain a vast affection for the liberty of the press. They never
proceed by information ! O, no; and then their Attorney-
General, Sir Thos. Denman, he also has a particular affection
for the liberty of the press. O yes, Denman is an honest

CHAP. III. fellow, and would not, on any account, touch the liberty of
1831. the press. Yet it has so happened, that this Whig govern-
July 7. ment, with their Whig Attorney-General, have carried on
more state prosecutions during the seven months they have
been in office, than their Tory predecessors in seven years.
The Tories—the haughty and insulting Tories—showed their
teeth, to be sure, but they did not venture to bite. Not so
with the Whigs. If they should happen to remain in office a
twelvemonth, all the gaols in the kingdom must be enlarged,
for they will not have room enough to contain the victims of
this Whig government. The government itself and its organs
are the most atrocious of all libellers. Their newspapers libel
right and left—but libel on their own side, and therefore are
allowed to libel with impunity. Look, for instance, at the
abuse which the *Times* is every day pouring on the House of
Commons, not only with the tendency but with the loudly
proclaimed purpose of bringing that branch of the legislature
into utter horror and contempt. Did Sir T. Denman prosecute ? No, no. That was on his side; and instead of
prosecuting when Sir R. Inglis brought the *Times* before the
house, he maintained that the libel was true, and should be
passed over. Not even the judges escaped. Not two months
before, the *Times* put forth that Mr. W. Brougham, a candidate for Southwark, said to the electors, in regard to the
Reform Bill—' Among the devices to defeat the measures of
ministers, a canvass is going on by the judges of the land,
who have degraded themselves and their station.' This was
pretty well, coming from the brother of the Lord Chancellor,
the first judge in the country. Then comes the *Times*, a
paper in close connection with the government, and, after
stating that the dignified neutrality which the judges have
observed, since the last days of Charles, was now at an end,
added, 'these judges expect a reformed parliament to ask
why they should receive £5,500 a year each, these hard

times.' Thus imputing to these learned personages the basest
motives. Next day, comes the *Courier*, the heirloom of all
administrations, saying that 'there has been a total disregard
of decency on the part of the judges ; and that such men were
not fit to preside on trials of a political nature ;' and then
asked, 'What chance has a reformer if tried before one of
these judges ? How is he to expect a fair trial ? We almost
wish that the judges did not hold their office for life.' "

After quoting the *Morning Chronicle*, and a paper called
the *Republican*,* he continued :—

" The Attorney-General has said in parliament that he
thought it better to leave such things to the good sense of
the people. Then why did he not leave my publication to
the good sense of the people ? Is this partial selection to be
endured ? Will the jury allow themselves to be degraded into
the mean tools of such foul play ? The Attorney-General
might recollect the circumstance of a person who is never a
hundred miles distant from Sir T. Denman, comparing the
late king to Nero, and calling the present king ' a royal slan-
derer.' But all these things are nothing, you may publish as
many libels as you choose, but only don't touch the faction.
That is my whole offence. For years I have been labouring
to lop off useless places and pensions, and that touches the
faction. These Whigs, who have been out of office for five
and twenty years—these lank Whigs—lank and merciless as
a hungry wolf, are now filling their purses with the public
money, and I must be crushed ; and to-day, gentlemen, they
will crush me, unless you stand between me and them."

He then went on to read portions of the impugned article,
which were not contained in the indictment, and argued that
the tendency of the article, as a whole, was the reverse of that

---

* Asserted by Mr. Hume in the House of Commons, to have been written
by a Mr. Lorimer, an anti-reformer.

which had been ascribed to it by the Attorney-General. He declared and endeavoured to show, that the only object he had in writing the article in question was to save the lives of the unfortunate men who were condemned to death by the special commission. He said that the Tories had ruled the country with rods, but that the Whigs scourged it with scorpions, and he concluded a very long speech by the following declaration :—

"Whatever may be the verdict of the jury, if I am doomed to spend my last breath in a dungeon, I will pray to God to bless my country ; I will curse the Whigs, and leave my revenge to my children and the labourers of England."

This speech was frequently interrupted by applause from the gallery, and when he sat down he was long and loudly cheered, in spite of the efforts of the officers of the court.

He then proceeded to call his witnesses. The first was Lord Brougham, who was summoned to prove that he had recently requested the publication of a paper by Mr. Cobbett, addressed to the Luddites, dissuading them from breaking machinery, and which it was thought would be useful at the present time, in dissuading the working classes from committing similar outrages. Lord Brougham testified that such was the case, but explained that the paper had not been published, on account of some objectionable expressions it contained, to the removal of which Mr. Cobbett would not consent. Lords Grey, Melbourne, and Durham had also been subpœned, and appeared on the bench. The defendant had called them for the purpose of questioning them with respect to the pardon of a labourer of the name of Goodman, whom he supposed and asserted to have been spared because he attributed his crime of arson to Cobbett's lectures; but Lord Chief-Justice Tenterden, the presiding judge, who throughout the proceedings had treated the defendant with marked courtesy, having decided that the questions were inadmissible,

Mr. Cobbett intimated that he would not detain them, and CHAP. III. they withdrew. Lord Radnor, who had known the defendant thirty years; Sir T. Beever, who had read his works fourteen or fifteen years, and knew him personally; Major Wyth, who had read his works thirty years, and several other persons who had been long acquainted with him, and had been readers of his "Register," deposed that from what they knew of the defendant he was not likely to incite the labourers to destroy the property of farmers and others, but on the contrary to dissuade them from such violences. A letter from Lord Sidney, and some extracts from the defendant's publications, were also read. The jury, not being able to agree in their verdict, after having been locked up for fifteen hours, were discharged. Ten of them were for a conviction, and two for an acquittal.

About this time some papers were laid before parliament which exhibited, in a very striking manner, the injustice and anomalies of the system which the Reform Bill proposed to abolish. From these papers it appeared that the boroughs of Beeralston, Bossiny, and St. Mawe's, each contained only one £10 householder; Dunwich, Bedwin, and Castle Rising two; Aldbrough, three; Ludgershall, four; Bletchingly, five; West Looe and St. Michael's, eight. Of the boroughs in Schedule B, Amersham would have twenty-five; East Grinstead and Okehampton forty-two each; Ashburton, fifty-four.* On the other hand, it was shewn that the large boroughs which were retained would have fewer voters under the proposed than under the old system, and that the constituencies of the new boroughs would not be unmanageably numerous. Thus that of Preston would be reduced from several thousands to 976; Birmingham would have 6,532;

1831.
July 7.

Anomalies of the old system exposed.

---

* It was intended that the boroughs in this schedule should have their constituency made up to at least three hundred by the annexation of adjoining districts.

CHAP. III. Manchester, 12,639; Leeds, 6,683.　Other returns presented
1831.　striking contrasts between the revenues derived from the
disfranchised and enfranchised boroughs.　Thus Beeralston
paid in assessed taxes £3. 9s.; Bramber, £16. 8s. 9d.; Bishop's
Castle, £40. 17s. 1d.; while Marylebone paid £290,376. 3s. 9d.;
Tower Hamlets, £118,546; Finsbury, £205,948; Lambeth,
£108,841; Leeds, £18,800; Manchester, £40,094; Birmingham,
£26,986; Greenwich, £21,341.

July 12.
The night
of divi-
sions.

It was now evident that the only hope for the opposition
was in delay.　Accordingly, when it was moved that the Speaker
do now leave the chair in order to go into committee, Lord
Maitland, the member for Appleby, urged that there was a
mistake in the population return of his borough, and moved
that his constituents be heard in person or by counsel at the
bar of the house.　Lord J. Russell admitted the statement of
the petitioner, that there had been a mistake, but thought
that the present was an improper time to argue the case, and
the house supported his opinion by a majority of 97.　Still
the question—that the Speaker do now leave the chair was
before the house, and this question was met by the opposition
with repeated motions for adjournment, on each of which a
discussion followed and a division took place.　At length
both parties agreed to go into committee *pro forma*, and
the house adjourned at half-past seven o'clock in the
morning to meet again at three o'clock the following day.
When Sir C. Wetherell, who led the opposition on this occasion, came out of the house he found that it was raining
heavily.　By G——, he exclaimed in a tone of vexation to a
friend who accompanied him, if I had known this they should
have had a few more divisions.*

---

* We cannot give a better idea of the history of this extraordinary night
than by the simple official statement of the divisions that occurred during
it:—" Reform of Parliament (England) Bill.—Order for committee read;
petition of the burgesses and others of the borough of Appleby read; motion

Thus the bill had at length got into committee with a CHAP. III.
majority able and determined to carry it through unim- 1831.
paired, but with a minority equally resolved to dispute The bill in committee.
the ground inch by inch, and if not to defeat, at all events
to delay to the very latest possible moment, the passing of
the hated measure. Thus they went on week after week
quibbling, wrangling, speaking against time. Each separate
borough was warmly and unscrupulously defended, sometimes
two or three times over. The speakers eulogised the purity
of its electors, argued that its peculiar franchises formed an
essential part of the British constitution, gave lists of the

made and question put:—' That the said petition be referred to the committee,
and that the petitioners be heard by themselves, their counsel or agents, and
be permitted to produce evidence before the said committee in respect of the
facts stated in the said petition.' The house divided:—ayes, 187; noes, 284.
Motion made and question proposed—'That Mr. Speaker do now leave the
chair.' Debate arising thereupon.

Mercurii, 13° Julii, 1831.

Motion made and question put:—'That the debate be now adjourned till this
day.' The house divided:—ayes, 102; noes, 328. Question again proposed—
'That Mr. Speaker do now leave the chair.' Whereupon motion made and
question put—' That the house do now adjourn.' The house divided:—
ayes, 90; noes, 286. Question again proposed—' That Mr. Speaker do now
leave the chair.' Debate arising thereupon, motion made and question put—
'That the debate be adjourned till Thursday.' The house divided:—ayes,
63; noes, 235. Question again proposed—' That Mr. Speaker do now leave
the chair.' Whereupon motion made and question put—' That the house do
now adjourn.' Motion by leave withdrawn. Question again proposed—
'That Mr. Speaker do now leave the chair.' Debate arising thereupon,
motion made and question put—' That the debate be adjourned to this day.'
The house divided:—ayes, 44; noes, 214. Question again proposed—'That
Mr. Speaker do now leave the chair.' Whereupon motion made and question
put—'That the house do now adjourn.' The house divided:—ayes, 37;
noes, 203. Question again proposed—' That Mr. Speaker do now leave the
chair.' Debate arising thereupon, motion made and question put—' That
the debate be adjourned to Friday.' The house divided:—ayes, 25; noes, 187.
Question again proposed — ' That Mr. Speaker do now leave the chair.'
Whereupon motion made and question put—' That the house do now adjourn.'
The house divided:—ayes, 24; noes, 187. Question—' That Mr. Speaker do
now leave the chair,' put and agreed to. Bill considered in committee;
committee to report progress; to sit again this day."

CHAP. III. eminent men who had represented it, and when all such
1831.   topics were exhausted they rang—over and over again—the
changes on anarchy, revolution, and military despotism; every
sentence and almost every word of the act was subject to
every imaginable criticism. To give an account of debates in
which the work of three weeks was spread over as many
months would be absurd. All that can be attempted is to furnish a general idea of the course which the discussions took,
and to recount, here and there, some incident which illustrates
the state of popular feeling, or which, for some other reason,
seems noteworthy. The house was chiefly occupied on the
July 13. evening of July 13th with the proposal of Mr. Wynn, that the
enfranchising clauses should be considered first, in order that
the number of places to be enfranchised being previously
settled, the house might gain the required number of seats,
and avoid disfranchisement by uniting small boroughs. After
a long debate this proposition was negatived by a majority of
July 14. 118. On the following evening, July 14th, Sir Robert Peel
proposed the omission of the word "each," in the first clause,
which enacted that each of the boroughs enumerated in
Schedule A should cease to return any member or members
to parliament, under the consideration of the house. The
adoption of his motion would have the effect of destroying
the sense of the clause, and thus either getting rid of it
altogether or of necessitating the substitution of a fresh
clause. On this motion a long and desultory debate arose.
It was of course rejected, but a whole evening had been spent
in discussing it, and reformers out of doors saw with apprehension and regret that the majority on this occasion had decreased to ninety-seven—not from the defection of reformers,
but their absence. The tactics of the anti-reformers were
clearly succeeding, and the friends of the bill out of doors
began to manifest great impatience and alarm.
        These feelings found a vent and manifestation in a manner

which illustrates the prevailing spirit. It has been already
mentioned that, on the night of divisions, Lord Maitland,
who represented the borough of Appleby, asserted that it
had been placed in Schedule A through a mistake in the
population returns of 1821, which had been taken as the
basis of the bill, and moved that his constituents should be
heard at the bar of the house against the Reform Bill,
so far as it affected their interests, and in support of the
allegations contained in a petition which they presented.
Among those who spoke and voted in favour of the motion
was Alderman Thompson, member for the city of London,
who was "intimately acquainted" with Appleby, and thought
that its population was sufficiently large to take it out of the
list of the proscribed boroughs. His constituents regarded a
vote with the anti-reformers as an act of treason against the
Reform party. A public meeting of the livery of London—
at that time a much more numerous and important body than
it is now—was called, and he appeared before it. He received
severe rebukes from several speakers, and was distinctly
told that he was sent to parliament to support the bill in all
its parts and stages. After listening very meekly to these
lectures he expressed his contrition, and pleaded that such a
prostration of body and mind had seized him, owing to the
fatigue arising from his close attendance at the House of
Commons, that he had committed an "inadvertence," and in
order to avoid similar mistakes in future he would vote
against every proposed alteration of the bill that was not
sanctioned by the government. The meeting, appeased by
his protestations and promises, administered some further
admonitions, which were received with due submission, and
concluded by passing the following resolution:—"That the
meeting of the livery of London, after a full and complete
inquiry into the vote of Mr. Alderman Thompson relative to
the borough of Appleby, and his explanations of the same,

CHAP. III.
1831.

are of opinion that he acted therein inadvertently, and Mr. Alderman Thompson having renewed his pledge to give entire support to the Reform Bill, this meeting feel themselves called upon to continue their confidence in Mr. Alderman Thompson as one of the representatives of the city of London in parliament." The *Times* and reformers generally thought such a spirit as had been displayed on this occasion highly creditable to the people. Anti-reformers, as the reader will easily conceive, thought much otherwise, and took care that neither the house nor the worthy alderman should soon forget the inadvertence that had been committed, or the manner in which it had been rebuked.

July 15.
Sir A.
Agnew's
motion.

The hero of the evening of July 15th was Sir A. Agnew. His object was the same as Mr. Wynn's—to save the boroughs marked for disfranchisement—but he proposed to effect this object by uniting several of them in the election of representatives. This motion served as the occasion of another long debate, which ended in its rejection by a majority of 111. This evening, however, the committee at length took one forward step, and agreed to the disfranchisement of the borough of Aldeburgh, the first on the list contained in Schedule A.

July 19.
Mr. Mac-
kinnon's
motion.

On the 19th, the next day on which the committee sat, the house was again brought back to a general question, by a motion from Mr. Mackinnon, member for Lymington, and one of the few anti-reformers who, not having a seat in the preceding parliament, had been returned at the last election. He moved that it be an instruction to the committee, that the boroughs inserted in Schedules A and B (that is to say the boroughs that were to be either entirely or partially disfranchised), be considered with regard to their population from the last census, and not from that taken in 1821, as proposed in the bill. As the census would probably not be ready to be laid on the table of the house for some time, it was clear that the adoption of this motion would cause

great delay, and render necessary a reconstruction of some of Chap. III.
the most important clauses of the bill; but it afforded some   1831.
boroughs a prospect of escape from disfranchisement, hence
the motion attracted at the time a good deal of public attention, and not a few reformers were disposed to support it.

"I hope," said Mr. Mackinnon in bringing it forward,
"that I shall not be charged with any unworthy motive, in
making the motion, as neither I nor any relation of mine is
connected with a close borough. The noble lord opposite has
laid it down as a principle, that boroughs with a population
under 4,000 and above 2,000, are to have one member; and
those with a population above 4,000, are to have two members. If that principle were acted on, and the census of the
present year taken as a criterion of the population of boroughs,
I believe that the result will be that six or eight boroughs
will be taken out of Schedule A and transferred to Schedule B;
that three or four boroughs now placed in Schedule B will be
taken out; and that one or two boroughs will be transferred
from Schedule B to Schedule A; and that one borough, not
at present in Schedule B, will be placed there. I am aware
of the argument which has been used against taking the
census of 1831 as the criterion of population, namely, that it
might be considered as not impartial. This argument, however, reflects but a poor compliment on those individuals who
are employed to make up the returns. I am sure that if the
noble lord opposes the resolution, the only answer he can
make must be of a similar kind to that which Cardinal
Ximenes, when preparing to overturn the constitution of
Spain, gave to a Spanish nobleman, who inquired by what
means the cardinal intended to effect his object. The cardinal replied, by pointing to a well organised and disciplined
body of troops, and, in like manner, the only argument which
the noble lord opposite can employ against the present motion
will be the majority at his back."

Lord J. Russell : " I think it unnecessary for me to say many words on the subject before the house, because I consider that after the house has consumed four days on the question of going into committee on the Reform Bill, and has already made some progress in the committee, the honourable member is too late with his motion. I conclude, from the various divisions that have taken place, that the house is ready to take the census of 1821. The reason why I think that census ought to be used in preference to the census of 1831 is this :—the house will remember that the Reform measure was brought forward in the beginning of March last, and the latest census the government could make use of was the census of 1821. That document, therefore, is the only sure document with respect to population which we possessed. If the government had chosen to wait for a new census, they might have taken that of 1831 ; but such a course would only have led to an alteration of the time of disfranchisement. I consider that much inconvenience would result from acting on the census of 1831, and the only advantage which the house could gain, would be to see that while some boroughs had increased in population, others had decreased. On the other hand, the census of 1821 was taken without any knowledge that it was to form the test of disfranchisement, and might therefore be considered as an impartial document. But what would be the result if the census of 1831 should be taken as the test ? Those boroughs in which no sort of fraud or mismanagement was practised would suffer; while those in which mismanagement has prevailed, by sweeping a number of persons into them, would be gainers, in consequence of the statement which ministers have published that 2,000 is to be the line of disfranchisement. I therefore think that the house will be of opinion that it will be better to proceed in the manner in which we have already begun."

Mr. Mackinnon's proposition was rejected by a majority

of seventy-five—the smallest majority in favour of any leading provision of the ministerial bill throughout the whole progress of the struggle in the House of Commons—and was subse- quently adopted by ministers themselves, and the measure which became law was based on the census of 1831.

The real business of the committee now fairly began, but did not go forward very rapidly. The whole evening was spent in a second wrangle over the borough of Appleby, which was at length condemned to political extinction by a majority of seventy-four.

On the following evening the progress was somewhat more rapid; twelve boroughs were doomed to parliamentary extinc- tion, notwithstanding all the efforts of the opposition to delay their fate. This rate of proceeding, however, did not by any means satisfy the impatience of reformers out of doors. They were beginning to complain of the forbearance and courtesy with which the opponents of the bill were treated by ministers, and to ask such questions as "Why not (as Mr. Hobhouse has already proposed) meet at ten o'clock in the morning?" "why not force the disfranchisement of nomination boroughs in the lump, instead of strangling the reptiles by the tedious and troublesome process of succession?" To all which questions ministers, heartily weary of the length to which the discussion had already gone, and contemplating with dismay the almost endless floods of talk that lay in prospect before them, lent a not inattentive or unwilling ear. Accordingly, on the 21st of July, the Chancellor of the Exchequer came forward with a plan, of which he had given notice the previous evening, "to enable the house to make a more expeditious progress with the Reform Bill." He proposed that the order for the day for the house resolving itself into a committee on the Reform Bill should precede all public business, and that the house should sit on Saturdays for the reception of petitions.

Sir Robert Peel, alluding to the pressure out of doors

CHAP. III. which had been brought to bear on ministers, exclaimed, with
1831. considerable warmth, "I am satisfied the noble lord would
July 21. have found it much better to depend on his own judgment and
discretion, instead of reading newspapers and obsequiously
adopting their tyrannical suggestions. The noble lord,"
he continued, with increasing warmth as he was encouraged
and excited by the loud applauses of his followers behind
him, "should have treated their proffer of advice with the
same contempt and indifference with which I and others view
the shameful and audacious menaces daily put forth, in order
to deter us from the conscientious performance of our duty.
Hitherto the noble lord has wisely trusted to his own discretion, and the result, I hope, has shown him that there is no
disposition in this house to interfere with the reasonable progress of the Reform Bill, or of any other measure which forms
part of the public business of the nation. We are assembled
in the month of July, and if people imagine that we will
consent to make a new constitution without enquiry or
deliberation, I can assure them they will find themselves
grievously mistaken. I will not sanction any improper or
undue delay; but, when I see that ten out of the sixteen
notices of motion to be considered in the committee, emanate from members who voted for the second reading,
and who it appears thought it necessary that it should under-
go the fullest discussion, I do think it rather hard to impute
factious motives to honourable members on my side of the
house, who have ventured to suggest other matters no less
closely connected with the details of the self-same measure.
I wish the house would consent to the amicable understanding on which they acted last session, to the effect that public
business should regularly commence at four o'clock."

It was eventually agreed that the house should go into
committee on the bill, daily, at five o'clock. Other business
intervened, and it was late on this evening before the Reform

Bill came before the house. However, some progress was
made; Downton, Dunwich, Eye, Fowey, Gatton, and Haselmere
were all disfranchised, and the Speaker at the conclusion of the
sitting announced that, in accordance with what appeared to
be the wish of the house, he would take the chair at three
o'clock, whenever the attendance of members enabled him to
do so. The only earnest contest took place in the case of the
borough of Downton, which had not, in the first instance,
been marked out for disfranchisement, and which had a
population considerably exceeding 2,000, but which had been
placed in Schedule A at the suggestion of the patron, Lord
Radnor, on the ground of the smallness of its constituency,
and of its being a nomination borough. Lord J. Russell,
after stating these circumstances, added, that the borough
might be allowed to retain its right of sending a member
without violation of any principle of the bill, and left it to
the house to decide freely on its fate. Thus encouraged,
Mr. Croker proposed its removal from Schedule A, and, after
considerable discussion, its retention in the clause was decided
by a majority of 30 only; there being 244 for the motion,
and 274 against it.

On the following day, the new arrangement was carried
out. At five o'clock the house went into committee on
the Reform Bill, and continued till about two o'clock, when
it proceeded to the other orders of the day, which were very
speedily disposed of. This first experience of its working
was highly satisfactory to reformers. Eighteen more
boroughs were added to the list of those condemned to disfranchisement. The event of the evening was an elaborate
speech from Mr. Croker, in which he pointed out that the
portion of the kingdom north of the Trent, would gain 110
members at the expense of the southern or agricultural
division. This was no doubt true, but the answer was that
the enormous increase of population which had taken place

in the northern part of the kingdom, and especially in the manufacturing districts, rendered it just and right that they should receive an increase in the number of their representatives which, after all, was far from being commensurate with their increased and still increasing population.

We have seen that eighteen boroughs were dispatched this evening, but reformers outside though glad to see this improvement, desired still greater rapidity. They complained that after a discussion extending over several weeks, the *first* clause had not yet been disposed of, and there were *sixty* more, and the House of Lords after all. The division lists were carefully scanned, and absentees on the reforming side admonished to be at their posts, if they wished to preserve the favour and support of their constituents. On the other hand, the Tories were delighted at these delays. They were beginning to recover hope, and uttered very confident predictions that the bill would never be carried. These vaunts increased the uneasiness and alarm of the reformers, and meetings began to be held in all parts of the country, for the purpose of petitioning the houses to proceed with the measure more rapidly. Coventry took the lead in this movement, and in ten hours, its petition, praying the house to be less dilatory in its proceedings, received 3,400 signatures.

These representations were not altogether ineffectual. On the night of the 26th, the remaining boroughs of Schedule A were disposed of, with the exception of Saltash, which was feebly condemned by the Chancellor of the Exchequer, defended by Lord J. Russell, and saved from disfranchisement by a majority of eighty-one. The borough of St. Germains was less fortunate. In this case the population of the town was considerably below 2,000, but that of the parish to which it belonged was above that number. In the first bill it had been placed in Schedule B; it was now removed into Schedule A, because it was found that there were only thirteen houses

in the town and parish that were assessed at £10 and upwards.
Mr. Ross moved that it should be reinstated in the position
which it had originally occupied; but he and a host of others
who followed on the same side, failed to convince ministers,
and after a long discussion the attempt to preserve its franchise
was negatived by a majority of forty-eight.

At length on the evening of July 27, the committee
reached the second clause of the bill, which enacted that for
the future the boroughs named in Schedule B of the bill
should return one member and no more to serve in parliament.
Sir Robert Peel at once rose, and proposed that the word
two should be substituted for the word *one*. In contending
for this change he developed more fully the argument urged
by Mr. Croker on the 22nd, that the agricultural interest was
very unfairly dealt with by the bill.

"I hold in my hand," he said, "a small map which has
been lately published, entitled, 'A Map; showing the places
in England and Wales sending members to parliament heretofore, with the alterations proposed to be made by the bill
amending the representation.' In this map I will draw a line,
not exactly across the centre of the country, but from the
indenture made in the coast by the Severn to the indenture
made in the opposite coast by the Wash. This line would
divide, with tolerable accuracy, the agricultural from the
manufacturing districts. Taking this line for my guide I
will attempt to prove that the bill will give an immense
preponderance to the northern or manufacturing districts.
I will now show how this bill affects these two great divisions
of the country. Schedule A comprised fifty-six boroughs
returning one hundred and eleven members. How are these
boroughs situated with respect to the districts north and
south of the line? The district north of the line loses only
five boroughs out of the fifty-six. The district to the south
of the line loses fifty-one. The district to the north of the

CHAP. III. line loses ten members, and the district to the south loses
1831.   one hundred and one. So much for Schedule A. I now come
July 27.   to Schedule B, in which forty-one boroughs are included.
Out of these forty-one boroughs, eight are to the north of
the line, and thirty-three to the south. By the combined
operation of Schedules A and B the manufacturing district
loses eighteen members, and the agricultural district loses one
hundred and thirty-four. I now come to the constructive
clauses. Here I find no compensation for the loss which the
destructive clauses occasion to the agricultural division.
Schedule C contains twelve new boroughs, each of which is
to return two members. Every one of these new boroughs,
with the exception of the metropolitan district and the town
of Devonport, is in the northern division. It is clear that
the return of members for the metropolitan districts will be
an injury instead of an advantage to the agricultural interest.
The bill creates twenty-six new boroughs with one member
each; and of these twenty-four are to the north of the line
and two to the south. I had hoped that these two at least
would be of some advantage to the agricultural interest, but
what was my disappointment when, in looking at the clause,
I found that in these instances the privilege of representation was conferred on Cheltenham and Brighton ? The
result of my statement is that the southern division of the
kingdom sustains a loss of one hundred and thirty-four
members, whilst the northern division sustains a loss of only
eighteen. On the other hand the southern district gains
seven members, and the northern district thirty-three. If
the house will accede to my proposition, and give two
members to the boroughs contained in Schedule B, the
agricultural interest will possess its due weight in the
representative system. At all times it is necessary to protect
the agricultural interest from the augmenting influence of
the manufacturing districts. The constituencies of populous

places have greater power of combining than the scattered
constituencies of agricultural districts. The influence of the
press and of clubs is much more powerful amongst the former
than amongst the latter body. I am aware that there are
anomalies in the present system of representation, but they
have existed for centuries. No such excuse can be made for
the anomalies that disfigure the new system. I and others
have argued that the destruction of nomination boroughs
would prevent the introduction of men of talent into the
house ; but I do not mean to deny that men of talent would
find their way into the house under the new system. On
the contrary, I think it will bring into the house men of
tremendously active talent, who will feel too strong a desire
to recommend themselves to their constituents to allow them
to interpose their reason between the deliberations of parliament and—I will not say popular clamour—temporary
popular feeling. I believe that under the system proposed
by government men of great experience in public life, but of
retired habits, would shrink from the election contests which
this bill will produce. Such are the combined considerations
on which I most earnestly entreat the house to pause, and to
inquire whether or no they might not consistently with the
principle of the bill suffer those forty boroughs, which are
included in Schedule B, to retain the right of sending two
members to parliament."

Lord J. Russell followed, and after some preliminary observations, thus replied to Sir Robert's arguments :—

" The right honourable baronet ought to recollect that by
the new system four additional members will be given to
Cornwall, Dorsetshire, and Wiltshire, and to several other
counties in the South and West of England. Cornwall,
which is one of the counties which ministers have thought it
necessary to despoil more than any other, having deprived it
of thirty members, will still be in possession of twelve

members, a very sufficient number, with which it will be better represented than it was when it sent forty-two members. Ministers have been accused of having unduly and unfairly enriched Durham in comparison with Cornwall. Now, how stands the fact? Cornwall contains 257,000 inhabitants, and Durham 205,000. The former returns twelve members, or, including Saltash, 13; the latter will send nine members to parliament, being in fair and exact proportion with the population. I do not mean to assert that all these counties receive exactly all that their wealth and population might demand. But ministers, instead of taking the course which the right honourable baronet recommends, that of carrying their scale more to the south and west—looked rather to the great population of the northern counties. They found that Lancashire contains more than a million of inhabitants, while Dorsetshire had only a population of 140,000. Therefore, Lancashire is allowed nineteen members, while Dorsetshire will send nine, being little more, in the former instance, than two to one. I contend, therefore, that the last charge which ought to be made against ministers is that of neglecting the interests of the southern and western counties, or overlooking the agricultural districts. They wish to give to those vast depots of manufacturing wealth, which during the last thirty years have been constantly increasing, the importance to which they are entitled. The individuals connected with them are in the habit of trading with every quarter of the world; they keep up the relations of this country with every portion of the globe; wherever they go they are admired for their mechanical skill, and envied for their increasing and secure prosperity. And yet, strange to say, they have never found admittance into this house, where they ought to have been assisting in the representation of the people of England, and legislating for a great, mighty, powerful and commercial country. In proceeding as they have done, ministers feel that the representation should not be the representation

of a particular class of men, strongly addicted to a specific set
of opinions. They think that if it were so an impetus and
a velocity might be given to the machine of government
not consistent with the established state of things. Therefore they have stopped their career at a particular point, and
laid down a line beyond which they will not go. There are
forty boroughs in this schedule which will send one member
each to parliament, and there are thirty others that will still
return two members; these latter do not contain any great
body of constituents, but still they will send members to
parliament to represent certain portions of the people who
have as firm a right to be represented as any other body.
We have left the boroughs in this schedule the right of
sending one member to parliament, not from any personal or
partial views, but because we thought it right and just to
stop where we conceived that total disfranchisement is no
longer necessary. The right honourable baronet has argued
that under the new system persons of very retired habits
would not find their way into this house, and he mentioned
Mr. Sturges Bourne in support of his argument. But really
a person must be of very retired habits if he could not
summon sufficient resolution to ask for the suffrages of the
electors. I can see no reason why Mr. Sturges Bourne could not
ask for the suffrages of the voters at Lymington, Chislehurst,
or any other place in Hampshire. I admit that if only such
great counties as Lancashire or Yorkshire were to be represented, then men who might be of great service to this house
would undoubtedly be excluded. But while such places
as I have mentioned exist, gentlemen of retired habits might
easily find their way into the house, and the country would
get rid of the great grievance of nomination boroughs;
the purchase of seats and the general system of bribery will
be done away, and members sent from insignificant and

inconsiderable places would no longer have the opportunity of overpowering and outvoting the real representatives of the people." The amendment was rejected by a majority of 67, there being 115 for, and 182 against it.

Notwithstanding this adverse decision of the house on the general question, the opposition strenuously and at great length defended each separate borough, and after each successive defeat again renewed the hopeless struggle with the same dogged and invincible obstinacy. Aldborough came first. Mr. Duncombe, who denominated it a rotten and stinking borough, proposed that it should be sent back to Schedule A, or in other words, entirely disfranchised. He was eventually persuaded to withdraw his motion, and it retained the place that had been assigned to it in the bill. The borough of Ashburton came next. Its two reforming members, Colonel Torrens and Mr. Poyntz, tried hard to avert its fate, but failed to convince the ministry or the house. An attempt to obtain an enquiry into the amount of the population of Chippenham, on the ground that there was a serious error in the population returns of the census of 1821 for that place, was equally unsuccessful. Eight boroughs, being a fifth part of the whole number designated by the bill for semi-disfranchisement, were disposed of this evening. The following evening six more were disposed of in nine hours. Never were procrastination and delay so systematically organised, or carried to such a pitch of perfection as in these discussions. There was a regular division of labour in the work of obstruction, which was arranged and superintended by a committee, of which Sir R. Peel was the president.* Each borough had its own band of

---

* In justice to Sir R. Peel it should be observed that his opposition was much more candid and less vexatious than that of most of those with whom he was associated.

defenders, whose business was not so much to endeavour to
save it, for of that there was no hope, but to consume time in
advocating its retention. And in order to promote delay, the
leaders of the opposition stood up again and again every
night, repeating the same stale statements and arguments,
and often in almost the same words. The *Spectator* computed the number of speeches which had been delivered in
committee between the 12th and the 27th of July, by some
of the leading anti-reformers, and found that Sugden had
spoken eighteen times, Praed twenty-two times, Pelham
twenty-eight times, Peel forty-eight times, Croker fifty-seven
times, and Wetherell fifty-eight times. It is needless to say
that the greater part of these speeches were inexpressibly
wearisome. Ministers, condemned to sit and listen, and
sometimes obliged to reply, were taunted by their opponents
for not answering their stale arguments, and severely lectured
by their friends out of doors for their mildness, courtesy, and
forbearance. These reproofs were undeserved, for they were
really doing their very best to push the measure forwards, but
they had to do with men who, knowing the advantages which
the forms of parliament afforded for delay, were determined to
profit by them to the very uttermost. We have an instance
of this on July 29th, when more than two hours were spent
in higgling with the opposition for a sitting on the day following (Saturday, July 31). The thermometer at this time
was ranging from 75° to 80°, and eight hours of each evening
were being given to the Reform Bill alone, besides the time
spent in other business. Ministers, as usual, carried their
point on a division; but the hours consumed in this unprofitable discussion nearly counterbalanced the gain. However, on
this evening, the rest of the boroughs in Schedule B were
disposed of according to the intentions of the government,
with the exception of two, Sudbury and Totnes, which were
postponed until the next meeting of the house, which was

CHAP. III. fixed for the 2nd of August—the 1st of that month being the
1831.   day appointed for the solemn opening of London Bridge by
the king in person.

The disfranchising clauses being now disposed of, the
house proceeded to the consideration of the third clause,
giving two members each to certain large towns therein
enumerated, which had hitherto been unrepresented. Even
Manchester, Birmingham, and Leeds did not receive the
right, so long withheld from them, of being represented in the
British Parliament, without a long discussion ; and when the
house adjourned, at a quarter to one o'clock, it had not gone
beyond these three towns.

August 2.   As the amendments proposed by reformers were laid hold
of by the opponents of the bill as occasions for delay, and as
excuses for amendments of their own proposed for the purpose
of obstructing the progress of the bill, a meeting of its
supporters was called on the 2nd of August, by Lord Althorp,
at the Foreign Office, and very numerously attended, for the
purpose of promoting the progress of the measure. At
this meeting, Lord Althorp appealed to the friends of the
administration, to withhold or withdraw motions designed to
effect partial changes in the provisions of the bill, in order to
allow it to pass through the house as speedily as possible.
He added the following warning, which, though addressed to
the absent opponents of the bill, was no doubt also intended
for some of its professed friends, in whose hearing it was
uttered :—" I beg it to be understood, that the enemies of
Reform are miserably mistaken if they hope to defeat the
bill by delay. They may originate discussions from day to
day, and throw obstacles in the way of the bill ; but of this
you may all rest assured—that rather than abandon the bill,
parliament will be kept sitting till next December, or next
December twelvemonths, if necessary."

Lord Milton was the only person present at the meeting

who openly dissented from the suggestions of his leader. He Chap. III.
said that wishing the measure to be final he thought it their 1831.
duty to make it as perfect as possible. The meeting however August 2.
adhered to the opinion of Lord Althorp, and the majority of
those present engaged, as far as lay in their power, to carry
out his sensible suggestions.

The same day a meeting of the livery of London was called
for the same purpose. It was decided that as the progress
recently made with the bill had been more satisfactory, and as
there was danger lest any petition should furnish the opposition
with pretexts for further delay, the matter should not be
proceeded with, but that the liverymen then assembled
should form a committee to promote the passing of the
Reform Bill.

On the night of August 3rd, Greenwich (with which August 3.
Deptford and Woolwich were united), Sheffield, Sunderland,
and Devonport were put on the list of towns to which
two representatives were to be given. The only division
that occurred was in the case of the town of Greenwich, the
enfranchisement of which was resisted by Sir R. Peel,
but sustained after a long debate by a majority of 107.
On the following evening, the progress of the bill, though August 4.
still far enough from being sufficiently rapid to satisfy ardent
reformers, was more satisfactory to them than it had been
hitherto. The opposition began to show signs of weariness,
they saw that their efforts were serving not so much to defer
the dreaded crisis, as to shorten their vacation. Besides
the 12th of August and the 1st of September were approaching, and many a keen sportsman was dismayed at the
prospect of being obliged to pass the shooting season in the
suffocating atmosphere of the House of Commons, instead of
breathing the pure air of his own moors and enjoying his
favourite amusement; and as most of the keenest sportsmen
sat on the opposition side of the house, this consideration was

CHAP. III.
1831.
August 4.

not without its influence on the anti-reform party. Accordingly this evening, to the no small consolation of all true reformers, five electoral districts, sending ten members to parliament, were sanctioned, and the third clause was completed. The fourth clause, giving one member to each of the towns and electoral districts which it contained, was entered on; but the house was prevented from proceeding further with it by the introduction of two preliminary questions, which were raised not by the enemies of the bill but by two of its warmest supporters. The first of these was brought forward by Mr. Littleton, and was intended to give two members to the town of Stoke-upon-Trent, but it was not pressed to a division. The second, which was moved by Lord Milton, proposed to give two members to all the places mentioned in Schedule D, to which the bill proposed to give only one. On this second amendment there was a debate and division, on which ministers triumphed by a majority of 128. One

August 5. more night served to dispose of all the places contained in this schedule, with the exception of Kendal, Walsall, and Whitehaven, which were reserved for future consideration. The principal debate of the evening related to the enfranchisement of Gateshead, which was objected to by Mr. Croker, on the ground that it was a mere suburb of Newcastle. To this objection the promoters of the bill replied that it was separated from Newcastle by the river Tyne, and was also in a different county. They added that the chief reason which induced ministers to propose its enfranchisement was a wish to strengthen the shipping interest, which was at present inadequately represented. A majority of 104 affirmed the ministerial proposition. The government also, in spite of the murmurs and remonstrances of the opposition, carried the adjournment of the house to eleven o'clock on Saturday morning; and at the same time announced that, in order to accelerate the progress of the bill, Saturday would be made

one of the regular business days until it had passed through all CHAP. III.
its stages. At the sitting thus gained, the enfranchisement of 1831.
the three reserved towns was adopted, and it was agreed that August 6.
Weymouth and Melcombe Regis, each of which had hitherto
returned four members to parliament, should for the future
send half that number. On the 9th, the fifth clause, containing August 9.
the electoral districts of England which were to return one
member, and on the 10th the sixth clause, which conferred August 10.
the same privilege on certain Welsh electoral districts, were
carried through the committee.   The union of Cardiff with
Merthyr-Tydvil was resisted, on the ground that the two
boroughs were twenty-five miles apart, but was affirmed by a
majority of forty-one. The seventh and eighth clauses excited
little discussion. The ninth clause, giving two representatives
to each of the three ridings of Yorkshire, was accepted without
a division, and the tenth clause, dividing Lincolnshire into
two districts for electoral purposes, and giving two members to
each of its divisions, was introduced the same evening, but,
after some conversation, its consideration was postponed. This
division of counties into two districts produced a great deal of
dissatisfaction in the reforming camp.   Loud were the complaints of some of the most zealous supporters of the bill. The
Times too, with its tremendous power over the public mind,
declared strongly against this proviso, alleging that it would
give the landed aristocracy an influence in the county elections,
and render the county divisions, to which the bill proposed to
give representatives, little more than nomination boroughs in
the hands of certain large landed proprietors.   The aversion
of reformers to the ministerial proposal was increased by
observing that, while it was opposed by many of the most
earnest of their own party, it was warmly supported by Sir R.
Peel, Mr. Goulburn, and other leading opponents of Reform.
In spite, however, of murmurs of friends, and opposition of
enemies, in spite of the shooting season now fairly arrived,

Chap. III. ministers steadily persevered. At the conclusion of the sitting
1831. of Saturday, August 13th, Lord Althorp explained, at con-
August13. siderable length, some modifications which ministers had
determined to introduce into their bill, either in consequence
of suggestions thrown out in the house, or of information
August16. received from without. On the 16th, another delay arose from
a friendly quarter, the greater part of the evening being
spent in a debate on a motion proposed by Mr. Hume for
giving the colonies a share in the representation. The
motion was rejected, but much precious time was lost in
the discussion, and the only progress made with the bill
this evening was that a member was given to the Isle of
August17. Wight. On the following evening a fresh delay was created
by another reformer, Colonel Davies, who opposed the fif-
teenth clause, on the ground of its being inconsistent with
some not very intelligible amendments which he desired to
introduce into the measure, but which ministers were
unwilling to accept. After a long debate, the clause was
carried by a majority of forty. The debate on the sixteenth
clause, which also came under consideration that evening,
was chiefly remarkable on account of a suggestion gravely
offered by Sir R. Peel, and declined with equal gravity by
Lord Althorp, that the further consideration of the bill
should be deferred for three months. Reformers outside
listened to these proposals in a mood in which derision
struggled for the mastery with indignation.

August18. The night of August 18th was memorable for the first and
last defeat suffered by ministers, in the course of all these
discussions and divisions. This defeat was sustained on an
amendment moved by the Marquis of Chandos on the sixteenth clause, still under the consideration of the house. The
object of the amendment was to give a vote to any farmer
occupying, on his own account, land at a rent of not less than
£50 per annum, without any specific tenure. It was opposed

by Lord Althorp, who contended that tenants-at-will, on whom CHAP. III.
it would have the effect of conferring the franchise, were com- 1831.
pletely dependent on their landlords. Many of the staunchest August18.
friends of the bill however dissented from this view, and announced their intention of supporting the amendment, which
was carried on a division by a majority of eighty-one. Alderman Venables, who voted with Lord Chandos on this occasion,
like Alderman Thompson, was called to account for his conduct
by the livery, and promised them that for the future he
would invariably support His Majesty's ministers. Friday August 19
and Saturday, the 19th and 20th August, were chiefly devoted and 20.
to the discussion of resolutions introduced by Lord Althorp,
for the purpose of adapting the clause under the consideration
of the house to the changes which the success of Lord
Chandos's amendment had made in it, which were adopted,
though not without considerable opposition, chiefly from the
ministerial side.

On the 24th of August, the house had reached that im- August24.
portant part of the bill which conferred the franchise on £10
householders. It was, however, chiefly occupied by amendments, of which reformers were the movers. The first of
these proceeded from Mr. Hunt, and had for its object to give
a vote to every householder, whatever might be the amount
of his rent. After a long debate, this amendment was, on a
division, supported by the single vote of its mover. Another
amendment, proposed by Colonel Davies, which was the first
of a series intended to secure to the boroughs a constituency
within their own limits, without any invasion of the county
constituency, was rejected by a majority of eighty-nine;
whereupon the colonel announced that he would bow to the
opinion of the committee expressed in the division, and would
not bring forward the remaining resolutions of the series of
which he had given notice. Two other amendments, also
emanating from reformers, were rejected that evening. An

Chap. III. amendment was introduced by ministers themselves, in fulfil-
1831.   ment of the promise they had made to remove the objection
August25. which had been raised against that provision, by which it
was required that a £10 householder, in order to be entitled
to a vote, should have paid up his rent, rates, and taxes.
They now proposed, and of course carried, a modification, in
virtue of which the occupant of a £10 house claiming to vote
would not be obliged to show that his rent should be paid;
and that, on the other hand, if he claimed to vote as being
assessed for taxes and rates on a house valued at £10, his
claim should be allowed if he had paid up his rates and taxes.
Mr. Hunt moved that payment of rent should not be required
in any case. He was coughed down, and found only nine
supporters. Mr. Campbell, afterwards Lord Campbell, moved
an amendment, the object of which was to prevent persons
who paid their rent more than four times a year from
acquiring votes. He argued that, if this were permitted, a
single landlord would be able to decide an election by giving
August26. notice to a large number of his tenants. This amendment
was lost by a majority of twenty-eight. Mr. Mackinnon also
moved an amendment, which proposed that the qualification
should be £10, £15, or £20, according as the town contained
under 500, under 1,000, or above 1,000 £10 houses. The
remainder of the twenty-first clause, after having run the
gauntlet of several other unimportant and unsuccessful
amendments, was passed with the changes that ministers
had introduced into it.

August27.   On Saturday, August 27th, Mr. Hume brought forward a
resolution designed to expedite the progress of the bill, but
which, like most other similar attempts, by occupying the
house uselessly, served to increase the evil it was intended
to remedy. After a long debate, in the course of which Lord
Althorp urged some very strong objections against the
proposed plan, it was withdrawn by its mover. The house

then went into the twenty-second clause of the bill, by which Chap. III.
all existing rights of election were preserved to freemen during 1831.
their lives, if they resided within seven miles of the place at
which they possessed votes. All beyond that distance it was
proposed to disfranchise. To this clause an amendment was
moved by Mr. Estcourt, having for its object the preservation
of all existing voting qualifications in places which were to
return members under the bill, provided that the persons to
whom they belonged were resident in or within a certain
distance of the places for which they had votes. This amendment, though strongly supported, was lost, but the clause
was not finally disposed of till the conclusion of the sitting on
Tuesday evening, when it was carried. Thus the house had
at length reached the end of the clauses which related to
what were called the "principles" of the bill. The rest
related to the settlement of boundaries of county divisions
and electoral districts, to the registration of voters, the
taking of the poll, and other matters of detail. These,
of course, were gone through more rapidly, yet even over
these the opposition continued to haggle. However, on
Saturday, the 3rd of September, the committee had made
so much progress that Lord Althorp was able to announce,
much to the satisfaction of members on his own side of the
house, that he hoped and trusted that the bill would have
gone through the committee before the coronation, which
was fixed for the 8th of September.

The progress on the day following that on which this
prediction was delivered was not such as to warrant any very
sanguine hopes of its fulfilment. But on Monday there was
a more rapid advance, eleven clauses being dispatched at that
sitting. On the evening following, the speed was still greater,
and the house passed from the forty-fifth to the sixtieth and
last clause, leaving, however, one or two provisions for further
consideration on the following evening, which, accordingly,

Chap. III. was duly given to them; and thus, at length, the consideration
1831.   of the bill in committee was completed, to the immense
satisfaction of the overwhelming majority of the house and the
country, and we doubt not, also, to the no small relief of the
patient and much enduring reader, who has followed us thus
far. It was now ready for its last reading and final adoption.
Thus the bill had passed through committee before the
coronation, and Lord Althorp's prediction was fulfilled.

The coro-   The coronation was performed as usual, only the cost was
nation.   greatly reduced, and the ceremony shorn of much of its ancient
pomp and time-honoured absurdity. At the banquet, which,
in accordance with the usual custom, followed, the king made
a declaration which served to increase his popularity through
the country, though not with many of those to whom they were
addressed: "I do not agree with those who consider the ceremony of coronation as indispensable, for the contract between
the prince and the people was as binding on my mind before.
No member of the House of Hanover can forget the
conditions on which I hold the crown; and"—added His
Majesty, with an energetic blow on the table—"I am not a
wit more desirous now than before taking the oath to watch
over the liberties and promote the welfare of my people."

Sept. 13.   Although, as we have seen, the Reform Bill had passed
Report of   through the committee, the contest was not ended, nor were
the com-
mittee.   the resources of obstruction and delay entirely exhausted. On
Tuesday, the 13th of September, Lord J. Russell brought up
the report of the committee, and called the attention of the
house to one or two alterations he proposed to make in it.
The consideration of the report occupied the house during the
evenings of Wednesday, Thursday, Friday, and Saturday, with
no other result than that Derbyshire, Carnarvonshire, Ashton-
under-Lyne, and Stroud, in Gloucestershire, with which last
borough Minchinhampton was incorporated, each gained a
member.

At last, on the evening of September 19th, the third reading of the bill came on ; and, in order that every man might be at his post, a call of the house was proposed but not enforced. The consequence was that the attendance was by no means large. After the presentation of petitions, and some other routine business, Lord J. Russell moved that the order of the day be read for the third reading of the Reform Bill. This having been done accordingly, he rose again and said, "I move that the bill be read a third time."

The anti-reformers expected that some discussion on this Third motion would take place, and very few of them were in their reading. places. Sir J. Scarlett, the only leading member of the opposition who happened to be present, attempted to speak against time, in order to give his friends an opportunity of coming up to the division, but he quailed before the vehement shouts of "divide" with which he was met, and after persisting for a few minutes, during which his voice was drowned by the clamour, he gave way, and the house proceeded to the division, when the numbers were :—

For the third reading 113
Against 58

Majority 55

These numbers sufficiently indicate that both sides of the house had been taken by surprise, and no sooner were the doors re-opened after the division, than the members who had been shut out came flocking in. Among them were Sir R. Peel and Sir C. Wetherell, who were received by the exulting majority with peals of derisive laughter, which lasted for some minutes. It was the first time the majority had fairly stolen a march on their opponents, and they were naturally not a little triumphant.

After the discussion of a rider, providing against the con- The bill is tingency of the king's decease before the bill could come into passed.

CHAP. III. operation, and the consideration and adoption of some unim-
1831. portant ministerial amendments, Lord J. Russell once more
Sept. 19. rose, and said :—" Sir, I now move that this bill do pass."
The opposition were not to be taken by surprise this time.
They were now in full force, and so, on the motion thus laconi-
cally proposed, a discussion, extending over the evenings of
the 19th, 20th, and 21st of September, ensued.   At length, at
five o'clock in the morning of the 22nd of September, the
house divided for the last time, when the numbers were :—

> For the question that the bill do now pass   345
> Against   239
>
> ———
>
> Majority   106

What will   Thus at length the bill, on which the House of Commons
the Lords   had been almost continuously engaged for nearly three months
do ?
of extraordinary labour, and unusually protracted sittings, at
last passed.   And now the eyes of all men were turned towards
the upper house. They had long been enquiring and were every
day asking more anxiously as the critical moment approached,
" What will the Lords do ? "   Reformers asked the question,
anti-reformers asked it, ministers asked it.   There could be
no doubt whatever, that if the peers consulted their own
opinions and inclinations, the bill would be flung out by an
overwhelming majority; but it was still fondly hoped, by the
administration and its supporters, that despair of ultimate success and dread of consequences would cause them to respect
the wishes of the majority of the lower house and of the
nation.   In order to secure this result, the friends of the bill
brought every possible influence to bear on the Lords.   The
press alternately soothed and threatened now the spiritual and
now the temporal peers.   Throughout the country, meetings
were being held and resolutions adopted which would, it was
hoped, convince the upper house that the people did not, as
the enemies of the bill industriously asserted, waver in their

attachment to it. At these meetings, which were both
numerous and enthusiastic, petitions were adopted, praying
the Lords, often in very outspoken language, to pass the
measure with all possible dispatch. A few extracts from
these documents will serve to show the state of public feeling
that prevailed throughout the country at this moment, and
they cannot be better introduced than by a quotation from a
requisition, requesting the Lord Mayor of London to call a
public meeting, from a number of eminent bankers, merchants,
and traders of that city :—

"We, the undersigned, request that your lordship will
summon, on the earliest convenient day, a meeting of the
merchants, bankers, and traders of the city of London to petition the House of Lords in favour of the Reform Bill ; to
impress upon their lordships the anxious and undiminished
solicitude with which the mercantile classes of London have
watched the progress of the bill through the Commons, and
to declare anew their heartfelt conviction that the tranquillity and happiness of the country in general, and the security
of commercial as well as other property, are deeply and fearfully interested in the speedy passing of this great national
measure."

The requisition to the churchwardens of St. Andrew's,
Holborn, is still more pointed. It requests that an early
meeting may be convened "to present an address to the
House of Lords imploring it, by the regard it ought to entertain for all the institutions of the country, and not least
amongst the rest that of its own order, at once to pass a
measure which has received the deliberative sanction and
interests of the people ; and, at the same time, freely, but
fearlessly, to point out to it the tremendous results which a
rejection of this bill must necessarily produce." The livery
of London, though their exclusive electoral privileges were
taken from them by the bill, adopted, with only a single

dissentient voice, a petition praying the Lords to pass it as speedily as possible.   In almost every parish of London and Westminster, and in all parts of the empire, meetings were held and petitions carried, assuring the Lords that the feeling in favour of Reform was strengthened rather than diminished, and praying them, by passing the bill, to avert convulsions, which might end in the overthrow of the institutions of the country.   One single sample will suffice to show, not, indeed, the temper of the generality of the petitioners, but the arguments which they employed.   It is taken from the petition adopted by the merchants, bankers, and tradesmen of the city of London, already referred to.

"We have heard," said the petitioners, "with indignation, the false assertion confidently put forth, that the people have become lukewarm or disinclined to the bill.   Fearfully alive to the apprehension that such calumnies might possibly mislead their lordships' judgment, they cannot rest content without impressing on their lordships, in the most solemn and emphatic manner, their unaltered attachment to the bill; their gratitude towards its authors and supporters ; and their impatience for its final consummation.   They beseech their lordships to consider that the demonstrations in favour of the bill have been unanimous throughout the kingdom ; that the enthusiasm on its behalf exhibited at the recent election was unparalleled ; that the majorities by which the House of Commons has pronounced its own Reform have been triumphant and overwhelming ; that the rejection or mutilation of a measure thus unanimously welcomed, and already half-assured, must spread universal disappointment and dismay; and as their daily support depends upon the undisturbed prosecution of their industry, they contemplate with unfeigned alarm the possibility of discontent and exasperation to such a degree as would paralyze commerce, deprive the labouring population of employment, and fatally endanger public credit.

They therefore respectfully but earnestly implore their lord- Chap. III.
ships to avert these perilous consequences." Again, the 1831.
inhabitants of Manchester pray the Lords not to " endanger
the safety of the nation by disappointing the highly raised
and just expectations of the people."

The people, thus up and doing, were not kept long in sus- Sept. 22.
pense.   We have already related that the bill passed the The bill carried up
Commons on the morning of the 22nd of September, and on to the
the evening of the same day it was carried up to the House of House of Lords.
Lords.   The Lord Chancellor took his seat and opened the
business precisely at five o'clock, but though it was well known
that the proceedings of the evening would be only of a formal
character, such was the interest felt in the bill, that long
before that hour there was a very numerous attendance of
peers, and the space before the throne was crowded with the
members of the House of Commons, who had been most active
and determined in their opposition to the measure.   No sooner
had the Chancellor taken his seat on the woolsack, than the
Deputy Usher of the Black Rod appeared at the bar, and
announced a message from the Commons.   The Lords, who
had hitherto been conversing in groups in different parts of
the house, now took their seats, and perfect stillness prevailed,
until the doors by which messages from the House of Commons are received were thrown open, and Lord Althorp and
Lord J. Russell entered, followed by more than a hundred
members, all staunch supporters of the bill.

The Lord Chancellor advanced to the bar, with the usual
formalities, and received the bill from the hands of Lord J.
Russell, who said with a firm voice :—"This, my lord, is a
bill to amend the representation of the people of England
and Wales, which the House of Commons have agreed to,
and to which they desire the concurrence of your lordships."
These words were followed by a loud cry of "hear, hear,"
from the deputation, which was met by a cry of "order" from

some of the peers. The deputation, instead of at once retiring, as is usual on such occasions, retained their position at the bar of the house.

The Lord Chancellor having returned to the woolsack, communicated to their lordships the nature of the message, in the form usually employed on such occasions; but such was felt to be the solemnity of the occasion, and such the deep feeling with which the Chancellor pronounced these words of course, that the formula which usually passes unnoticed was listened to with deep and breathless attention.

Earl Grey was not in the house at the moment when the message was brought up, and, in consequence of his absence, an embarrassing pause ensued. At length he entered, and said:—"My lords, I was not present when the bill for effecting Reform in the representation of the people was brought from the House of Commons, I beg, however, to move—'That the bill be read a first time.' Having made this motion, it will be necessary to fix a day for the second reading of this bill; and in doing this I have no other wish than to consult the convenience of your lordships. I think the second reading of the bill should not be taken sooner than Friday se'nnight nor later than Monday se'nnight. It will perhaps meet the convenience of all parties if I fix the reading for Monday se'nnight."

This proposal having been agreed to, the members of the House of Commons retired.

Sept. 25.
Dinner to Lords Althorp and J. Russell.
The majority of that house celebrated the successful termination of their long labours by a dinner, given on the 25th of September, to Lord Althorp and Lord J. Russell. It was attended not only by almost all of those who gave the dinner, but also by several peers, who had been created on the occasion of the coronation, and who had, of course, been selected on account of their warm support of the bill, as well as by the Lord Mayor and others. Coming, as this banquet

did, at the close of the long and arduous struggle, in which

those who gave it had borne so painful and laborious a part, and while the ultimate fate of the bill was still in suspense, it was an event of more than ordinary significance. We shall not, however, record anything more in reference to it than the words in which Lord J. Russell acknowledged the compliment paid to him when his health, coupled with that of Lord Althorp, was proposed by the president, Sir F. Burdett, and drank by the company with the most enthusiastic acclamations.

"I always felt," he said, "that although duties like those in which we have been engaged naturally invite the exercise of man's best powers, yet that the exertion which is absolutely necessary for the discharge of those duties,—the mere physical exhaustion it produces,—the calumnies with which men, though actuated by the purest motives, are perpetually assailed,—the embarrassments which, from whatever cause, are constantly thrown in the way of the best and most salutary measures,—and the frequent disappointments and reverses that occur when the goal is almost attained ;—I always felt, I say, that however honourable and praiseworthy might be the duty, yet that these obstacles were almost sufficient to deter a man from the prosecution of that duty, and make him shrink from that which he owes it to his country to perform, if he had not the conviction that if he behaved with a good conscience towards his country, and had the good fortune to render any service to his country, would not have to complain of want of approbation from all who are capable of appreciating honest intentions ; but that he would receive from all well-wishers of his country credit—and, perhaps, as I receive now, undue credit—for his exertions in the service of the public. The measure, however, which we have had at length the good fortune to carry through the House of Commons, is one, the object of which is of that noble and

CHAP. III. elevated character, that it was likely to induce much greater
1831.   exertion and determination than any measure of an ordinary
Sept. 25. political nature; for it is not a measure of temporary and
transient benefit, but one which will secure permanently the
liberties of the people,—not a measure which will give triumph
to a party, but one which will place upon a fair and impreg-
nable basis the welfare and happiness of a nation."

Asserted   It must not be supposed that while the reformers were
reaction. thus celebrating their triumph in the House of Commons,
and exerting themselves to obtain a crowning victory in the
House of Lords, that the anti-reformers were idle. They too,
as has already been intimated, had been eagerly asking the
question, "What will the Lords do?" And they were straining
every nerve to secure that the answer given to that question
might be, as they very confidently affirmed it would be,
that they would throw out the bill. Already, Lord Eldon,
whose advanced age and long tenure of the great seal gave
him great influence in the House of Lords, had declared,
amidst the marked applauses of the Duke of Cumberland,
the king's brother, and many other anti-reforming peers, that
they would do their duty; and every one perfectly well knew
what that expression meant in his mouth. In Dublin, in
Nottingham, in Kingsbridge, and many other places, the
anti-reformers were busily engaged in getting up petitions,
which, if not numerously were "respectably" signed, and were
sure to be thankfully and respectfully welcomed by the
majority of the assembly to which they were addressed. At
this momentous crisis, too, Lord Ashley, an anti-reformer,
came forward to contest the representation of the county of
Dorset with Mr. Ponsonby, who was already in the field, and
it was hoped by anti-reformers that his personal popularity
and family influence would win him a triumph, which would
give some colour to the assertions they were industriously
propagating, that the nation was cooling down in its zeal for

Reform, and that a reaction had begun. They were also
making great use of the queen's name, while the reformers
on the other hand were strongly arguing that Lord Howe, her
Chamberlain, and other officers of her household, who were
members of the House of Peers, should be required either to
support the bill or resign their offices.

At length the anxiously expected 3rd of October arrived,
and now the question—"What will the Lords do?" must
receive its answer. After the presentation and discussion of
a large number of petitions, most of them in favour of the
bill, but some of them in òpposition to it, the order of the day
for its second reading was read, and then, amidst deep silence,
Earl Grey advanced to the table to address the house in
support of it. It was a solemn moment—one of the most
solemn that has ever occurred in the history of the British
senate. The eyes of the whole nation—we may almost say
of the whole world—were fixed on the Lords, and they felt it.
And the premier was now standing before them to propose to
an assembly—the majority of which he knew regarded him
with a hostile respect—a measure which he had taken up in
his youth, which he had supported when the struggle for it
seemed hopeless and almost Quixotic, through all the best
years of his long public life, and which he was now at length
enabled to bring forward as the first minister of the crown.
There he stood, with that nobly formed brow which plainly
betokened a meditative mind and a spotless soul, an eye
sparkling with intelligence, and that patrician countenance
and bearing which awed at the same time that it attracted,
and which indicated boldness and firmness associated with
wisdom and prudence. There was a majesty in his manner
that proclaimed the statesman. The solemnity of the moment
was felt by all, but by none more than the earl himself.
The recollections of the past and the responsibilities of the
present rushed into his mind with overpowering force.

He assayed to speak, but his agitation deprived him of utterance, and notwithstanding the sympathetic and encouraging cheers which proceeded from every part of the house he was compelled to resume his seat. After reposing himself for a few moments, he rose again, spoke in a very low tone, which grew louder as he proceeded, until each word became distinctly audible in every corner of the house. Less rhetorical than his great colleague Lord Brougham, he was not less eloquent, and the matter of his speech secured a continuance of that rivetted attention which his demeanour, character, and subject had commanded before he commenced.

"In the course of a long political life, which has extended to half a century, I have had the honour of proposing to this and the other house of parliament, amidst circumstances of much difficulty and danger, in seasons of great political convulsion and violence, many questions affecting the government of the political interests of this country, as well as the government of its domestic concerns. If at such times, speaking as I did in the presence of some of the greatest men that have ever graced this country, I experienced awe and trepidation it was, as your lordships will readily believe, nothing to the emotions which affect me now, when I am about to propose to the consideration of your lordships a question involving the dearest interests of the nation—a question for the consequences of which I am more responsible than any man—a question which has been designated as subversive of the constitution, as revolutionary, as destructive of chartered rights and privileges, and as tending to produce general confusion throughout the empire; but which I solemnly and deliberately feel to contain changes that are necessary, to be a measure of peace and conciliation, and one on the acceptance or rejection of which I believe depends, on the one hand, tranquillity, prosperity, and concord,—on the other, the continuance of a state of political discontentment from which those

feelings must arise which are naturally generated by such a
condition of the public mind. Those members of the house
who have observed the political conduct of so humble an
individual as myself are aware that I have always been the
advocate of Reform. In 1786 I voted for Reform. I supported
Mr. Pitt in his motion for shortening the duration of parliaments. I gave my best assistance to the measure of Reform
introduced by Mr. Flood before the French revolution. On
one or two occasions I originated motions on the subject.
Although I have reverted to these facts in my previous political
career, I do not stand here to advocate the measure of Reform
on the ground that I have never swerved from maintaining
the necessity and expediency of its adoption; I am bound to
entertain the conviction that in proposing a measure, affecting the mighty interests of the state, the course I take is
called for by justice and necessity, and essential to the safety
of the country. Your lordships cannot have forgotten the
agitation which prevailed throughout the country at the
commencement of the last session—the general discontent
that pervaded every part of the empire—society almost disorganised—the distress that reigned in the manufacturing
districts—the influence of the numerous associations that
grew out of that distress—the sufferings of the agricultural
population—the nightly alarms, burnings, and popular disturbances, approaching almost to the very skirts of the
metropolis—the general feeling of doubt and apprehension
observable in every countenance. Noble lords will, no doubt,
recollect these events; but I recollect in addition that there
prevailed a general growing desire for the adoption of some
measure of Parliamentary Reform. If the anxiety to urge
forward that question had ever slept, it was only in appearance
and partially, never really or completely. On the arrival of a
season of difficulty, the question was stirred anew,—a circumstance which, of itself, demonstrated the necessity of having

it speedily settled. But granting that a measure of Parliamentary Reform is necessary, why have ministers gone to the extent of this measure which, in the language of many, is revolutionary in spirit and subversive of the best principles of the British constitution ? I hope to answer this question satisfactorily, and to prove to your lordships that there is nothing in the measure that is not founded on the principles of the British constitution,—nothing that is not perfectly consistent with the ancient practices of that constitution,—and nothing that might not be adopted with perfect safety to the rights and privileges of all orders of the state, and particularly to the rights and privileges of that order to which your lordships belong. Is it possible that the boroughs called nomination boroughs can longer be permitted to exist? When the people see the scenes which disgrace every election,—when they witness the most gross and scandalous corruption practised without disguise,—when the sale of seats in the House of Commons is a matter of equal notoriety with the open return of nominees of noble and wealthy persons to that house,—when the people see these things passing before their eyes as often as a general election takes place,—and when, turning from such sights, they read the lessons of their youth, and consult the writings of the expounders of the laws and constitution, where they find such practices stated to be at once illegal and inconsistent with the people's rights, and where they may discover that the privileges which they see a few individuals converting into a means of personal profit, are privileges which have been conferred for the benefit of the nation ? It is with these views that the government has considered that the boroughs which are called nomination boroughs ought to be abolished. In looking at these boroughs we found that some of them were incapable of correction, for it is impossible to extend their constituency. Some of them consisted only of the sites of ancient boroughs, which, however, might

perhaps in former times have been very fit places to return
members to parliament; in others, the constituency was insig-
nificantly small, and from their local situation incapable of
receiving any increase; so that, upon the whole, this gangrene
of our representative system bade defiance to all remedies but
that of excision." After dwelling at great length on the provisions of the measure, after replying to the objections which
had been urged against it, and after referring to the dangers
which would arise from its rejection, he then proceeded:—

"I especially beg the spiritual portion of your lordships
to pause and reflect. The prelates of the empire have not a
more firm friend than I. But if this bill should be thrown
out by a narrow majority, and the scale should be turned
by their votes, what would be their situation? 'Let them set
their houses in order.'* I have said, and I am not the man to
recall what I have said, that by this measure I am prepared
to stand or fall. The question of my continuance in office
for one hour will depend on the prospect of my being able to
carry through that which I consider so important to the tranquillity, to the safety, and to the happiness of the country. I
must repeat, that no danger which might be attendant on the
rejection of this measure could be obviated by the introduction of one of less efficiency. At all events, if such a measure
is introduced, it will not be by me. I am convinced that the
people will not cease to urge their rights, and if your lordships should reject this bill, it is more than probable that
you will hereafter have to consider a measure in which much
greater concessions will be demanded. Most fervently do I

* This phrase, as we shall see by the sequel, gave great offence to the
prelates. It must be admitted that they had some reason to complain, when
we consider the whole of the passage from which it was quoted. "Set thine
house in order, for thou must die and not live."—2 *Kings*, xx., 1; *Isaiah*
xxxviii., 1. I almost think, judging from Earl Grey's general character,
that he used the expression inadvertently, without remembering the context
Certainly it was not his habit to employ such menaces.

CHAP. III. pray that the Almighty Being will so guide and direct your
1831. lordships' counsels, that your ultimate decision may be for
October 3. the advancement of his glory, the good of his church, the
safety, welfare, and honour of the king and the people."

Lord
Wharn-
cliffe's
speech.
Lord Wharncliffe, one of the most moderate of the opponents of the bill, and who candidly admitted the desirableness
and necessity of a considerable Reform in parliament, followed, and, at the close of a long speech against the bill,
moved that it should be rejected. At a subsequent period
of the evening, finding that the terms of this proposition were
unusual and might be regarded as insulting to the House of
Commons, he desired to substitute for it the customary
formula, that the bill be read a second time this day six
months. Ministers resisted this change, wishing to retain
the advantage which it gave them in debate. However, after
a long discussion, they yielded to the majority, and allowed
the amendment to be couched in the usual terms.

October 4.
Lord Mel-
bourne's
speech.
Lord Melbourne—courteous, candid, sensible, and inof-
fensive—addressed the house on the second day of the
debate. He said that he had opposed Reform as much
as any man. He had opposed the extension of the suffrage
to the great towns of Manchester and Birmingham; but he
had done so because he felt that if that measure were granted,
it must lead to further measures, and his whole speech seemed
to show that he was induced to support the bill rather by the
danger of refusing concession to the demands of the people
than by any love of Reform. In the course of his observations, he said that he could not concur in the censure which
had been passed on the House of Commons, for the time and
consideration they had bestowed on the bill. It was perfectly
impossible that they could have done otherwise, and he did
not think that any time had been needlessly consumed, or
that the delay had been at all extravagant, considering the
great importance of the measure adopted by them.

In the course of the same sitting, the Duke of Wellington
spoke strongly against the measure. On all occasions, but
especially on this, he was sure to be listened to with attention; but this attention was a tribute paid rather to his high
character and his fame as a warrior, than to his capacity as
a statesman or his merits as a speaker. The commencement
of his speeches was indeed usually effective, from the strong
common-sense view which he took of the question before the
house, but, unhappily for himself and his audience, he never
knew when to stop, and often destroyed the favourable impression he had made in the beginning of his address by
continuing to speak after his ideas were exhausted. His
speeches were rendered still more tedious by a defective
elocution, caused by the loss of several of his teeth, which
often prevented many consecutive sentences from being
heard, even by the most attentive listener. He explained at
length and defended his conduct with reference to the question
of Reform ; he stated his objections to the present measure ;
he gave it as his opinion that under the system it established,
the king would not be able to carry on the government of
this country, on the principles on which governments had been
conducted at any former period, and declared his intention of
voting against the second reading of the bill.

Lord Brougham delivered his opinions on Friday, October
7th; but as they have been published in the well-known collection of his speeches, we do not think it necessary to attempt
to give an account here of one of the most able and eloquent
addresses ever delivered in either house of parliament. He
concluded it by imploring the house not to reject the bill.

Lord Lyndhurst—inferior to Lord Brougham alone in the
power of his eloquence, and greatly his superior in tact and
mental agility—rose to reply. He expressed the feeling of all
present when he characterized his great rival's speech as an
eloquent and splendid display, never surpassed on any former

occasion even by his noble friend himself. He dwelt at great
length on what he denominated the revolutionary violence of
the measure; and in reference to the argument that inasmuch
as they assented to the principle of the bill they should
read it a second time, he replied that they assented to its
object but they opposed its principle. After mentioning
several objections he entertained to the measure, the noble
lord thus proceeded :—

" But all these objections vanish into insignificance when
compared with the aggregate consideration I am now about
to mention. The bill takes 157 members from the aristocratic part of the House of Commons. It gives back 65 in
the shape of county members; but it gives also 50 members
to the populous towns, to be elected by such a constituency
as I have described. What would the representatives of such
places be ? We may judge by the persons who are at present
the favoured candidates. The difference is not a difference
of 50 members, but a difference of 100, for 50 are taken
from the aristocratic part and given to the democratic part of
the house. But then there are 35 more to be taken away,
so that, in fact, the aristocratic part of the house will lose 135
members. The same consequences will result in Scotland,
where the democratic part of the members will utterly
overwhelm the aristocratic part. Then look at Ireland.
Three-fourths of the representation of Ireland will be in the
power of the Catholics. I must say that I think the whole
will form what the noble duke near me has described;
namely, a fierce and democratic assembly." He then proceeded to state what he conceived would be the consequence
of this change. He believed that Earl Grey and his associates after having opened the floodgates would be carried
away by the torrent—that a republic would be established—
that the Protestant Church in Ireland would be destroyed,
and church property in both kingdoms confiscated.

"This," he concluded, "is the crisis of your lordship's
fate, if you now abdicate the trust reposed in you, you will
never be able to resume those trusts, your rights, your titles,
and the liberties of the country will be trampled in the dust.
The guardianship of the constitution has been entrusted to
you, and if it should be despoiled while in your custody, the
blame will rest with you and with you only. But if, on the
contrary, you preserve it unimpaired, you will receive the
thanks of all reasonable men of the present generation, and
your memory will live in the gratitude of posterity, to whom,
by your instrumentality, the invaluable blessings of the
British constitution will have been transmitted, uninjured
and undiminished."

Lord Tenterden, the Chief Justice, gave utterance to the
prevailing wish and opinion of the legal profession when he
announced that it was his intention to vote for the rejection
of the bill. Dr. Howley, Archbishop of Canterbury, followed
him. No prelate had ever more worthily filled the throne of
Lanfranc, Anselm, A'Becket, and Laud, and none had ever
more fully commanded the reverence of the House of Lords.
Briefly, hesitatingly, and with evident deep feeling, he declared
that he should have supported a moderate Reform, but that
this bill he regarded as destructive. "If," he concluded, "it
should be your lordships' pleasure to pass this bill, I shall
rejoice if I find my apprehensions groundless ; and if, on the
contrary, your lordships should deem it expedient to throw
the bill out, and that popular violence—which I do not anticipate—should result from this proceeding, I will cheerfully
bear my share of the general calamity, and I shall have the
consolation, for the few years or days I may have to live, of
reflecting that I have not been actuated by sinister motives,
but that I opposed the bill fairly and in perfect purity of
heart, believing it to be mischievous in its tendency and
dangerous to the fabric of the constitution." It was evident

from the assenting cheers of the bishops behind him, that the
venerable prelate uttered the prevailing sentiments of the
episcopal bench.   These declarations of the heads of the
legal and clerical professions, though not unexpected, were
ominous of the fate of the bill.   The Duke of Sussex, the
king's brother, on the other hand, declared that he should
vote for the bill, and at some length stated the reasons for
his vote.   He was followed by his brother, the Duke of
Gloucester, who briefly announced his intention to vote
against it.

The morning of the 8th of October was already far spent,
when Lord Grey at length rose to reply.   He retorted, with
telling effect, upon Lord Lyndhurst, the charge of inconsistency, which that noble lord had insinuated against him.
After some remarks in defence of the bill, he thus concluded :—

"I have observed symptoms of an intention to attack
government with a view to overthrow it.   All I can say is this,
that to this measure, or to a measure of the same extent, I
am pledged.   A noble and learned lord has said that if I
abandon office it would be a culpable abandonment of the
king.   It is for me to consider what I will do.   I certainly
will not abandon the king, as long as I can be of any use to
him.   I am bound to the king by obligations of gratitude,
greater, perhaps, than any subject ever owed to a sovereign,
for the kind manner in which he has extended to me his
confidence and support, and for the indulgence with which
he has accepted my offers and best endeavours to serve him.
But I can only be a useful servant to the king whilst I am
able to carry measures which are necessary to the security of
the country, as well as to my own character.   If I should once
lose my character, the king had better have any man in the
world for his servant rather than me, for as for abilities I
pretend not to them, nor to the other qualifications which

long habits of office give. All that I can pretend to is an
honest zeal, a desire to do my duty in the best way I can,
sensible of my deficiencies, but feeling that there is no
personal sacrifices I am not bound to make for my king,
whose friendship to me can never be obliterated from my
heart, whatever may happen, to the last moment of my
existence. Place was not sought by me. I can appeal to
the history of my whole life to prove that I do not desire
office. I found myself in a situation in which I thought that
I could not shrink from serving my country and my king,
and I accepted office very much against my inclination. I
have lived a long life of exclusion from office. I have no
official habits. I possess not the knowledge that official
habits confer. I am fond of retirement; and in domestic
life I live happy in the bosom of my family. Nothing
but a strong sense of duty would have tempted me to
embark on these

'—— stormy seas,
Bankrupt of life, but prodigal of ease.'

I have quitted my retirement from a sense of duty to my
country and my king, whom I shall continue to serve as long
as His Majesty may be pleased to require me; but if parliament and the country withdraw their confidence from me,
and I find that I can no longer be a useful servant to the
king, I will resign office, and when in retirement, I shall, at
least, be able to look back to having done my best to serve
both king and country."

These words extorted loud cheers of assent and approval
not only from the supporters of the ministry, but from the
Duke of Wellington and many of the opposition peers, and,
at the conclusion of the speech all sides expressed their
sympathy by clapping of hands and stamping of feet—marks
of approbation which, if not altogether unprecedented in the
House of Lords, were very unusual.

CHAP. III.   After a few words of explanation from the Duke of
1831.   Wellington and Lord Lyndhurst, the house divided, when
October 8.
The   there appeared :—
division.
            For the amendment—Present .   . 150
                              Proxies   .   49—199
            Against   .   .   Present .   . 128
                              Proxies   .   30—158

            Majority against the second reading .   .   41

The house then adjourned, and noble lords went home, no
doubt seriously reflecting on the consequences of what they
had done, at twenty minutes past six o'clock in the morning.

Meanwhile, the French were engaged in abolishing the
hereditary peerage ; a fact which, though not much referred
to, was, no doubt, a good deal in the thoughts of noble lords,
producing different results according to the various constitutions of their minds and the different ways in which it was
regarded.

CHAPTER IV.

NEVER, perhaps, had the whole English nation been in such a state of feverish and excited expectation as on that Saturday the 8th day of October, 1831, on the dawn of which we left the peers walking out of their own house after having thrown out the Reform Bill. The news spread through the country with the speed of lightning, producing wherever it came, alarm, disappointment, or indignation.. Every man felt as if he were walking on ground from which a volcano might burst forth. The people could do nothing, think of nothing, talk of nothing, but "the bill." The very women and children caught the contagion of the prevalent feeling, and were ardent reformers or strong anti-reformers. By the Tories the intelligence was welcomed with an exultation which was largely chastened with alarm. But the former feeling they were compelled to repress, for the reformers were not in a mood to tolerate its manifestation. By these latter, the tidings were received with a deep feeling of exasperation, which only needed a leader and a distinct aim in order to produce great results. A stirring word thrown among the multitude at that moment might have produced a revolution. But no such word was spoken—indeed the leaders of the movement, while desiring that the popular enthusiasm should be sustained, as being necessary to the success of the bill, were also anxious that it should be curbed, and fully alive to the destruction that might result from its possible excesses. However, expressions of disappointed hope and fixed resolve

CHAP. IV. were not wanting.   In London and in many other towns the
1831.   shops were closed, and the bells of the churches were muffled.
The shopkeepers of Spitalfields decided to keep a political
fast day, and to close their shops on the following Wednesday.
A run for gold was commenced, and caused no little alarm
to the governors of the bank.   About 200 members of
the House of Commons met at Willis's Rooms, and unanimously determined that resolutions should be submitted
to the House of Commons, affirming that it was expedient
to declare their unaltered and undiminished attachment to
the great measure of Reform, and their determined purpose
to support the king's ministers in the present crisis ; a resolution which, as we shall presently see, was speedily carried
out.   The same evening, and within twelve hours of the
fatal division, the common council met, and passed similar
resolutions.

Popular
indigna-
tion.

But while these efforts were being made to secure the
ultimate success of the bill, the popular indignation against
the authors of the nation's disappointment was being loudly
and strongly vented. The reforming press, at once expressing
and stimulating the general feeling, threw off all the restraints
it had hitherto imposed on itself, in the hope of soothing the
anti-reforming lords into compliance with the nation's desires,
and now reproached and denounced them in unmeasured
terms.   The abolition of the House of Peers was frequently
suggested.   Still more violent was the language employed by
the orators who addressed the meetings which were now again
being held in every part of the metropolis and of the United
Kingdom.   The whole force of the popular rage was directed
against the majority of the House of Lords.   On Monday,
October 10th, a great crowd assembled along the line of road
from Whitehall to Parliament-street.   The obnoxious peers
and members were protected from personal violence by a very
strong party of the new police, but they were received with

roars of execration, which, it was said at the time, would CHAP. IV.
have drowned a peal of thunder. The cheers which greeted 1831.
the reforming peers and members were equally loud. The Oct. 10.
bishops especially were objects of popular detestation, and
could not appear in the streets without danger of personal
violence. Many of the temporal peers were assaulted on their
way to or from the house. The Duke of Newcastle, who was
peculiarly obnoxious to the reformers, was personally assailed,
and his house was attacked by an infuriated mob. The
Marquis of Londonderry, riding in a cabriolet, was stopped,
violently struck, and would probably have been murdered,
but for the presence of mind of the driver, who whipped the
horse forward into a gallop, and saved his master from the
exasperated populace. The anti-reforming peers, irritated
by the treatment to which they had been exposed, and
ascribing it, in some measure, to the language employed by
Earl Grey and other ministerial speakers in the late debate,
loudly complained of the alleged remissness of the government
in not suppressing violence, which tended to intimidate the
opponents of the bill, and to prevent them from voting
according to their convictions. This impression produced a
scene in the House of Lords on the evening of the 11th of Oct. 11.
October, almost rivalling in the violence of the language Scene in the House
employed that which occurred on the eve of the dissolution. of Lords.
Of all the assailants of the church at this time few, if any,
surpassed Lord King in the frequency or bitterness of their
invectives. If ever there was a good hater he was one, and
the clergy, and especially the bishops, were the objects of his
peculiar aversion. He took every opportunity of attacking
them, and with no little ability and effect. At this period of
their deep unpopularity his assaults were more bitter and
persistent than ever. On the evening in question he presented
a petition from a parish in Suffolk against an alleged unjust
exaction of tithes, and, in doing so, made some very severe

reflections on the conduct of the clergy. Lord Ellenborough called him to order, but he persisted in the same line of offensive remark.

The Earl of Suffield, who followed him, strongly censured the conduct of the bishops, observing that if they had, as usual, supported ministers instead of opposing them they would have carried the bill. He was interrupted and called to order by Lord Carnarvon. Hereupon the Lord Chancellor interfered, and, after giving his opinion on the question of order, added—"Good God, my lords, the charge against the right reverend prelates of anything like self-interest in their conduct in this house, is the very last imputation that can be made against them. It may be true that the bench of prelates have recently departed from their habitual course of supporting all administrations—it may be true that they have just opposed the government in a great national measure— it may be true that they have thought of tripping up His Majesty's government—"

Lord Ellenborough : " I rise to order.

Earl Grey : " I very much regret that the topic has been introduced. To discuss the motives of the prelates is not consistent with order, and I think the noble earl has rather overstepped the order of the house."

The Earl of Suffield: "I regret that I should ever deviate from the order of debate. I will not question either the votes or the motives of the right reverend prelates, but surely I have a right to review their recent conduct as a matter of fact. I will say then as a fact, that the votes of the right reverend prelates have always been in favour of ministers, and now, for the first time, when government stands in need of their votes in favour of a great national measure intended for the general benefit of the country, I find the bench of bishops have turned against the government. This I state as a fact, and I will state more—"

Lord Wynford : " Order, order, order."

The Bishop of London : " I concur in the extreme inconvenience of introducing such topics of discussion, but I will not sit still and suffer to pass unnoticed the observations proceeding from the woolsack. I did not take any part in the late memorable debate, nor have I expressed any observations or uttered any opinions on the object of it, but when the noble lord on the woolsack went so far as to indulge in a vein of sarcasm on the bench of bishops—when he even insinuated, or rather asserted, that the bench as a body had been influenced by a desire to trip up His Majesty's government, I speak with perfect confidence that no such thought has ever entered their minds. So far as the interests of the church are concerned, not one of them has had any occasion to blame His Majesty's present ministers. Whether the bench by their votes on a recent occasion have pursued a course of wisdom is a different question ; but I venture to assert that it has been a course of conviction and integrity."

The Bishop of Landaff said a few words.

The Bishop of Exeter, by far the ablest and the most courageous of all the prelates, and one of the most eloquent speakers in the House of Lords, next rose to vindicate his brethren from the attack that had been made on them. Usually his speeches were as remarkable for the calmness and courtesy of their manner and delivery as for the force and fullness of their matter; but on this occasion he spoke with a warmth very unusual to him, and in a tone of great excitement. " The bishops," he exclaimed, "have opposed this measure because, in their consciences, they cannot approve it; and they are ready to brave the censures of the mob, even when urged and instigated by those whose duty it is to restrain its ebullitions. I defy any noble lord to state a single instance in the history of this country, in which any members of this house have been so vilified and insulted as the bishops have

been within the last year, and that, too, by men of the highest
station in His Majesty's councils. I do not apologise for my
warmth ; for I should be ashamed of myself if I could be
cool on such a subject. If the attack on the bench of bishops
had been made in a moment of excitement, to that excitement I should have submitted ; but upon the mere presentation of a petition, and that a petition of no consequence,
a noble lord has abused the Church as the great arch-disturber
of all order, and another noble lord charged the bishops
with being bound together in a conspiracy against the
liberties of the country, and against 'all that could constitute
the welfare and happiness of the people.'"

Earl Grey: "What the right reverend prelate has uttered
is the most unprovoked, the most intemperate, and the most
unfounded insinuation that I have ever heard from any
member of this house. The right rev. prelate said that every
man who has spoke from this side of the house has spoken in
a tone of sarcasm and reprobation of the recent conduct of the
bishops. I ask if that observation is true, and if it could
with truth be applied to the few words that have fallen from
me ?"

The Bishop of Exeter here attempted to explain, but was
compelled to resume his seat by loud cries of "Down," "Down."

Earl Grey continued: "I appeal to every noble lord
whether there was anything in what I said at all like what
the right reverend prelate attributed to me ? Did I not
reprobate the discussion altogether? Did I not state it as my
opinion that the discussion was altogether inconsistent with
the orders of the house—and did I not do all I could to stop
it ? On what ground then could the right reverend prelate
make an attack so intemperate and so utterly without any
pretext or foundation ? I ask the right reverend prelate
whether it has ever been my custom to say anything whatever offensive to the church, or anything that was not in

support of it ? The right reverend prelate said he had heard CHAP. IV.
from a person holding the highest situation in the govern-   1831.
ment, frequent attempts to degrade, insult, and vilify the   Oct. 11.
church. Whether the right reverend prelate alluded to me
or to my noble friend on the woolsack, I know not, but of
this I am perfectly sure, that of neither could the observation be made with any justice or truth. The right reverend
prelate was not content with this want of truth, but he
uttered it with an appearance of a spirit that but little became
the garment he wears. It was the grossest injustice I ever
heard. He said that those who were charged with the care
of the public peace, and were bound to support the institutions of the country, had actually been the instigators of a
mob to insult the bench of bishops. I cannot conceal the
contempt and indignation with which I heard the charge.
I dare the right reverend prelate to state, if he can, one single
syllable of truth to support the falsest and most calumnious
accusation which I ever heard. If any man could be capable
of such conduct, no reprobation could be sufficiently severe
against him. So far from encouraging proceedings such as
the right reverend prelate alludes to, I am one of the very
first who would exert the full powers of the government to
protect those whose votes were hostile to me. I call on the
right reverend prelate to support what he has said by
proofs."

The Bishop of Exeter: " As I am called upon to produce
proofs of what I asserted, irregular as it may be to refer to
the debates which have recently taken place, yet under the
peculiar circumstances of my case, I hope for the indulgence
of your lordships, in being allowed to refer to the proceedings
in question. It must be within the recollection of every noble
lord who hears me, that in the first night of the debate on the
bill, the noble lord, without any one thing to excite him from
the bench of bishops, had thought himself justified in calling

CHAP. IV. on the bench seriously to take to mind what would be their
1831. position with the country if there was a narrow majority of
Oct. 11. lay lords against the bill, and if it were discovered that the
bishops had voted with that narrow majority. To call upon
any set of men—to call upon one of the great states of the
realm (as they are called by the sages of the law and by the
law itself)—to call upon them by way of menace of popular
indignation, has the tendency, a tendency which the noble
lord perhaps little suspected, to excite the odium of the
people. Has not that odium been excited, and have not the
bench of bishops been exposed to its effects? The noble lord
assumed the character of a prophet, and told the bishops
"to set their houses in order." It is true that the noble lord
did not conclude the sentence. He left that for us to do.
But it was impossible not to know that he referred to words
in which the prophet had threatened destruction. The noble
lord in the same speech took special care to remind the
bishops that certain important questions were in agitation,
which might take the turn which would prove favourable or
unfavourable according to the conduct of the bench on that
night. What are those questions? If the noble lord meant
that schemes of confiscation were in contemplation—that the
bold among the multitude would be encouraged, and the multitude goaded on to more immediate execution—then indeed
I could conceive that the conduct of the bishops on that night
might have the effect of driving the multitude to such purposes. Have I said anything which the proofs I have
produced have not fully substantiated?"

Earl Grey: "I ask the right reverend prelate why he did
not make the serious charges he has now brought forward
when the words he imputed to me were fresh in the recollection of the house, and when he could have made those
charges in a regular manner? For my part, I think that the
right reverend prelate's proofs correspond very little with his

assertions. The right reverend prelate charged His Majesty's
ministers with having purposely done all in their power to
encourage tumult and excite the mob to acts of popular
violence."

The Bishop of Exeter : "Most solemnly do I declare that I
do not think I have used any such words. Upon my honour
and conscience I did not use those words."

Earl Grey : "The right reverend prelate in his anger was
not likely to recollect what words he did use."

The noble lord then went on to re-assert his charges against
the bishop, and concluded by saying : "The right reverend
prelate has uttered a foul and calumnious aspersion, totally
unfounded in truth, nor has he in the least benefitted himself
by the explanation he has entered into."

The Duke of Wellington: "The question before the house
is merely the reception of a petition. A noble lord has
attacked the bench of bishops for having always servilely
supported every government of arbitrary principles, whilst on
the Reform Bill they deserted the government because its
principles were liberal. I call upon the noble lord to state
what he means by a government of arbitrary principles, and
which administration he accused of having such principles.
I have been at the head of administration for some time, and
I choose to ask the noble lord on what his charge is founded.
For the last ten months there has been but one division in
this house upon which the bishops could give their votes
against ministers, and if upon the Reform Bill the bishops
have departed from their usual course of giving their support
to the treasury benches, it is because the bill is such that
they could not conscientiously support it. It is not fair to
bring such charges against a body of men, on the ground of
difference of opinion."

The Duke of Newcastle and the Marquis of Londonderry stated that they had been attacked by a violent and

CHAP. IV. riotous mob, and bitterly complained that they had not
1831.   received the protection to which they were entitled.
Oct. 11.   Lord Melbourne assured them that the first desire of His
Majesty's government in general, and of himself in particular,
was to afford every possible protection both to the persons
and properties of all His Majesty's subjects. He deeply
lamented the excitement which prevailed in the metropolis
at present, and sincerely lamented that any noble lord or other
individual should have been exposed to acts of outrage and
violence.

Some further conversation took place on the subject, in
the course of which Lord Wharncliffe gave testimony to
Lord Melbourne's zeal and activity as secretary of the home
department. The conversation was interrupted by the
entrance of a message from the House of Commons, bringing
up the Consolidated Fund Bill, and the subject was dropped.

Oct. 12.   On the 12th of October, an immense procession, composed
Proces-   of delegates from nearly every parish of the metropolis,
sion.   marched to St. James's, to present an address to the king. It
was computed that it was composed of 60,000 persons, almost
all of them adult males. The leaders of the several bodies
of delegates, of which the procession was made up, were
introduced to Lord Melbourne, the Home Secretary, who
expressed his regret that he had not sooner been made
acquainted with their wish to present addresses, as he had
no doubt that, under the circumstances, His Majesty would
have waived the usual court etiquette, and received the heads
of the delegations in person. As it was now too late to do
this, he recommended them to give the addresses to the
county members, Messrs. Byng and Hume, who would, no
doubt, gladly present them. This suggestion was at once
followed, and after an interval of about an hour, Mr. Hume
re-appeared, and assured the parties who had entrusted the
address to him, that he had presented it to His Majesty,

informing him that it had been passed at a meeting of nearly
40,000 persons, and that it prayed him to retain his present
ministers, to use all constitutional means to promote the
passing of the Reform Bill, and to remove from his court and
household all those persons who were opposed to the measure.
Mr. Hume added, that he had the happiness to say that His
Majesty had distinctly promised that the prayer of the
petition should be complied with, that every effort should
be exerted to ensure the success of the Reform Bill, that
all persons about his court who were opposed to the bill
should be removed from the offices they held ; and that he
also emphatically stated that he had the highest confidence
in his present ministers.   After making this announcement,
which was received with tremendous cheering, Mr. Hume
exhorted the assemblage to disperse peaceably.

This advice was followed by most of those to whom it
was addressed, but some of the vast crowd which had
either formed part of the procession, or who had congregated
to witness it, were bent on mischief.   The house of the
Duke of Wellington and the Marquis of Bristol were attacked
and the windows demolished.   Several collisions took place
between the police and the mob in various parts of the
metropolis.   The Duke of Cumberland was dragged from his
horse on his way back from the House of Lords, and rescued
with difficulty by the exertions of the police.   Poor hot-headed
Lord Londonderry was the object of another assault.   He
was on his way to the House of Lords, when he fell in with
a mob of some 4,000 persons.   He proceeded through them
some distance without being recognised, when a man called
out—" There goes the Marquis of Londonderry."   He was
instantly assailed with hisses and pebbles, whereupon he
pulled out a pistol, but was prevailed on by a friend who
accompanied him to abstain from using it, and to retire
to the Horse Guards, where a large body of troops was

CHAP. IV. drawn up, but before he could take refuge behind them he
1831.   was struck by a stone, which inflicted a severe wound on the
right temple.

While these things were being done in the metropolis,
the same spirit was manifested elsewhere. It is true that
Sudbury, famous in the annals of corruption, rang its church
bells and fired cannon to celebrate the rejection of the bill,
but these demonstrations could not be made elsewhere with
safety, if indeed at all. At Derby, when the intelligence
arrived, it was received, as it was almost everywhere, with
tokens of sorrow and disappointment. The church bells were
muffled and continued throughout the night to send forth
their mournful music. There was, however, at first no disturbance, and in all probability none would have occurred, if
a few of the more foolish and violent anti-reformers had not
thought proper to give three cheers in the market-place for
the glorious majority of forty-one. This silly demonstration
stung to madness some of the hotter reformers, and a serious
tumult was the consequence. The houses of several of the
principal anti-reformers were assailed and their windows
smashed. The mob excited by this first breach of the peace,
attacked several other houses in the same manner, and did not
always discriminate between reformers and anti-reformers.
They also besieged the borough gaol, but it was successfully
defended. A young man, of the name of Haden, was killed
by a stone which struck him on the face, and several rioters
were killed and wounded. The arrival of the military prevented
further mischief.

At Nottingham, the violence of the mob was even greater
than at Derby. The castle, which was the property of the
unpopular Duke of Newcastle, was burnt to the ground.
Colwick Castle, the seat of Mr. Musters, was also fired, but
the flames were speedily extinguished. Mrs. Musters, whose
maiden name was Chaworth, the first love of the celebrated

Lord Byron, and the lady to whom his earlier poems were addressed, fled in terror from the burning mansion, and took refuge in a summer house, but the fright produced an illness which terminated fatally a few months after. At Beeston, a factory was burnt down; the house of correction was also attacked, but saved by the timely arrival of the 15th Hussars. At Loughborough, there were serious disturbances. Belvoir Castle was attacked. On the whole, however, the disappointment, though severe, was borne with creditable patience, but this was in a great measure owing to the determination of ministers to retain office. The question of resignation had been very seriously considered. While they were deliberating upon it they received a message from the king, now thoroughly alarmed at the state of the country, begging them to retain their places; it was also intimated to them that this was the wish of the majority of the peers. Had they resigned at this moment, there can be no doubt that outrages of far greater violence and far more general would have been committed, and they must have been immediately reinstated or a revolution would have taken place. Their resolution to retain office was justly regarded as a pledge that the struggle would be renewed as soon as possible, and they hastened to confirm this expectation, and to promise another measure of equal efficiency with that which had just been rejected. These declarations were imperatively called for. The danger was imminent, and ministers knew it, and did all that lay in their power to tranquillize the people, and to assure them that the measure was only delayed, not finally defeated.

Lord Brougham, especially, on Wednesday, October 12th, in his place in the House of Lords, referring to the outrages which had been committed, condemned them in the strongest terms, declaring that the authors and abettors of such acts were the worst enemies of Reform. "The people," he continued, "who are zealously, anxiously, and devotedly desirous

CHAP. IV. óf the passing of that great measure should not permit them-
1831.   selves, on account of any temporary disappointment in that
Oct. 12. respect, to be betrayed into proceedings which could alone
be expected from the bitterest foes of the success of that
momentous measure which they have so much at heart,—
they should not allow any temporary defeat which their
hopes and wishes may have experienced to' drive them into a
course of proceeding inconsistent with the public tranquillity,
and destructive of the peace of society. I call upon them, as
their friend, and as the friend of Reform, not to give way to
any such unfounded disappointment. I tell them that
Reform is only delayed for a short period. I tell them that
the bill will pass,—that the bill must pass,—that a bill
founded on exactly similar principles, and equally extensive
and efficient with the bill which has been thrown out, shall,
in a very short period, become part and parcel of the law of
the land."

Oct. 10.   This timely declaration did much to allay the irritation
Lord Eb-   that prevailed, and to reconcile the people to a delay
rington's   which they hoped would not be of long duration. Mean-
resolution. while the House of Commons lost no time in speaking out.
The resolution of the meeting held on the Saturday on which
the bill was rejected, was carried with effect on the Monday
following. Lord Ebrington then moved, and Mr. Dundas
seconded, the following resolution, which was carried the
same evening by a majority of 131:—"That while this house
laments the present state of a bill for introducing a Reform
into the Commons house of parliament, in favour of which
the opinion of the country stands unequivocally pronounced,
and which has been matured by discussion the most anxious
and the most laborious, it feels itself imperatively called on
to re-assert its firm adherence to the principal leading
provisions of that great measure, and to express its unabated
confidence in the integrity, perseverance, and ability of the

ministers, who, in introducing and conducting it, so well consulted the best interests of the country."

The outrages which had been committed and the prevailing popular excitement were brought under the notice of the
House of Commons on the evening of October 12th, in reference to a great meeting which had been held at Birmingham,
and which was said to have been attended by 150,000 persons.
At this meeting very violent language had been held in
reference to the rejection of the bill by the House of Lords.
One of the speakers exclaimed :—" When Hampden refused
the payment of ship money, his gallant conduct electrified all
England, and pointed out the way by which the people, when
unanimous and combined, might rid themselves of an odious
and oppressive oligarchy. I declare, before God, that if all
constitutional modes of obtaining the success of the Reform
measure fail, I will be the first man to refuse the payment of
taxes, except by a levy on my goods. I now call upon all who
hear me and are prepared to join me in this step to hold up
their hands." These words were received by the vast multitude with indescribable enthusiasm ; and when the speaker
called on those present to hold up their hands in token of
their determination to refuse the payment of taxes, a forest
of hands was immediately raised, amidst the most tremendous
cheering. He then added :—"I now call upon those who are
not prepared to adopt this course, to hold up their hands, and
signify their dissent." Not a single hand was lifted up, and
the shouts and cheers were redoubled.

At the same meeting, a vote of thanks was passed to Lord
Althorp and Lord J. Russell, and forwarded to them by Mr.
Thomas Attwood, a banker, of Birmingham, who, as president
of the Birmingham Political Union, occupied the chair at this
meeting. In acknowledging this compliment, Lord J. Russell
used the following expression :—" It is impossible that the
whisper of a faction should prevail over the voice of a nation."

Sir H. Hardinge, amidst the loud assenting cheers of the opposition, denounced this phrase as insulting to the House of Lords, and as improperly identifying the government with the Political Unions, and especially that of Birmingham, under whose auspices the meeting had been assembled.

Lord J. Russell, after stigmatising in the strongest terms the outrages that had been committed, and especially those which had been directed against the mansion of the Duke of Wellington, to whom the country was so much indebted for his past services, defended the expressions he had employed in his letter to Mr. Attwood, and explained that he did not mean to apply the phrase "whisper of a faction" to the whole majority of the House of Peers, but only to a small self-interested portion of that majority.

Lord Althorp, referring to the charge of his having written a letter to the Birmingham Political Union, declared that he had written no letter whatever to the body known by that title. He admitted that he had addressed a letter to the chairman of a meeting at Birmingham, consisting of 150,000 persons, expressing his sense of a vote of thanks with which so large a portion of his fellow-countrymen had thought fit to honour his conduct; and he could not think that in doing so he had acted by any means in a manner unworthy of his station. In acknowledging to the chairman of the meeting the honour thus conferred on him, he had taken the opportunity to recommend that gentleman to use his influence for the prevention of acts of violence, or illegal and unconstitutional excesses. He had also stated to him that the rejection of the Reform Bill was a great calamity, for as a calamity he and his colleagues regarded it.

Sir C. Wetherell vehemently condemned the letters of Lord Althorp and Lord J. Russell, and gave notice of a motion for an address to the king, praying His Majesty to issue a special commission to try the offenders concerned in the

outrage of burning down the Duke of Newcastle's castle in Chap. IV.
Nottinghamshire. The following evening Sir C. Wetherell was 1831.
not in his place at the time when this motion should have come
on. However, late in the evening he proposed it in the shape
of an amendment to another motion. In supporting his
proposition he indulged in his usual strain of vehement
invective against his opponents, and especially against the
members of the administration. In the course of the discussion
which followed, the Attorney-General stated that no person
concerned in the firing of Nottingham Castle was yet in
custody, and therefore there were no prisoners whom the
proposed commission could try. Of course, the proposal was
negatived.

The public mind was now completely reassured with Impatience
respect to the retention of office by the ministry and the of the
nation.
renewal of the attempt to carry the bill, but this fear was
succeeded by an apprehension that concessions would be
made to the Lords, and that much of the efficiency of the
bill would be lost. The nation was also anxious to have the
matter at once brought to an issue, and, in its impatience of
delay, did not consider sufficiently the fatigues and anxieties
to which both the government and the legislature had been
exposed, and the absolute necessity that existed for a short
respite from their labours. This impatience was increased by
a circumstance which arose out of it. Earl Grey returning
from the house of a friend, at a quarter-past eleven o'clock at
night, found Dr. Carpue and seventeen other reformers, who
had been delegated from different parishes in the metropolis,
and who, without any previous notice, had come to communicate to him the opinion of their friends, and particularly to
recommend that after a prorogation of seven days the Reform
Bill should be again brought forward and proceeded with
until carried. Lord Grey, justly offended at their impertinent
intrusion, rebuked them in his mild, lofty, aristocratic way,

CHAP. IV. and sent them away greatly displeased at the reception they
1831. had experienced. In this mood they reported that parliament
would be adjourned over Christmas,—that Lord J. Russell's
bill would not be revived,—that no extensive creation of peers
would take place,—and that a bill would be brought in which
would satisfy the Tories and the bishops, who were now willing
to submit to what they called a moderate measure of Reform,
and which the delegates and reformers generally thought
likely to prove much more remarkable for its moderation than
for its efficiency. Reports of dissensions in the ministry itself
were also rife; it was said that the Chancellor thought the
bill much too violent, and that he headed a party in the
cabinet who were labouring to bring the premier over to these
views.

Oct. 17.   These reports were so widely disseminated and were
Lord
Brougham's producing so much discontent and alarm that it was thought
explana-
tions. necessary to give them an authoritative contradiction. The
ministry had already insisted on the dismissal of Lord Howe,
the queen's chamberlain, and other officers of Her Majesty's
household, who, in their own persons, or those of their near
relatives or connections, had opposed the bill. Earl Grey,
both in a letter to Sir J. C. Hobhouse and in a speech in the
House of Lords, contradicted the rumours that had been
circulated; and Lord Brougham, with the same object, gave
the following explanations of the plans and intentions of
government in his place in the House of Lords on the evening
of Monday, October 17th:—" I rise in consequence of attempts
which have been pertinaciously made to induce the opinion
that there is a difference of opinion between my noble friend
Lord Grey and myself on the subject of Reform, to declare,
in the presence of my colleagues, that there has never been
the slightest difference of opinion between my noble friend
and myself respecting even the most minute particulars of
the bill,—I will not say the principle—for as to that we were

all agreed—but the minutest details of the measure. I shall
now pass to the difficult and delicate question of the recess. Notwithstanding the impatience of some worthy individuals, whom I believe to be extremely well disposed towards the government, and most zealous for the success of the bill, but who, in recommending a prorogation for a week, certainly do not display a zeal according to knowledge,—I must avow my opinion that for the session to commence after so brief an interval, and for the Chancellor—I mean the Chancellor in another house—to begin his labours again, and for my noble friend who has introduced the bill to renew his advocacy of the measure, I must pronounce my opinion that this would be physically impossible, after having given three months, day and night, to deliberation and discussion. None feels more than I do the impossibility of continuing such exertions. It was just twelve months last Friday since I began hard work in London, and during all that time I have enjoyed no respite or relaxation, with the exception of two days at Christmas and Easter, and even they were chiefly spent upon the road. During that period I have been occupied from six or seven in the morning until twelve and one at night, and if any man is so unreasonable as to say that I ought not to be allowed to enjoy a little repose, with that man I will not pause to reason. I will throw myself on the good sense and kind feeling of my countrymen, and I am confident that they will not bring in a verdict of guilty. Whatever advice may be offered as to the time of prorogation, the people of England may rest assured that it will be given on a solemn principle of public duty, and with a view to the carrying of that great measure, to which none can feel more devoted than myself and my colleagues. The public will see, when the measure is again before parliament, the wisdom with which we have acted; and that the period that will intervene is no longer than is required, I will not say in justice—but in mercy."

CHAP. IV.   At length, on the 20th of October, the indispensable
1831.   business of the session having now been transacted, the king
Oct. 20.   in person prorogued the parliament to Tuesday, the 22nd day
Proroga-
tion of par-   of November, with the usual formalities. The royal speech
liament.   on this occasion contained the following passage : — "The
anxiety which has been so generally manifested by my people
for the accomplishment of a constitutional Reform in the
Commons house of parliament, will, I trust, be regulated by
a due sense of the necessity of order and moderation in their
proceedings.

"To the consideration of this important question, the
attention of parliament must necessarily again be called at
the opening of the ensuing session ; and you may be assured
of my unaltered desire to promote its settlement, by such
improvements in the representation as may be found necessary for the securing to my people the full enjoyment of
their rights, which, in combination with those of the other
orders of the state, are essential to the support of our free
constitution."

Asserted   Meanwhile, the anti-reformers, who had been terrified at
reaction.   the first violences which followed the rejection of the Reform
Bill, and who feared that their oft-repeated predictions of
revolution were about to receive an immediate fulfilment,
finding that the crisis had passed without any very serious
disturbances, and seeing that the people bore their disappointment with patience and calmness, began to take heart,
and to assert that a reaction had commenced, and that the
people were sick of the bill. They saw with delight, while
reformers marked with silent regret, that Lora Ashley, the anti-
reforming candidate for the county of Dorset, had beaten his
opponent, Mr. Ponsonby, a moderate reformer, by some thirty-
six votes—that at Liverpool, the moderate reformer, Lord
Sandon, son of Lord Harrowby, one of the leading opponents
of the bill, had triumphed over Mr. Thornley, the thorough-

going reformer, by a majority of 849 at the end of the second day, when Mr. Thornley retired from the hopeless contest— that in Pembrokeshire, Mr. Greville, the Reform candidate, had withdrawn from the contest with Sir J. Owen, an anti-reformer, at the end of the second day, finding himself in a minority of 108. On the other hand, it was some consolation to them to find the county of Cambridge returning the Reform candidate, Mr. Townley, by a majority of 536 over his opponent, Captain Yorke.

But while the Tories were congratulating themselves on the elections they had gained, and triumphantly pointing to them as proofs of commencing reaction, they were very seriously disquieted by the proceedings of the Political Unions which, as already mentioned, had been established in Manchester, Liverpool, Birmingham, and other large towns, and were every day being formed in new towns, and agitating for Reform more and more strongly. An union of this kind had recently been formed in the metropolis; and these associations were receiving a sort of military organization, and were acting together in concert for the promotion of Reform. The *Times* and other ministerial journals applauded the movement, and urged reformers to establish similar bodies in every part of the kingdom. The proceedings of existing unions and the formation of new unions were carefully and triumphantly chronicled. The embodiment of a "Conservative Guard," to resist the "rich opponents of Reform and the ragged promoters of disturbances," was strenuously advocated; and on the last day of October, we find Sir F. Burdett occupying the chair at a great meeting of the inhabitant householders of the metropolis, convened for the purpose of forming a National Political Union, whose great object should be to obtain good government, and preserve social order through a full and efficient representation of the people in the Commons house of parliament. These unions, all along

CHAP. IV. a source of constant alarm to the anti-reformers, were now
1831. beginning to be regarded with no small uneasiness by many
sincere reformers, who feared that they might prove unmanageable, and dictate to parliament and the government
changes far more violent and organic than any which had been
hitherto proposed. The king himself had long been strongly
impressed with this feeling, and continually urged his ministers to suppress these formidable associations, while it was
still possible to do so. The ministers themselves began to
participate in these disquietudes, and accordingly, on the
2nd of November, a proclamation was issued, in which they
were denounced as unconstitutional and illegal.

Oct. 29.
The Bris-
tol riots.
This proclamation was not issued too soon. Before it
appeared an event had occurred which greatly augmented
the prevailing alarm. The city of Bristol was the theatre of
an outbreak which filled the kingdom with consternation.
The office of recorder in this city was held by Sir C. Wetherell,
and in virtue of that office he exercised within the county of
Bristol (for Bristol was at that time a county as well as a city),
all the functions of one of the judges of the realm, and was
received, when he came down to hold the assizes, with honours
similar to those which were usually paid to the judges. It
was his duty to hold the usual gaol delivery at this time.
Having been, as we have seen, the most active, persevering,
and prominent of all the opponents of the bill, he was
peculiarly obnoxious to its supporters outside, whose hostility was not disarmed by the experience of the wit and
humour he displayed in resisting the measure, and which
rendered him almost a favourite with the reformers inside the
house. The Bristol mob was notoriously one of the fiercest*
in England, and Sir C. Wetherell was at that moment of
strongly excited political passions the most unpopular man

* See Macaulay's History of England, vol. ii., page 99.

in England. It was, therefore, anticipated that some hostile CHAP. IV. demonstrations would be made on the occasion of his visit, 1831. and some of the citizens of Bristol tried to dissuade him from Oct. 29. holding the gaol delivery, which might, from the state of the calendar, have been postponed without much inconvenience. The representations thus made were referred to the Home Secretary, Lord Melbourne, who did not think it necessary to interfere, but left Sir Charles to act according to his own judgment. Each probably thought that the event would prove favourable to his party. Sir C. Wetherell no doubt hoped that all would pass off quietly, and that he should be able to refer to his reception at Bristol, as another proof of the reaction, which, by dint of continual assertion, he and his friends had really begun to believe in, and Lord Melbourne was probably not sorry that he should have an opportunity of witnessing and showing to the country the full extent of his unpopularity, not expecting that the demonstration would proceed beyond hootings and execrations. Precautions, however, were taken which were thought sufficient to meet any emergency at all likely to arise, and to preserve public order. The whole police force of the city was mustered. The sailors of the port refused to be sworn in as special constables for the protection of Sir Charles, but a considerable number of citizens were enrolled, and a handful of troops had been sent to the vicinity and placed at the disposal of the magistrates, with the express understanding that they were not to be called in except in case of necessity. Sir Charles made his public entry into the city on the 29th of October. He appeared in a carriage drawn by four grey horses, many hours earlier than the customary time, at Totterdown, and much nearer the Guildhall than the place at which he was usually received. It was hoped that by this means the opening of the commission would have been quietly effected before the arrival of the recorder was known. Sir Charles

CHAP. IV. here quitted his own carriage, and took his seat in that of the
1831.   high sheriff, amidst the yells, groans, and hisses of the mob
Oct. 29.   which had already assembled, notwithstanding the precautions
that had been taken.   The carriage was escorted by a large
number of special constables, and on each side of it was a
gentleman mounted on horseback.   It was preceded and followed by the usual cortege of mayor's and sheriff's officers.
As the procession advanced, stones began to be thrown at the
carriage, and the crowd became denser, louder, and more
violent.   Females of the lowest class were present in great
numbers, and were observed to be particularly violent in
the expression of their feelings, and in endeavouring to excite
the men to make an attack on the recorder.   Some of the
attendants were severely injured by the stones aimed at
the carriage.   At length the Guildhall was reached, but the
pressure of the crowd was so great that it was only after a
severe struggle which lasted some minutes that Sir Charles
was at length conducted into the building, and took his seat
on the bench.   The doors of the hall were then thrown open,
and in a very short time the area set apart for the general
public was crammed with spectators.   The recorder was
naturally agitated in consequence of the violent efforts he
had been obliged to make to force an entrance, but in a few
minutes he recovered his composure, looked round the court,
and smiled and nodded to some of his acquaintances.

The opening of the commission was commenced in the
usual form, but amidst noise, confusion, and interruption,
which rendered it quite inaudible.   Mr. Serjeant Ludlow,
the town-clerk, rose in the midst of the tumult and exclaimed,
" I believe there is not an individual present who has
come here for the purpose of insulting the commission of the
king.   As for Reform—" No sooner had the word escaped
from his lips than there broke forth from the mob such a
shout in favour of the measure referred to that he was unable

to proceed, and Sir C. Wetherell, well aware of the imprudence
of introducing the topic on such an occasion, and under such
circumstances, endeavoured to induce him to desist. When
the outcry had in some degree subsided, the serjeant continued, saying,—" The question of Reform has nothing to do
with the proceedings of this day." The reading of the commission proceeded amidst continued outcries, which rendered
it completely inaudible. When it was concluded the recorder
addressed one of the officers of the court, and directed him to
observe those who were making disturbances, adding that if
any person doing so were pointed out he would at once commit
him. This threat only served to increase the uproar, amidst
which the preliminary formalities were completed, and the
court adjourned to the following Monday, October 31st. Sir
Charles then quitted the bench amidst groans and yells
directed against himself, mingled with cheers for the king.
He remained for some time in the robing room, probably
hoping that the mob, tired of waiting, would quietly disperse.
If this was his expectation, he was completely disappointed.
A dense crowd filled the whole of the way leading from the
Guildhall to the Mansion House, and hooted and hissed him
as before, except in the front of the commercial rooms where
a compact body of his admirers had posted themselves, and
greeted him as he passed with loud cheers. He reached the
Mansion House after considerable delay, but without injury.
On his arrival there, a few stones were thrown at the carriage,
by one of which a lamp or a window was broken, but no further damage was done, and he entered the Mansion House in
safety. The constables who had attended him were left
outside, without any magistrate to direct them or persuade
the populace to disperse. Stones were occasionally thrown by
the mob, and skirmishes now and then took place, and some
of the rioters were taken into custody. In these encounters the
constables did not exhibit the forbearance that was desirable.

CHAP. IV.
1831.
Oct. 29.

They used their staves much too freely, and one of the crowd was killed by a blow on the head which he received. This increased the exasperation of the mob, and a cry was raised,—"To the back," meaning the back of the Mansioh House, where there were several piles of firewood, A large portion of the mob acted on the hint, and in a few minutes reappeared in the square armed with sticks. Seeing this the constables made a charge, and the crowd fled before them, throwing away their sticks, which were gathered up and removed, thus showing how easily the disturbance might have been quelled at this period. The mob finding that the pursuit was not followed up, speedily returned, and from half-past twelve to four o'clock they remained face to face with the constables, skirmishing with them and throwing stones at them. In these conflicts the advantage remained with the constabulary, and it seemed likely that the mob, after having vented their wrath against the recorder, and testified their zeal for Reform, would gradually disperse. But unfortunately, at four o'clock, half the constabulary force were allowed to retire for the purpose of obtaining refreshments, with the understanding that they were to return at six o'clock, and release those who remained. The mob, encouraged by this diminution in the number of the defenders of the Mansion House, became more daring in their attacks, and began to gain the upper hand. The mayor, who was himself a reformer, now came forward, accompanied by some of the magistrates, and begged the people to desist from these unlawful proceedings and retire quietly to their houses; he implored them not to impose on him the necessity of reading the riot act and calling in the military. While he was speaking several large stones were thrown at him, one of which passed close to his head, and the person standing next to him was struck, and had his hat knocked off. As the crowd still continued to increase in number and violence,

at five o'clock the riot act was read, whereupon the rioters
made a rush on the constabulary and completely routed them.
Most of them were disarmed and severely beaten. One was
compelled to throw his truncheon through the Mansion House
windows, others fled, and one of these last was chased into
the flat dock, and with great difficulty saved from being
drowned. A few took refuge in the Mansion House, which
was at once attacked by the triumphant mob. The windows
and sashes of the building were shivered, the shutters beaten
to pieces, the street door broken open, and the rioters forced
their way into two rooms on the ground floor. During this
attack, Sir C. Wetherell escaped in disguise, clambering over
the roofs of the adjoining houses, and quitting the city as
quickly as possible. Unfortunately his departure, the knowledge of which might have put an end to the disturbances,
was not publicly announced till the following noon. The mayor
and the other occupants of the Mansion House barricaded
themselves as well as they could in that part of the building
which the mob had not yet entered, but into which they were
endeavouring to force their way. To effect this object, the
rioters tore up the iron palisades in front of the house and
some young trees growing near, and converted them into
weapons of offence and destruction. Walls were thrown
down to furnish bricks, which were hurled through the upper
windows, and straw and other combustibles were placed in
the dining-room for the purpose of burning down the building.
In a few minutes more the house and its inmates would
probably have been burnt, had not the military made their
appearance at this critical moment. The mob quickly
evacuated the building, but did not desist from their attacks
on the outside, and they were encouraged by the appearance
of a large additional body of rioters, composed of some of
the worst characters of the neighbourhood, whom the tidings
of the riot had brought into the city in great numbers.

CHAP. IV. The mob received the troops with loud cheers. Such was
1831. the state of affairs when Major Mackworth, aide-de-camp
of Lord Hill, the Commander-in-chief of the Forces, reached
the Mansion House ; he found it filled with special and
other constables who had taken refuge in it, and who
added to the confusion that prevailed without being of any
service. With the consent of the mayor he formed them
into four divisions, one of which he posted in the rear of the
Mansion House, another at the side, and the third in front.
Colonel Brereton, who commanded the troops, co-operated
with his soldiers in enabling him to make these dispositions.
The fourth and smallest body remained in the house, and
took charge of the prisoners. Thus in less than five minutes
the Mansion House was cleared of its assailants, and so
remained till the following morning. Nine prisoners were
captured by the civil force and safely conducted to the gaol.
Colonel Brereton came into the Mansion House for orders,
and was directed to clear the square and the adjacent streets,
but did not carry out his instructions. Meanwhile the soldiers
and constables continued to be annoyed by stones thrown at
them, and two of the former were brought into the Mansion
House seriously wounded. The colonel, however, continued
to trot his men up and down the square, shook hands with
the rioters till his arm was tired, harangued, entreated,
threatened, exhorted them to disperse, and even waved his
cocked hat when they shouted for the king and Reform.
But all was in vain. The mob, it is true, listened respectfully
to the colonel, cheered him and his soldiers, sang "God save
the king," but would not take his advice and go home.
However, he still hoped, good-natured man, to prevail by fair
means. From time to time he went to report to the magistrates, who were sitting in the Mansion House. He told
them that he hoped to disperse the mob by riding about the
square; they however thought that the tumult was increasing,

and they found that the rioters were renewing their efforts to
force their way into the kitchen and other parts of the
building. At length Serjeant Ludlow, astonished at his
temporising conduct, plainly asked him whether he had
received any orders which prevented him from obeying those
he had received from the magistrates; and on being answered
that his orders were to place himself under their directions,
the serjeant at once distinctly required him to clear the
streets. Colonel Brereton then commanded a charge, and
the rioters were driven from the square and neighbouring
streets in great confusion, but without any wounds being
inflicted. Nevertheless many of the mob took refuge in
narrow passages and on board ships lying in the harbour,
from which they annoyed the cavalry with stones and other
missiles. An officer went to the Mansion House to complain
of this, and to obtain permission to fire, and one of the
special constables offered to go with twenty-five others and
dislodge these assailants. This plan was disapproved by
Colonel Brereton, who assured the magistrates that if the
people were let alone they would soon be quiet and go to
their homes ; he added that he would be answerable for the
peace of the city, and would patrol it during the night. This
promise he fulfilled; but the soldiers continued to be annoyed
as before, and one of them, who was struck by a stone,
levelled his carbine at his assailant, and shot him dead on
the spot. Other rioters received sabre wounds.

At an early hour of the morning of Sunday, October 30th,
the people again began to assemble in the square, and by
seven o'clock the mob already amounted to several hundreds;
but they seemed to be drawn thither by curiosity, and manifested no disposition to renew the disturbances of the preceding
day. Major Mackworth, therefore, finding a handful of soldiers
patrolling their tired horses before the Mansion House,
thought it would be better to send them home, as they

seemed to serve no other purpose than that of attracting a crowd, but he found it impossible to do so, because the 250 constables whom he posted the night before for the defence of the Mansion House had now dwindled down to twelve, and the mayor was the only magistrate remaining within the building. Colonel Brereton, however, thought differently, and ordered the soldiers to their quarters. Their departure was a signal for a fresh attack. During the night the house had been barricaded as well as circumstances would admit, but the mob soon forced their way into it. The only persons left in the building were the mayor, Major Mackworth, the under-sheriff, and seven constables, all without firearms or other means of defence. Major Mackworth then told the mayor that he thought the time had now arrived when he was justified in providing for his own safety.

"Do you really think," asked the mayor, " that I shall be justified in quitting my post ? "

" Even as a soldier," replied the major, " I think it right, and it has clearly become your duty."

The little party then made their way out of the top of the house, through one of the front windows, and hiding themselves from the view of the mob behind the parapets of the houses, they crawled along till they reached the Custom House, kicked out a pane of glass, raised the sash, quietly descended, escaped into a back street, and made their way without molestation to the Guildhall.

The mob were now in full and undisputed possession of the Mansion House. Some occupied themselves in destroying and flinging out into the square the furniture of the rooms which they had not been able to enter on the Saturday. Others descended into the cellars, which contained about three hundred bottles of wine, of which nearly a third part was carried off and drank, or wasted in the square. A disgusting

scene followed.   Persons of all ages and of both sexes were
seen greedily swallowing the liquors, while scores lay on the
ground in a state of drunken insensibility.   Others excited,
but not stupefied, spread themselves over the town, adding
to the confusion and consternation which everywhere prevailed.   The troops were now brought back, but the people,
flushed with victory, maddened with wine, and exasperated
by the death of the man who had been shot the night before,
received them with a shower of stones, bottles, and bricks.
The rioters evacuated the upper part of the Mansion House,
but those in the cellars still continued their carouse.   One of the
aldermen now appeared, read the riot act, and endeavoured
to persuade the mob to retire.   He then desired Colonel
Brereton to order the troops to fire.   This, the Colonel, however, flatly refused to do, alleging that it would be of no
avail, and would render the mob so infuriated that they
might overcome the troops, and the city be given over to
slaughter.   He urged that it would be better policy to try to
keep the rioters in good humour till the following morning,
when reinforcements would probably arrive.

The mayor sent summonses to the churchwardens of the
different parishes, and caused placards to be posted at all the
places of worship and public-houses, giving notice that the
riot act had been read three times ; that all persons tumul-
tuously assembling would be guilty of capital felony ; entreat-
ing his fellow citizens to meet at the Guildhall, to assist the
magistrates in quelling the riots, and announcing the departure
of Sir C. Wetherell.   Only a very small number of citizens
answered the mayor's appeal by coming to the Guildhall, and
the few who appeared said that they would not risk their
lives unless supported by the military.   At this juncture
Colonel Brereton requested the magistrates to authorise the
withdrawal of his soldiers, stating that they were harrassed
and fatigued, and incapable of rendering any further service.

He added, that the mob were so exasperated against the 14th, in consequence of their having fired, that their lives would be in danger if they remained. The magistrates strenuously remonstrated against this proposal, which, if carried into effect, would leave the city at the mercy of the rioters, telling the colonel that if he removed the troops he must do so on his own personal responsibility. Finding him determined, they said that if they could not sanction the course he thought fit to adopt, they would not embarrass him, and they informed him where he would find quarters for his troops. The colonel then proceeded to carry out his intentions. It appears, however, that they were unwilling to go, and expressed the utmost readiness to act. As they withdrew they were followed by a large body of rioters, who continued their assaults on them, until provoked beyond endurance, they faced about and fired on their assailants. Notwithstanding, the mob continued to follow them to College Green, where a considerable number of persons had assembled in the expectation that Sir C. Wetherell, according to custom, would attend divine service in the mayor's chapel. Here the soldiers again faced about and fired. Still the mob pressed on them closely, and assaulted them as before, until they reached their quarters, when the soldiers once again turned and fired. These vollies were probably intended rather to intimidate than to injure the rioters, as only one person was killed and seven or eight wounded. Amongst these, was a poor fellow who had taken no part in the disturbances, but was shot through the arm as he was standing on the opposite side of the quay.

Colonel Brereton, whose conduct evidently arose from no want of personal bravery, rode back to the square, followed and cheered by a large number of men and boys. He addressed them, promising that there should be no more firing, assuring them that the 14th should be immediately

sent out of the city, and exhorted them to return to their
homes. Meanwhile the dragoons and the people occupied
the square without coming into collision. At length a portion
of the mob, stimulated by wine, and impatient of inaction,
went to the Bridewell to liberate the prisoners, who had been
conducted thither on the Saturday evening. They procured
sledge hammers from a smith's shop in the neighbourhood,
and at once proceeded to beat in the doors. About thirty
citizens and constables were dispatched by the magistrates,
but found themselves powerless to contend with the large
mob that was assembled, and were dispersed and maltreated.
They were followed by a small party of dragoons, who
advanced at a slow pace. At their approach the populace
fled in all directions, and they took up their position in front
of the building without difficulty, but they made no attempt
to disperse those who remained outside, or to clear the
building of the rioters, who, to the number of about 100, had
forced their way into the interior. Encouraged by this
inaction, the runaways soon returned, and the troops were
withdrawn amidst the cheers of the people, which some of
them acknowledged by waving their gloves ; the rioters then
lost no time in completing the work of destruction, the doors
that still resisted were beaten in, the prisoners liberated, and
the governor's house set on fire.

While these things were being done at the Bridewell,
another large body of rioters proceeded to the city gaol. This
was a strong modern structure which had been erected about
ten years before at a cost of nearly £100,000. It might easily
have been held against the mob by the turnkeys and other
officers, but here, as at the Bridewell, resistance seems not to
have been attempted. A vast mob surrounded the building.
Hammers were procured from an adjoining shipyard. The
massive locks were dashed to atoms, and the rioters forced
their way into the yard and the governor's house, which they

CHAP. IV. speedily gutted, throwing the furniture into the new river,
1831.   which, at the time, was ebbing fast and rapidly bore away
Oct. 30. the articles that were flung into it. The mob then released
the prisoners, and set fire to the building, which was speedily
wrapt in flames. As before, the troops arrived, but too late
to be of any service,—they did nothing, attempted nothing,
and went away. Major Mackworth thought them too tired
to do anything effectual. As they retired they acknowledged
the applause of the mob by taking off their caps.

The mob now finding that they encountered no serious
opposition, divided into parties, and proceeded to the toll
houses at Prince's-street bridge, at the Wells, at St. Philip's.
These they also set on fire, having previously allowed the
occupants to remove their furniture. A party of the rioters
went to the Gloucester county gaol, which is in the immediate
vicinity of Bristol. Here, too, the prison doors were force [1],
the prisoners released, and the building fired. The fire at the
Bridewell, which had gone out, was about the same time
rekindled, so that the three prisons and the toll houses were
all in a blaze together.

The next object of attack was the bishop's palace. The
bishop himself appears to have entertained some fears that
it might be assailed, for he had quitted Bristol this very
morning, after preaching at the Cathedral, and had caused
some of the more valuable and portable articles of furniture
which his mansion contained to be removed. At first the
number of rioters who attempted to break into it was so
inconsiderable that the few persons who were on the premises
were able to hold them in check. The mayor, being informed
that the palace was in danger, came to the spot accompanied
by a handful of citizens, whom he was able to collect at the
moment, and the military who were protecting the Mansion
House followed. The mob profited by their absence, and at
once attacked the unfortunate Mansion House, which they

forced, and set on fire. The party at the palace, seeing
that it was not at the moment seriously threatened, and
finding that the Mansion House was on fire returned to the
square. But they were now too late to be of any service
there. Already the whole of the back of the building was in
flames, and the front was occupied by a set of wretches
engaged in firing the various rooms, and who appeared at
the windows receiving the soldiers with loud shouts of
triumphant derision. The fire spread with appalling rapidity,
and many of these reckless creatures, unable to escape, were
consumed by the flames they had themselves assisted to
kindle. In about twenty minutes the roof fell in, and
brought down the whole front of the building with a
tremendous crash.

The soldiers remained idly gazing at the destruction which
they came too late to avert. But, while useless in the square,
they might have been of great service had they remained at
the bishop's palace. No sooner had they quitted it, than a
fresh body of assailants arrived, overpowered the servants
who were left in charge of it, set it on fire, and in a short
time reduced it to ashes. An attempt was also made to burn
down the Cathedral, but was frustrated by the efforts and
persuasions of five respectable inhabitants, who, to their
honour be it recorded, were all dissenters.

The Mansion House being now destroyed, it was thought
useless to keep the soldiers any longer in the square. They
were therefore ordered to the Guildhall, where their commanding officer and the magistrates had been sitting, which
had been attacked on the previous night, and which it was
feared would be the next object against which the efforts of
the rioters would be directed. But a portion of the mob in
the square were bent on further mischief, and finding no one
to resist them, they fired the house adjoining the Mansion
House, and by twelve o'clock at night the whole mass of

buildings between the Mansion House and Middle Avenue were in flames. Among these was the Custom House, a very large building, which was so speedily fired in different parts, that many of the incendiaries were unable to escape, and perished in the burning building. All this mischief was effected by a small party, chiefly boys. They went about their work in a very systematic and business-like manner, giving the inmates of each house half an hour's notice before firing it. The leaders were armed with axes, and some of them carried pots of turpentine and brushes, with the help of which they produced the complete conflagration of a house in a few minutes. With their axes they cut holes in the floors of the burning houses, to allow the air to enter and cause the flames to spread more rapidly. The fire extended to the houses in the adjoining streets, and as many of the principal wine and spirit vaults were in this quarter, they burnt with great fury. Others flung themselves from the windows, and were severely injured by the fall; among these was a woman, who shortly after expired. Three men were burnt to cinders. Two leaped from the roof and were killed on the spot; two boys, who had attempted to escape, were seen frying alive in the molten lead which rained from the roof to the pavement. Altogether, the rioters had fired the Mansion House, the bishop's palace, the Excise Office, the Custom House, three prisons, four toll houses, and forty-two private dwellings and warehouses.

But what were the respectable inhabitants doing while their city was in flames? Major Mackworth tells us that he went that evening to the council house, and found some two hundred persons there, under the presidence of an alderman, engaged in a very stormy discussion. They were all crying out "we are willing to act but we have no one to direct us." The major, one would think, was just the man they wanted. He was an officer of experience, cool, clear headed, and knew

as we have already seen, how to bring a handful of men to
bear with effect on a mob. However, he found that they
would not act to any good purpose, and retired disgusted with
their folly and party spirit, not however without arranging to
meet them in College Green, at six o'clock on the following
morning, when he promised to endeavour to organise them
into a body capable of being of some service. As for the
Dragoons, harrassed as they had been by repeated and useless marches, coming too late, or, if coming in time, not
ordered to act, they had been of little use, and were now
thoroughly wearied. The mayor, however, roused by the
conflagration in the square to a sense of the necessity of
acting vigorously, sent at twelve o'clock a letter to Colonel
Brereton, authorising him to take whatever steps or give
whatever orders he might think fit, to restore and preserve the public peace, as well with the troops he had at
present under his command, as with any others that might
subsequently arrive. In consequence of this communication,
the 3rd Dragoons, who had been withdrawn to their quarters,
were brought back into the square.

On Monday morning, Major Mackworth punctually presented himself at his place of rendezvous, but not a single
citizen met him there. He therefore went in search of the
Dragoons, whom he found quietly patrolling the square with
Colonel Brereton at their head. Two sides of the square
were in flames, and the rioters, numbering about a thousand
persons, were forcing their way into the corner house on the
side of the square nearest to the shipping; the major at once
saw that if this house were once fired, the shipping which
was closely moored in the very heart of the city would soon
be in a blaze, and the greater part of the city would be
destroyed. He therefore at once said to Colonel Brereton,
"we must instantly charge," and without waiting for an
answer, he gave the word "charge and charge home."

Colonel Brereton then charged at the head of his men, and the rioters fled in all directions; many of them were cut down and ridden over; some were driven into the burning houses, from which they never returned; and the Dragoons, after sabring all they could come at in the square, re-formed, and charged down a neighbouring street, then returned to the square once more, and rode at the miserable mob in all directions.

Still they were but a handful of some twenty-five men, and the mob dispersed in one place, re-assembled in another. Major Mackworth, therefore, clearly saw the necessity of obtaining reinforcements, and being the only one of the party in plain clothes, he galloped to Keynsham, about six miles distant, whither the 14th Dragoons had been led, and brought them back to the city, from which they had been hooted the day before, but in which they were now welcomed as deliverers. On the road, they were joined by a dozen of the Bedminster Yeomanry, and entered the city, charging the rioters vigorously. One troop pursued the Kingswood colliers, who had been very active in the work of destruction, two miles along the Gloucester road. The other executed charges in the city, cutting down all who resisted, and retook the gaol. And now troops and yeomanry came flocking in from all quarters. Major Mackworth, who had handed over the 14th to their commanding officer, Major Beckwith, organized the yeomanry, the pensioners, and the special constables, and the tranquillity of the city was restored. It should be mentioned, in justice to the Bristol rioters, that notwithstanding all the drunkenness and excited passions that prevailed, no act of personal violence or brutality to any individual could be laid to their charge.

Disturbed state of the country.
The disposition which these disturbances manifested was by no means confined to Bristol. There was perhaps not a town in the empire in which accidental circumstances might

not have produced similar disturbances. Nay, it was by no means improbable that the insurrection might have spread from Bristol to other places, and have become almost universal. It was the consciousness of this fact that secretly paralysed Colonel Brereton, and prevented the magistrates from giving their directions with that decision which would have ensured obedience. Had they positively and peremptorily in writing required him to act, he probably would have acted, and perhaps the riots would have been suppressed, not, indeed, without bloodshed, but with far less loss of life than actually occurred. But they recommended rather than ordered, and tried to shift the responsibility of acting off their own shoulders on to those of the military commander. We need not be surprised at their hesitation, nor at the still greater and more culpable backwardness of Colonel Brereton. The political atmosphere was everywhere charged with electricity, and this all men felt. About the same time that this terrible destruction of life and property took place at Bristol, there were riots at Bath, riots at Worcester, riots at Coventry, riots at Warwick, and in other towns. The destruction of the bishop's palace at Bristol was by no means a solitary instance of the detestation with which the bishops and clergy, but especially the bishops, were regarded at this moment. The Bishop of London was absent from the division on the second reading of the bill. His absence did not exempt him from the hatred with which his order was regarded. He had been announced to preach at St. Ann's, Westminster, but finding that on his appearance in the pulpit the congregation would leave the church, or perhaps even maltreat him, he did not fulfil his engagement. At a somewhat later period, Dr. Ryder, Bishop of Lichfield, a man of the highest character, after preaching a charity sermon at St. Bride's Church, was grossly insulted, and in danger of being killed by the infuriated populace, who surrounded the sacred building, and waited for the bishop's

CHAP. IV. departure from it. The Archbishop of Canterbury, the saintly
1831.   and venerated Howley, coming to Canterbury to hold his
primary visitation was insulted, spit on, and with great
difficulty, and by a very circuitous route, brought to the
deanery, amidst the yells and execrations of a violent and
angry mob. The Bishop of Bath and Wells being expected
to visit the latter city, a popular commotion was apprehended,
and troops were sent thither for his protection.   On the 5th
of November, the bishops in many of the towns, and especially
the cathedral towns, were substituted for Guy Fawkes, and
received the honours usually bestowed on that worthy.   The
Bishops of Winchester and Exeter were hanged and burnt in
effigy close to their own palaces. The latter prelate, who,
from his abilities and the decided stand he had made against
the bill, was peculiarly exposed to popular odium, was
represented on this occasion, as we are informed by the papers
of the period, by a figure thus made up :—"A head composed
of a hollow turnip, with a candle in the centre, in which were
cut the nose and mouth, but no eyes,—showing that though
the head possessed light, the bishop was blind to the past
and the present scenes around him. The faggots being
adjusted, they were set fire to, and the light soon discovered
the vitals composed of the liver and lights of a sheep and a
heart one mass of corruption."—*Morning Chronicle.* Nor
was this feeling confined to the persons of the clergy. It
engendered a savage Vandalism towards those sacred
buildings, which we, with all our mechanical advantages
vainly strive to rival. The author of this work, then a boy,
well remembers the fierce shout of applause which rent the
air at a large public meeting at Canterbury, when one of the
speakers suggested that the noble cathedral of that city
should be converted into a stable for the horses of the cavalry.
Such were the disastrous consequences of identifying the
church with a party in the state, and that too the party which

was engaged in resisting progress, passionately demanded by Chap. IV.
the mass of the people, and essential to the safety and well-   1831.
being of the state.

The intelligence from France served to increase the Parlia-
prevailing uneasiness and alarm. Before the country had ment re-
assembles.
recovered from the consternation which the Bristol riots had
produced, intelligence arrived that disturbances of a far more
serious and alarming character had broken out in Lyons, the
second city in France. The anti-reformers, half in terror,
half in triumph, pointed to these outbreaks, as evidences of
what might be expected if the Reform Bill should pass.
These events, too, had an unfavourable influence on many
timid though sincere reformers, and particularly on the king,
who daily became more and more alarmed. Still the great
body of the nation were as fully resolved as ever not to rest
until they had obtained a measure of Reform as strong and
as effective as that which the Lords had rejected. With this
determination was associated a strong desire to humiliate the
upper house ; in fact, this latter feeling had become almost if
not quite as earnest as the wish for Reform itself. In the
meantime trade and manufactures were everywhere suffering
most seriously from the prevalent alarm and agitation, and
the industrial stagnation greatly increased the popular
discontent and the general impatience to have the bill re-
introduced into parliament as speedily as possible. It was
rumoured that ministers did not intend to assemble parliament
before January, and the *Times* and the other Reform journals,
expressing the wishes and opinions of the great majority of
the people, vehemently deprecated this delay. At length, to
the great satisfaction of all but the anti-reformers, it was
authoritatively announced on the 21st of November that
parliament would re-assemble on the 6th of December, on
which day accordingly it met, and the session was opened by
the king in person, with the usual formalities. The speech

CHAP. IV. which His Majesty delivered at the opening of the session

1831. contained the following passages :—

Dec. 6.
King's
speech.
    "I feel it to be my duty, in the first place, to recommend to your most careful consideration the measures that will be proposed to you for the Reform of the Commons house of parliament. A speedy and satisfactory settlement of this question becomes daily of more pressing importance to the security of the state and the contentment and welfare of my people.

    "The scenes of violence and outrage which have occurred in the city of Bristol and in some other places have caused me the deepest affliction. The authority of the laws must be vindicated by the punishment of offences which have produced so extensive a destruction of property and so melancholy a loss of life, but I think it right to direct your attention to the best means of improving the municipal police of the kingdom, for the more effectual protection of the public peace against similar commotions."

Dec. 12.
Re·intro-
duction of
theReform
Bill.
    On Monday, December 12th, Lord J. Russell brought forward the third Reform Bill. In asking leave to introduce the bill, he spoke in a tone which showed that the recent occurrences had caused him to regard with considerable alarm the consequences that might result from another disappointment of the people's wishes, and his speech was evidently designed to allay the excitement which prevailed out of doors, as well as to persuade his hearers that the danger which attended a prolonged resistance was greater and more imminent than any danger which could arise from concession. Of the new features introduced into the bill, he gave the following statement :—"With regard to the principle of disfranchisement, we formerly took the census of 1821, and a certain line of population; but, since that time the census of 1831 has been nearly completed. It is however liable to the objection of being made at a time when disfranchisement

was connected with a small population, and persons might
have been gathered together in certain of these small
boroughs, in order to make up the required number of 2,000.
We have, therefore, preferred to take as a test the number of
houses instead of the number of persons. And as we do not
wish to place towns with several mean houses in a situation
of greater advantage than towns with a smaller number of
better houses, we have not taken the number of £10 houses
only, but the number of all houses rated to the assessed taxes,
up to April last. Ministers have obtained much information
from gentlemen whom we sent down to draw the limits of
boroughs; and from this mass of information, Lieutenant
Drummond, who is at the head of the commission, has been
instructed to make out a series of a hundred boroughs, beginning with the lowest, and taking the number of houses and
the amount of their assessed taxes together. From this
return Schedule A has been framed. It was necessary then
to draw an arbitrary line somewhere, as to the number of
houses and amount of taxes below which a borough should
be deemed too inconsiderable to enjoy the right of electing
members. We have hence taken the number of fifty-six
which was found in the bill of last session, and the result is,
that some boroughs which formerly escaped disfranchisement,
will now be placed in Schedule A, while others will be raised
out of it, and placed in Schedule B. The boroughs which
will be placed in Schedule A, in consequence of this change,
are Aldborough (Yorkshire), Ashburton, Amersham, East
Grinstead, Okehampton, and Saltash. There is another
borough, regarding which there are some doubts as to its
limits. Supposing Ashburton* to be one of the fifty-six, then
the boroughs that are to be raised out of Schedule A
into Schedule B, are Midhurst, Petersfield, Eye, Wareham,

---

* It was subsequently transferred to Schedule B.

Woodstock, and Lostwithiel. Schedule B, which in the last bill contained forty-one boroughs, will be reduced to thirty. It was formerly proposed to diminish the house by twenty-three members, but it has now been thought desirable to conciliate those who objected to the diminution, by leaving the present number of its members undiminished, more especially as this can be done without sacrificing any of the principles of the bill. It is proposed that of these twenty-three members, ten should be given to the most considerable towns in Schedule B; that one should be given to Chatham, so as to render that town independent of Rochester; and one to the county of Monmouth. Tavistock will be one of the towns removed from Schedule B. I have desired every information respecting that borough to be collected, and it will be laid before the house; and if any gentleman should still say that there has been unfair dealing with regard to it, I can only say that such an assertion will be false and unfounded. The remaining members will be given to the following large towns, to which the late bill gave one member each:—Bolton, Brighton, Bradford, Blackburn, Macclesfield, Stockport, Stoke-upon-Trent, Halifax, Stroud, and Huddersfield. With regard to the £10 qualification, ministers have never had the slightest intention to change it, either in amount or value. The right was formerly limited to those who had not compounded with their landlords for the rates, and who had resided in the house for twelvemonths. Under the new bill, all persons of full age, and not legally disqualified, occupying a house, warehouse, or shop, separately or jointly, with land of the yearly value of £10, would be intitled to vote. The former bill continued the franchise to all existent resident freemen and apprentices, and others with incorporate rights. The present bill will continue the franchise to all freemen possessing it by birth or servitude, for ever, provided they reside within the city or borough, or within seven miles of the place of voting."

Such were the principal changes announced by Lord J. Russell. Sir R. Peel, after expressing his readiness to postpone all discussion till the second reading, dexterously availed himself of the fact admitted by Lord J. Russell, that most of these changes had been suggested in the debates which had taken place in committee. "I congratulate the house," he said, "on the great escape they have had from the bill of last session, and I must express my deep gratitude to those to whom we are indebted for that escape from a danger which I never fully appreciated till now. The advantages of those maligned delays and objections are now visible throughout every part of the bill. There is scarcely an amendment which has been offered from this side of the house that has not been adopted; and these amendments are now all urged by the noble lord as so many improvements in the plan. I am not surprised to find the noble lord so severe on the late bill, but I own I was not prepared for such a sacrifice to the *manes* of the last parliament, as the adoption of General Gascoyne's resolution. It is now declared to be the deliberate conviction of the king's government, that the objections we made to the former bill were well founded. I cannot therefore but rejoice at the delay which has taken place." A long debate ensued, in which the opposition pleaded earnestly for the delay of the second reading, and taunted ministers with having borrowed all the improvements in the bill from their side of the house. At the same time they announced that they still regarded it as a dangerous and revolutionary measure, and were determined to resist it to the last. Many reformers expressed their strong dissatisfaction at the changes made in the bill. Cobbett, on the other hand, who was by no means partial to the government, publicly stated that he considered that they had fully redeemed the pledge they had given in promising that it should be at least as efficient as that which the House of Lords had

Chap. IV.

1831.
Dec. 12.
Sir R.
Peel's
observa-
tions.

CHAP. IV. rejected, and declared that it was even a better measure.   In
1831.   spite of the protestations of the opposition, the second reading
was fixed for Friday, December 16th.

Dec. 16.   On that day, accordingly, the question was brought for-
Second
reading.   ward by Lord Althorp.   He contented himself by simply
proposing it, adding that when it was disposed of he should
move that the house at its rising should adjourn till Tuesday,
the 17th of January, 1832.   All parties were now disposed
to shorten a discussion, the prolongation of which would serve
not to delay the progress of the bill but to abridge the vacation.   Lord Porchester, however, moved its rejection, in a
speech in which he stigmatised this measure as more objectionable than its predecessors, and after two nights' debate
the house divided on Sunday morning, when the numbers
were as follows :—

> For the second reading   324
> For the amendment   162
> Majority   162

This majority of exactly two to one was greater by more than
fifty votes than that which passed the preceding bill, and
exceeded by twenty-six votes that by which its second reading
was carried.

What will   And now the country was more and more occupied with
be done
with the   a consideration which for months past had been engaging its
Lords ?   attention.   The question now was no longer,—" What will the
Lords do ? but what will be done with the Lords ?"   The
extreme Radical party clamoured loudly for the abolition of
the hereditary branch of the legislature, but the great majority
of reformers were continually urging on ministers that a large
creation of peers ought to be made, and much was to be said
in favour of this expedient.   During the last fifty years the
enemies of Reform had been almost without interruption in
possession of power, and it was affirmed that they had filled the
House of Lords with peers who were the ardent defenders of

the abuses and corruptions which the bill aimed at removing. CHAP. IV.
It was pointed out that of the peers created before 1790,   1831.
one hundred and eight voted in favour of the bill and only
four against it ; while of the peers who owed their elevation
to Mr. Pitt, fifty voted for the bill and one hundred and fifty
against it. The bishops too, who owed their elevation to the
bench to anti-reform premiers, had almost unanimously
opposed the bill. It was urged, therefore, that ministers owed
it to themselves, and to their party, to create such a number
of peers as would restore the equilibrium of the house in
reference to the Reform question. At first, ministers did not
lend a ready ear to these suggestions. The king was strenuously opposed to such an exercise of his prerogative. Lord
Grey was almost equally averse to it, and most of the other
members of the cabinet, who were either peers themselves or
closely connected with the peerage, were very unwilling to
take a step which must destroy the independence of that
branch of the legislature. Still there appeared to be no other
means of carrying the bill, and strong as were the objections
of the ministers to create peers, they were justly still more
apprehensive of the consequences which would result from
the frustration of what they themselves had denominated the
just demands of the people. But the subject was frequently
discussed, at first with the idea that the creation of ten or
twenty peers might suffice. One by one the ministers became
convinced of the necessity of the measure. Lord Brougham
was the first convert, and, once convinced, he advocated it
with all the ardour and impetuosity that belonged to his
character. Earl Grey held out long, the Canning section of
the cabinet still longer, but finally all were brought to the
conclusion that the creation of a large body of peers, though
much to be deprecated and regretted, was the only means of
preventing far more terrible evils. Still the repugnance of
the king remained to be overcome, and it was rather

CHAP. IV. strengthened than diminished. He had, indeed, in the first
1831. instance, cordially approved the bill, and had fully intended
to support ministers in their endeavours to carry it, but he
had candidly informed them that he would not consent to
swamp the House of Lords for the purpose of carrying it.
He had indeed tardily and reluctantly agreed to create the
small number of peers which it was thought would suffice to
carry the second reading, but beyond this he would not go.
If therefore the bill should pass that stage, and the Lords
should materially alter the character of the bill, as, from the
avowed opinions of the majority, there was every reason to
expect that they would, the ministers would be obliged either
to violate the pledges they had given by accepting alterations
which would, in their own and the popular opinion, impair
the efficiency of the measure, or finally abandon their bill
and retire from office. The question, therefore, was for the
present left in abeyance. The ministers could only resolve
to deal with the difficulty when it arose, and to try to work
upon the prudence or the fears of the majority of the peers,
in the hope of averting the necessity for a creation which
they themselves still continued to regard as a great, though
perhaps necessary, evil.

Close of
the year
1831. Thus, amidst the anxieties of reformers on the one hand,
and the dread of revolution on the other, amidst incendiary
fires now again prevailing,* and Asiatic cholera spreading
through the country,† amidst distress of trade and dread of
coming bankruptcy, amidst the horror created by the crimes
of Burke, Hare, and Williams,‡ the year 1831 went gloomily

* Numerous incendiary fires occurred in the neighbourhoods of Bedford,
Cambridge, Canterbury, Devizes, and Sherbourne, in November and December; there were no fewer than eleven between the 23rd and 28th of the latter
month.

† It did not appear in the metropolis until the beginning of February.

‡ These wretches committed murders for the purpose of selling the
bodies of their victims to surgeons for dissection, and their teeth to dentists.

out; but the majority of the nation now thoroughly exaspe- CHAP. IV.
rated by the obstinacy of the anti-reform peers, hailed with a 1831.
grim consolation, the abolition of the hereditary peerage in
France, and hoped that this example would be speedily
followed in England.

The new year opened with a series of trials arising out of 1832.
the disturbances which followed the rejection of the Reform The new
Bill by the House of Lords. Special commissions were sent year.
down to Bristol and Nottingham, to try the rioters of those
neighbourhoods, great numbers of whom were convicted, and
some capitally punished. Colonel Brereton and Captain
Warrington were tried by court martial. The former avoided
conviction by committing suicide; the latter was sentenced
to be cashiered, but, by the recommendation of the court, was
allowed to sell out. Later in the year the Mayor of Bristol was
tried before the Court of King's Bench, but was honourably
acquitted, the jury giving it as their opinion, that in a situation of great difficulty, and when deserted by those from whom
he was entitled to expect aid and encouragement, he had
conducted himself with great firmness and propriety. The
parties chiefly to blame were the householders of Bristol, who
neglected to come forward when summoned by the mayor to
aid him in the preservation of the peace of the city. It is
satisfactory to know that they were compelled to pay a rate
of ten shillings in the pound on their rentals, to defray the
cost of the damage, which would have been prevented had
they done their duty. Four men, named Davis, Kayes,
Gregory, and Clarke, were executed at Bristol; and three,
named Beck, Hearson, and Armstrong, at Nottingham.*

---

* A circumstance, strikingly illustrative of the extent and character of
the social and political exaltation which prevailed at this period, may here be
mentioned. On the 18th of January, there was a meeting of Mr. Owen's
" Association for the Removal of all Ignorance and Poverty from the British
Nation," the Rev. Dr. Wade in the chair. £1,500 were collected; and it was announced that thirty-four bankers in London had agreed to receive subscriptions.

CHAP. IV.

1832.

Re-assemblage of parliament.

Parliament re assembled on the 17th of January, and ministers announced that they would go into committee on the Reform Bill on the 20th. Messrs. Croker and Goulburn complained that information which had been promised to the house, and which was necessary to enable members to form an opinion on the new provisions which had been introduced into the bill had not been forthcoming at the time for which they were promised ; and that such papers as had been furnished, were drawn up in a manner calculated rather to perplex and mislead than to inform. Lord J. Russell and Lord Althorp admitted that there was some foundation for these allegations, and explained the manner in which the delay had arisen. They would not, however, consent to a postponement of the committee, but promised that the papers should be printed as speedily as possible, and that the discussion of those parts of the bill which could not be understood without these documents, should be deferred until time had been given for their consideration.

The Reform Bill passed in the House of Commons.

Accordingly, on the 20th, it was moved that the house should go into committee on the Reform Bill. Mr. Croker repeated his arguments for delay, and was supported by Sir R. Peel and others. He subsequently moved an amendment that the house should go into committee on the 24th, but was of course defeated on a division ; and the house went into committee. Then the old game of procrastination and delay was played over again by the opposition. The first great battle was fought on the question whether the number of fifty-six should be retained in Schedule A. Defeated on this question, the opposition contended in vain for an alteration of the number of boroughs contained in Schedule B, now reduced to thirty. A long discussion took place respecting the returning officers of the boroughs. Colonel Sibthorp endeavoured to save his county of Lincoln from division. Both these attempts were defeated. On the general questions of

these divisions of counties, many of the usual supporters of Chap. IV.
the government opposed them, wishing that four members 1832.
should be given to the undivided county, rather than two to
each division; but, on the other hand, many of the opposition
supported the ministerial proposition, and after a protracted
debate, it was sustained by a majority of 215 to 89. But it
would be tedious and useless to enumerate even the principal
of the various and almost innumerable discussions that were
raised. Suffice it to say that the opposition repeated their old
artifices and their stale arguments and declamations about
democracy and revolution, and that by steady persove-
rance ministers at length succeeded in triumphing over all
procrastination and opposition; that the bill passed through
committee on the 14th of March, was read a third time by a
majority of 355 against 239, and finally passed the House of
Commons on Friday, March 23rd.* On the following Monday,

---

* On the 20th of March, in the course of the debate on the third reading
a scene occurred, the like of which has not happened since the days of
'Praise God Barebones" parliament. On that evening, Sir C Wetherell had
delivered one of his usual tirades against the bill, and was answered in a somewhat acrimonious tone by the Attorney-General. He was proceeding with his
speech when (the morning of March 21st, the day appointed to be observed
as a fast day on account of the cholera, having now arrived) Mr. Spencer
Perceval, member for Tiverton, broke in upon him with the following rhap-
sody :—" In whose name do you sit here? In his name, at the mention of
whom, with bitter taunts—(cries of 'question')—and think ye for one moment
that sitting here, in that forgetfulness of him from whom alone all counsel,
wisdom, and might—(' question.') (Lord Althorp rose and said—' I apprehend
the honourable member means to move an adjournment.') ('Adjourn,' 'Go on.')
Mr. Perceval continued—Think ye if that thing be true which is written—
'Except the Lord build the house, they labour in vain that build it; except
the Lord keep the city, the watchman waketh but in vain;' think ye, if that
scripture be true, that this your work can be blessed, or that the fruits which
ye expect from it can come to good? How standeth the account of the house
with its God at this time? (Loud cries of ' Adjourn.') Twice have ye, the
Commons of England, been called upon, but twice have ye been called upon
in vain, to humble yourselves before your God, and to seek his blessing in
contrition and repentance. (Loud cries of ' Question,' and considerable
confusion, amidst which several members quitted the house.) Ye depart, do

CHAP. IV. Lord J. Russell, attended by a large number of members,
1832.   once more carried it up to the House of Lords, there it was
read a first time on the motion of Earl Grey, and it was

ye, when the name of your God is mentioned? Ye would have sat till
five o'clock, and till six o'clock in the morning, had not his name been
mentioned, listening to the tongues of men tinkling like idle cymbals. (Mr.
Hunt rose to order, and moved an adjournment). Mr. Perceval continued—I
stand here to warn you of the righteous judgment of God which is coming
on you, and which is now near at hand. Do ye think that I stand here
relying on my own strength to keep ye attentive, or that I have power of
myself to force five hundred of ye to listen to my trembling accents? (Hear,
hear). Ye have in the midst of you a scourge of pestilence, which has crossed
the world to reach ye. Ye brought a bill into the house to retard its approaches,
and ye refused in that bill to insert a recognition of your God. The people
are the only god before whom ministers bow down in degraded worship.
[Here several members surrounded Mr. Perceval, and professing the great
respect which they felt for him, requested him to desist from his extraordinary
mode of proceeding]. The people of Scotland, more religious than their
neighbours, called for the insertion of the name of God, and when the people
called, that name was inserted in *their* bill. Ye have appointed a fast; but
I tell ye that that fast is, in the eye of God, a solemn mockery, which he
will not away with. I tell ye that it was not in the heart of the king's
council to humble themselves before God; and I tell them that he is not a
God to be mocked at. It was not because they trembled at their offences,
because they saw in the cholera a scourge hanging over the-land, or in the
disturbances of the country signs of God's approaching judgments, that they
reluctantly determined to appoint a fast; and therefore I tell them that this
mockery of religion, God will not away with. Commons of England, ye have
cast God of your own accord from you, and I tell you that in consequence this
work which ye have now in hand cannot be blest—the curse of God is upon it.
It hath been hanging over the country as a curse from the first day on which
the bill was introduced, and a curse it hath been upon the country from that time
to this. (Cries of 'Adjourn.') I tell ye that this land will soon be desolate; a
little time and ye shall howl one and all in your streets. I tell ye that the
pestilence, which God is now holding in, will be let loose among ye, and that
the sword will follow it. The church of the land shall be laid low, for she hath
corrupted her way before God. Ye may think me mad and ridicule me as a
man beside himself; but an hour is coming, and that shortly, when ye shall see
whether what I speak cometh from myself or from God. Ye sworn servants
of your king, have been anxious only to draw him into your net, but he is the
Lord's anointed, and ye shall not encircle him. I call upon ye to flee from your
forgetfulness of God and from the stone that threatens you."—Lord Sandon:
"There are strangers in the gallery."—The Speaker ordered the strangers to
withdraw —Mr. Perceval sat down suddenly, and the debate was adjourned.

agreed that the second reading should be moved on Thursday,
April 5th, but at the request of Lord Wharncliffe, who hoped
that by mutual concessions, the rejection of the second
reading might be avoided, it was subsequently postponed to
the following Monday.

Lord Wharncliffe, in making this request, had spoken on
behalf of a small body of peers headed by himself and Lord
Harrowby, which for the moment held the balance between
the contending parties in the House of Lords, the members of
which, under the names of "waverers" or "trimmers," became
for a short period the heroes of the day. When the Reform
Bill was thrown out by the peers, Lord Wharncliffe led the
opposition, and proposed its rejection in a form which he
found it necessary to alter, because it might be regarded as
insulting to the House of Commons. Lord Harrowby also
had spoken very strongly against the principle of the bill; and
all the waverers either voted against the second reading, or
were absent from the division. Their opposition to the bill
had, however, been expressed in terms much less uncompromising than those employed by the Duke of Wellington and
most of the Tory speakers, and approved by the majority of
the peers. Lord Wharncliffe, especially, had admitted that
a very large measure of Reform must be conceded, and both
he and Lord Harrowby voted against the second reading,
not with a view to prevent all reform but to obtain a miti-
gated measure of it. They hoped, therefore, that when the
bill was re-introduced, it might be modified in such a manner as to meet their views, and enable them to support the
second reading; and they were the more desirous that this
should be the case, because they dreaded above all things a
large creation of peers, in case the bill should be again
rejected on the second reading. The king himself entertained
very similar views, and hoped, by means of the waverers to
escape from the embarrassing situation in which he foresaw

CHAP. IV. that he would be placed. Lord Grey, too, was no less anxious
1832. to avoid a large creation of peers. Negociations were therefore carried on, commencing soon after the rejection of the
bill, between the king and the waverers, through the
medium of Sir Herbert Taylor, His Majesty's secretary,
with the full cognizance and approval of the premier. But
Lord Grey and the government were deeply pledged to introduce a measure fully equal in efficiency to that which the House
of Lords had rejected, and the very object of the waverers was
to diminish that efficiency in the sense in which the term
was understood both by the ministry and the nation. All
therefore that the government could do, with every desire
to meet and conciliate them, was to make such alterations
in the bill as, without rendering it less acceptable to the
nation, or more palatable to them, might afford them
an excuse for supporting the second reading when the bill
came again before the House of Lords. And this is the
true key to almost all the alterations which were made in the
measure on its third introduction. Some of the features to
which Lords Wharncliffe and Harrowby had particularly
objected were withdrawn, but they were balanced by other
concessions to the popular feeling, such as the enfranchisement of a greater number of large towns. This was all the
waverers could gain by their long negociations, and though
they were very far from being satisfied by the attempts made
to conciliate them, they resolved to vote for the second reading
in the hope of preventing a fresh creation of peers; and of removing some of those portions of the bill which they regarded
as most dangerous. Accordingly, when it was introduced,
Lords Harrowby and Wharncliffe stated that they still strongly
objected to it as it stood, but that they thought that some
concession should be made to public opinion, and that they
would vote for the second reading, and accept the principle
of the measure, but would endeavour to improve its details in

committee, and expunge those portions of it which they
regarded as too democratical. At the same time they
intimated that if they should fail in this attempt, they would
vote for the rejection of the bill on the third reading. The
Bishop of London was still more explicit. He not only
promised to vote for the second reading, but declared that he
would not support any amendment that would go to alter the
bill, so as to mutilate or destroy its essential principles, and
by that means bring it into such a state that the Commons
would refuse to agree to it. These frank declarations were
met with equal frankness by Earl Grey. He said that the
expressions of his noble friends, and especially those of the
Bishop of London, afforded him great satisfaction; that he
was apprehensive that some alterations might be proposed to
which he could not accede, but he promised that he would
give due consideration to the proposals in the true spirit of
conciliation. On the other hand, the Duke of Wellington
announced that he could not follow the example of Lords
Wharncliffe and Harrowby; the bill was not Reform, but in
many respects it was revolution; and Lord Grey himself had
insisted that it was really, truly, and in principle, exactly the
same measure as that to which they had refused to give a
second reading. This declaration faithfully expressed the
feelings and opinions of the great majority of those by whose
votes the bill had been previously rejected.

Such was the state of parties in the upper house when, on
Monday the 9th of April, the question of the second reading
was brought forward. Lords Harrowby and Wharncliffe justified at great length the course which they had already
announced that they would take, and the Duke of Wellington,
in accordance with his previous declaration, gave the bill the
same uncompromising opposition as before.* In order to

---

* Before the debate commenced the Duke of Buckingham favoured the
house with the outlines of a plan, which he gave notice that he should propose

Chap. IV. encourage the anti-reforming peers to vote against it he
1832. contradicted the assertions which were so generally propa-
April 10. gated, and so confidently made, that the king was in favour
of the bill. "It cannot be denied," he said, "that the
parliament was elected under circumstances of real excitement, which has ever since been kept up by the circulation
of reports that the king wishes for a Reform in parliament
such as the present bill proposes. Now, my lords, I do not
believe a word of any such thing. My opinion is, my lords,
that the king follows the advice of his servants ; it is also my
opinion that the part taken in the king's name on this subject
will make it very difficult to do otherwise than Reform parliament. I am fully persuaded, my lords, that it is a mistake
to suppose that the king has any interest in this bill, and I
am satisfied that if the real feeling of the king were made
known to the country the noble earl would not be able to
pass the bill. I am satisfied that if the country and the
parliament were convinced that the king was not fully
determined to go with his ministers it would be impossible
to pass such a bill as this."

This declaration, which it was felt that the duke would
not have hazarded if he had not the best authority for making
it, plainly intimated that the king was not favourable to the
bill as it stood, and would not be sorry to see it greatly
modified. Besides, looking at the question as a parliamentary
strategist, that is to say with a view to the influence which
the division would have on the greater or less amount of
Reform to be ultimately conceded, the duke thought—and,
perhaps, rightly thought—that it would be better to refuse
the second reading than to go into committee on it, even

if the ministerial measure should be rejected on the question of a second
reading. As, however, the event which the noble duke contemplated did not
occur, and his plan went no further, it is not necessary to give any account
of it.

though the rejection should be followed by a large creation
of peers. He probably reckoned on the known repugnance of the premier to a measure which would inflict a
blow on the independence of his order, from the effects of
which it might never recover. The duke, also, no doubt,
wished to carry on the game of delay, which was being played
by his party, and by rendering necessary another recommence-
ment of the contest, to produce a weariness which might lead
all men to desire a compromise. His opinion was strenuously
supported by Sir R. Peel. On the other hand, many of the
lords believing that the minister had obtained the king's consent to a creation of peers in case the bill should be rejected
on its second reading, and feeling that the independence of
their house, and their own individual importance would be
seriously affected by a large addition to their number made
under such circumstances, were disposed either to absent
themselves or vote with Lords Harrowby and Wharncliffe for
the second reading. Earl Grey and the ministers generally did
their best to encourage these dispositions. The premier,
especially, held out hopes of considerable concessions in committee. In his reply, at the conclusion of the debate, referring
to a portion of the speech of Lord Lyndhurst, he said :—

"The noble and learned lord says that ministers are
pledged to consent to no alterations in the bill. Now,
although I think fifty-six boroughs are not too many to
disfranchise, and that ten pounds is not too small a sum to
which to extend the suffrage, these propositions are no part
of the principle of the bill, and both of them may be altered
with perfect consistency with that principle. But the noble
and learned lord says that I will not consent to any alteration
in the bill. To that objection I will make the same answer
that I made in October,—that it does not depend on me, for
that it depends on your lordships. When the bill goes into
committee I shall certainly feel it my duty to resist any

CHAP. IV. alterations which I may think inconsistent with the main
1832. object which the bill proposes to carry into effect. But if it
April 13. can be shown that any injustice has inadvertently crept into
any of the schedules,—if it can be shown that any qualification
not so small as ten pounds will be less open to fraud and
abuse,—I will not resist the correction of such circumstances.
It is, at the same time, perfectly true that I should strongly
oppose any diminution of the number of fifty-six boroughs
which it is proposed to disfranchise, and any increase of the
ten pounds which it is proposed to fix as the minimum of
qualification. *But the decision on these points will depend
on the house, and not on me.* My opinions are as I have
stated them to be, but it is in the power of the house to
make such alterations as may, in their opinion, render the
provisions of the bill more accordant with the principles of it."
At the conclusion of this address the house divided, when the
numbers were:—

Content—present . 128—Proxies . 56 . 184
Non-content „   . 126   „   . 49 . 175

Majority in favour of the second reading   9 *

May 7. Thus, by the assistance of the waverers, the second
The Com-reading of the bill was carried, though by a majority so
mittee. small † as plainly to show that the opposition would have the
game in their own hands. The house adjourned at the
beginning of the following week for the Easter vacation, and
did not resume its sittings until the 7th of May, when it
resolved itself into a committee on the bill. Lord Grey on this
occasion manifested the same conciliatory disposition as before,

---

* The number of the bill's supporters on this occasion, as compared with
the last, had increased from 158 to 184, while the opposition had diminished
from 199 to 175.

† The majority of those *present* at the division was only two, and proxies
could not be used in committee.

and he moved the omission from the first clause of the bill Chap. IV.
of the words " fifty-six," thus leaving, for the present, unde-   1832.
termined the number of the boroughs to be disfranchised,   May 7.
and giving at least the appearance of freedom to the debates
that were to follow.

The opposition, however, were not disarmed by this con-   Lord Lynd-
cession. Lord Lyndhurst took the lead on the occasion, by   hurst's
motion.
moving that the consideration of the disfranchising clauses
should be postponed until the enfranchising clauses had first
been considered; so that instead of making enfranchisement
a consequence of disfranchisement, disfranchisement might
follow enfranchisement. The noble lord, and those who supported him, made many protestations of their desire to give
the bill a friendly and candid consideration, and of their
willingness to disfranchise a large number of boroughs.
Lord Wharncliffe, in particular, distinctly stated that while
he thought it to be his duty to vote with Lord Lyndhurst,
he was determined to go the full length of disfranchising at
least the number of boroughs contained in Schedule A. In
fact, the proposal was put forward as being simply a question
of the order in which the clauses of the bill were to be considered in committee; and it might seem to be a matter of
little importance whether the order proposed by the ministry
or that contended for by their opponents should be adopted,
but the real question at issue was, whether the control of the
committee was to be in the hands of the friends of Reform,
or of those who had all along been its open and avowed
enemies, and who, if they were now prepared to allow the bill
to pass in any shape, notoriously yielded because they durst
no longer resist the plainly declared will of the nation.
Ministers, therefore, wisely resolved to take the first opportunity of bringing this question to an issue. Accordingly,
after several of them had strongly contended that the proposal of Lord Lyndhurst was opposed to the principles of the

CHAP. IV. bill, Earl Grey distinctly warned the house that he should
1832.   regard its success as fatal to his measure ; thus intimating to
May 7. the opposition lords that if they voted for it they must be
responsible for the consequences of the rejection of the bill.
In spite of this warning, Lord Lyndhurst's motion was carried
by a majority of 35, there being 151 in favour of it and 116
against it.

Lord Ellen-   Earl Grey at once moved that the house should resume,
borough's
programme adding that he should also move that the further consideration of the bill should be delayed till Thursday the 10th.
This notice was equivalent to an intimation that the ministry
would either obtain the king's permission to create peers or
resign their places. The opposition sincerely deprecated both
these alternatives. They had resolved to make considerable
concessions, and hoped to force the government to meet them
half-way. This, however, the administration would not and
could not do. The opposition therefore determined, as a last
resource, to place the plan of Reform before the country,
hoping that they would be able to gain a considerable amount
of adhesion to it. Lord Ellenborough, therefore, who moved
the amendment for the rejection of the bill on the second
reading, on the formal motion being made by Lord Lyndhurst
for the postponement of clause B, rose and gave a programme
of the Reform which he and his friends were prepared to
support. "I will merely say that having, in conjunction with
other peers, given the most serious consideration to the great
principles of the bill—having well considered the claims possessed by the towns included in Schedules C and D*—having
likewise considered the reasonableness under existing circumstances of carrying into effect the changes which these
clauses, taken in conjunction with other parts of the bill,
would create —having reflected on the proposal to give

---

* The enfranchising Schedules.

additional members to the counties,—and having at the same Chap. IV.
time very strong objections to Schedules B and E,* the result   1832.
of the amendments to be proposed would have been to give   May 7.
enfranchisement to an extent such as would have made it
necessary (unless an inconvenient increase of the members
of the house were resorted to) to disfranchise the boroughs
contained in Schedule A, which, with Weymouth, would
cause a reduction of 113 members.   Another proposal would
have been to prevent persons from voting for counties in
respect of property situated in boroughs, and to adopt a more
clear and certain mode of ascertaining the genuineness or
value of holdings, while both the £10 qualification should be
adopted, and the scot and lot right of voting retained."

Such was the programme of the plan of Reform which
terror and the fear of worse had wrung from the anti-reform
peers.   It was put forward with the double view of inducing
the ministry to accept the offered concessions, or of appealing
to the country if they declined them.   So far as the administration was concerned, the hope of influencing them, if
seriously entertained, was completely disappointed.   Earl
Grey, with cold politeness, rejected the overture thus made
to him.   He sarcastically congratulated the noble lord and
the house on the progress he had at length made in the
principles of Reform, and especially on his expressed intention
not to touch the £10 qualification, and to preserve the scot and
lot right of voting where it at present existed, thus rendering
this "democratic measure still more democratic."   The house
accordingly resumed, and the further consideration of the bill
in committee was postponed to Thursday.

Nothing now remained for the ministry but to recommend Resigna-
such a creation of peers as would enable them to carry the ministry. tion of the

* The former containing the places to be deprived of one member, the
latter those to have outlying districts annexed to them.

CHAP. IV. bill through the House of Lords without important modifica-
1832. tions. The king had, as we have already intimated, all along
entertained the most decided objections to this step. He
had with great reluctance so far yielded as to consent to the
creation of peers if it should be found absolutely necessary
to carry the bill, and he wished that every possible expedient
should be tried to avoid this dire necessity; and, as we have
seen, it was probably the knowledge of his feelings on
this subject more than anything else which had induced the
waverers to consent to the second reading of the bill. When,
therefore, it came to be a question of the order in which the
clauses of the bill were to be taken, the king was fully justified,
according to the understanding which existed between himself
and his advisers, in refusing to follow their advice. But
besides this, a great change had come over the king in regard
to the Reform Bill. It is due to him to say that there is every
reason to believe that he had in the first instance given it his
cordial approval, that he had frankly and honestly supported
his ministers in their endeavours to carry it, and had at the
same time candidly stated to them the length to which he was
prepared to go with them, and the point at which he was
resolved to stop. But, in following the discussions on the
measure, he had been gradually more and more influenced by
the predictions of revolution, which were uttered by men who
enjoyed a high reputation for political sagacity, and by the
parallel which was often drawn between the commencement
of his reign and that of the unfortunate Louis XVI., which
seemed to be verified by the increased agitation which pervaded
the country, and by the rapid wane of his popularity. He
saw, too, with great dissatisfaction the growing feeling which
prevailed against all hereditary authority. Thus the Reform
Bill, if it had not become absolutely odious to him, was
certainly viewed by him with much less complacency than
he had formerly felt towards it, and this feeling extended to

the ministry by which the bill was introduced, and whom
he naturally regarded as the authors of the unpleasant—not
to say dangerous—dilemma in which he found himself.
When, therefore, Lord Grey and his colleagues required him
to choose between a creation of peers large enough to enable
them to carry the bill unimpaired or their resignation, he
at once accepted the latter alternative, cordially thanking
them at the same time for the services they had rendered
to himself and the country during the period of their administration. In all this there is nothing that is not perfectly
intelligible,—nothing to justify the charge of systematic
dishonesty and duplicity which has been brought against this
monarch, but which was certainly never believed by those
whose constant official intercourse with him afforded them
many excellent opportunities of forming a correct judgment
of his character, and whose penetration was unquestionably
sufficient to fathom a deeper mind than that of William IV.

On the evening of May 9th, Earl Grey announced in the May 9.
House of Lords the king's acceptance of the resignation
of his ministry, and moved that the order for going into
committee on the next day should be discharged, adding
that he did not think it necessary to fix another day for the
purpose.

The Earl of Carnarvon, one of the most violent opponents Altercation
of the measure, stigmatised in very strong terms the conduct between
Lords Car-
of the ministers. "My lords," he exclaimed, "the noble lords narvon and
opposite may act as they think fit; we know the grounds, the Grey.
slight grounds, which their defeat of Monday evening afforded
them for one of the most atrocious propositions with which
a subject ever dared to insult the ears of a sovereign. We
have heard, what I naturally expected to hear, that His
Majesty, who was among the first to recommend Reform,
upon broad and constitutional principles, finding himself
reduced to the alternative to which his ministers ventured to

reduce him, has acted as became a sovereign of the House of Brunswick, and by so doing has established an additional title to the respect and affection of his subjects. But, my lords, it shall not go forth to the public that, because the noble lords opposite have determined to abandon this measure, this house is unwilling to enter into the discussion of its merits. I therefore move that your lordships proceed with the consideration of the Reform Bill in committee on Monday next."

Earl Grey replied to this attack with a severe dignity, which on such occasions no one could more effectually assume, and to which his lofty figure, his commanding attitude, and aristocratic bearing, gave peculiar force and effect.

"My lords," he said, "I am too much accustomed to the ill-timed, violent, personal, and unparliamentary language of the noble earl who has just sat down to be much affected by the disorderly attack which he has made on my colleagues and myself. Nor is it for the defence of myself, personally, against the imputations which the noble earl has thought proper to cast on me, that I again rise to address your lordships. I trust, my lords, that in the estimation of your lordships and the public, my character is such that I may without presumption consider myself as sufficiently guarded from the danger of suffering by such imputations. The noble earl has been pleased to qualify the advice which I thought it my duty to tender to my sovereign as atrocious and insulting; and there were other noble lords on that side of the house who appeared to agree with the noble lord in that opinion. All I can say is, that I deferred giving that advice until the very last moment; until the necessity of the case and my sense of public duty imposed upon me an obligation which appeared to me to be imperative. But I appeal to your lordships, whether, until that period shall arrive, I am called upon to notice the accusation."

But the majority were not in a mood to listen to nor
follow the ex-premier, and after some further altercation, the
motion of the Earl of Carnarvon was agreed to, and the house
separated.

In the House of Commons, Lord Althorp made an announcement similar to that which had been made by Earl
Grey in the House of Lords. Lord Ebrington immediately
gave notice that on the following day he would move an
humble address to His Majesty on the present state of public
affairs; he added that he should also move that the house
should be called over on the occasion.

In pursuance of this notice, Lord Ebrington, on the following day, May 10th, moved the following resolution :—

" That this house, in conformity with the recommendation
contained in His Majesty's most gracious speech from the
throne, has formed and sent up to the House of Lords a bill
for the Reform in the representation of the people, by which
they are convinced that the prerogatives of the crown, the
authority of both houses of parliament, and the rights and
liberties of the people are equally secured.

" That to the progress of this measure this house considers
itself bound in duty to state to His Majesty that his subjects
are looking with the most intense interest and anxiety, and
they cannot disguise from His Majesty their apprehension
that any successful attempt to mutilate or impair its efficiency would be productive of the greatest disappointment
and dismay.

" This house is therefore compelled, by warm attachment
to His Majesty's person and government, humbly, but most
earnestly, to implore His Majesty to call to his councils
such persons only as will carry into effect, unimpaired in
all its essential provisions, that bill for the Reform of the
representation of the people which has recently passed this
house."

CHAP. IV. After a long discussion on the resolution, the house
1832. divided, when the numbers were :—
May 10.
          For the motion   288
          Against   208
                                         ———
          Majority   80

State of   If the state of the nation was alarming at the rejection of
the nation. the last bill it was much more so now. It soon became evident
that so far from there being any reaction, the feeling in favour
of the bill had become more intense and general. At no place
was it more distinctly manifested than at Birmingham, which
at this time exercised a more powerful influence on the
destinies of the bill than the other great towns of the empire,
not only on account of its central position and comparative
proximity to the metropolis, but also as being the heart of a
district densely peopled by a rugged and robust race who were
united almost to a man in determined support of Reform.
On the very day on which Lord Lyndhurst's motion was
carried, a meeting had been held, in anticipation of the
rejection or mutilation of the measure by the House of Lords,
at which 200,000 persons were said to have been present,
and at which very violent language was used, and very
violent resolutions were adopted. When, therefore, the
news of the resignation of Earl Grey's ministry reached
Birmingham, it produced a ferment. Everywhere it was
resolved not to pay taxes, and not to purchase property
which might be distrained for the payment of taxes. This
determination was announced in notices placed in most of
the windows in the town, and would unquestionably have
been carried out not in Birmingham only but throughout the
empire, and not only by the lower classes but also by many of
the upper and middle classes. Lord Milton desired the tax-
gatherer to call again, intimating that he might find it
necessary to refuse payment, and when afterwards asked in

the House of Commons whether he had really used this Chap. IV.
language he replied "certainly." It was a significant fact that 1832.
four Catholic priests and a large number of Quakers joined
the Birmingham Union at the moment when it seemed almost
ripe for rebellion.

On the 10th of May, the common council of the city of Meetings.
London resolved that "they who have advised His Majesty
to put a negative on the proposal of ministers to create peers
have proved themselves enemies of the sovereign, and have
put in imminent hazard the stability of the throne and the
tranquillity and security of the country." They also petitioned
the House of Commons to refuse the supplies until Reform
should have been secured. The same prayer came from Manchester, Birmingham, Leeds, and in fact from almost every
part of the kingdom. Everywhere the strongest determination was expressed, and the most violent proposals and the
most outrageous language were welcomed with the loudest
applauses. At a meeting of the inhabitant householders of
Westminster, Mr. O'Connell elicited tremendous cheering by
reminding his audience that Charles I. had been beheaded
for listening to the advice of a foreign wife. The prayer of
all the myriads of open meetings that were being held was
that the Grey ministry might be immediately reinstated and
the bill passed annihilated. Of all the speeches made at this
conjuncture, there is probably one only from which the reader
will desire to have any extract, and that is the speech of the
Rev. Sidney Smith. Everyone has heard of that worthy
divine's celebrated comparison of the House of Lords to Dame
Partington, when the bill was rejected in 1831; and many no
doubt will read with interest the following extract from his
speech at Taunton at the crisis we have now reached, in which
she is again referred to. "One word before we part for an old
and excellent friend of ours, I mean Dame Partington. It is
impossible not to admire spirited conduct even in a bad cause,

CHAP. IV. and I am sure Dame Partington has fought a much longer
1832.   and better fight than I had any expectation she would fight.
Many a mop has she worn out, and many a bucket has she
broken, in her contest with the waves. I wish her spirit had
been more wisely employed, for the waves must have their
way at last; but I have no doubt I shall see her some time
hence in dry clothes, pursuing her useful and honourable
occupations, and retaining nothing but a good humoured
recollection of her stiff and spirited battle with the Atlantic."

Efforts to   While these efforts were being taken to reinstate the
embarrass
the coming Grey ministry, efforts were also made to embarrass their
Adminis-   successors. One of these was a run on the banks. The
tration.
streets of London were covered with placards on which
were printed in huge letters—"Go for gold and stop the
duke." At the Manchester Savings Bank alone 620 persons had given notice for the withdrawal of deposits to the
amount of £16,000. Preparations were being made for
a recourse to arms, and there can be no doubt that if the
resistance to the popular will had been carried much further
than it was, a civil war would have broken out, or rather
an immense and irresistible armed mob would have marched
on London, and would have dictated their own terms to the
king, the government, and the legislature. What these terms
would have been it is idle now to conjecture, they would
certainly have gone far beyond the passing of the Reform
Bill, and probably would have involved the overthrow of the
monarchy and a complete change in the form of government.

Attempts   In the meantime, the king had sent for Lord Lyndhurst
to form a   to advise him respecting the course he should adopt under
ministry.
the circumstances in which he found himself placed. Lord
Lyndhurst recommended that the Duke of Wellington should
be sent for. The duke, though his conduct on this occasion
exposed him to much obloquy and aggravated his unpopularity,
appears to have acted in a highly honourable manner. We

may doubt his judgment in bringing on the crisis which he CHAP. IV.
was summoned to deal with, but we cannot refuse our admira- 1832.
tion to the self-abnegation and courage which he displayed
on the occasion. Entertaining the opinions he had all along
avowed on the subject of Reform, it was only natural that he
should endeavour to defeat so strong a measure as that which
the government had brought forward, or, finding that impossible, that he should seek to render it as little objectionable
in his eyes as he could venture to make it. But now that the
crisis had occurred, his predominant desire was to save his
sovereign from the humiliation of being compelled to solicit
Earl Grey to return and of consenting to the creation of peers.
The duke, however, felt that after the strong declaration he had
made against all Reform, after the uncompromising opposition
he had offered to the measure now before the House of Lords,
he was not the man to carry it through, even in a modified
form, or to accept office in an administration by which it was to
be taken charge of. He could not but be aware of the danger
to which he exposed himself, and of the imputations which his
opponents would not be slow to heap on him. He therefore
recommended that Sir R. Peel should be sent for and requested
to form a government, promising at the same time that whether
in or out of office, he would give every support in his power
to the new administration. Sir R. Peel, however, felt that
after the uncompromising opposition he had offered to the
bill, he could not accept an office from which he was certain
to be ignominiously precipitated in less than a week after his
acceptance of it, unless he supported all the essential features
of a bill he had so strongly denounced. The frightful responsibility which the state of the country imposed on an unpopular minister, might well make a man of much greater
courage than he possessed, shrink from a position in which he
would probably have to choose between civil war and revolu-
lution, without having time or opportunity allowed him even

CHAP. IV. to explain his intentions. Besides, the Catholic Emancipa-
1832. tion struggle was still fresh in his remembrance and in
the recollection of all men, and if he were now to accept
office and carry the Reform Bill, it would appear that the
accusation that he had been actuated by a sordid love of
the patronage and emoluments of office was really well-
founded. Men, whose opinion is entitled to some weight,
think that if he had accepted office at this juncture, he
might have retained it. Looking at the state of the country
at that moment, it appears to me that he must have been
hurled from power almost before his ministry was formed, and
perhaps the constitution would have fallen with him. But
be that as it may, there can be no doubt that both on public
and private grounds he exercised a very wise discretion in
declining the tempting offer. At the same time he promised
that if a ministry were formed from the political party to which
he belonged, he would give it all the support he could, and
his whole life shews that this promise would have been
honourably fulfilled.

Failure   Sir Robert Peel having declined to take office, there was
of the at- no other man in the anti-reform ranks who possessed suffi-
tempts to
form an ad- cient weight to form and lead an administration, except the
ministra-
tion.   Duke of Wellington. All the reasons which could be urged
against Sir R. Peel's acceptance of office might with equal
force be urged against his accession to power, with the
additional objection of the loss his ministry would suffer both
in weight and in strength by Sir R. Peel's refusal to join it.
But the duke's devotion to his sovereign and his sense of
duty prevailed over every other consideration, and seeing
that no one else could be found competent to form such a
ministry as the king desired, he accepted the thankless and
dangerous task. The king's eldest natural son had been
created Earl of Munster by Earl Grey, at the solicitation of
his father: he had however quarrelled with him, and had

been forbidden the court, but he now returned, and was said
to have taken an active interest in the formation of the new
administration. But all these efforts were unsuccessful. The
perils and difficulties of the situation were insuperable. Even
Sir R. Inglis and Mr. Davies Gilbert, two of the strongest
Tories in the country, denounced the attempt to form an anti-
reform ministry, which should pass the Reform Bill, even in
a modified shape. And on the 13th of May, the duke, having
exhausted all his efforts and resources, quailed before the first
sighings of the storm he had raised, and wisely yielded
before it burst forth. Mr. Baring, who throughout these
transactions had acted as the mouthpiece of the proposed
ministry in the House of Commons, announced, in his place
in that house, amidst the loud cheers of the majority, that
the commission given to the Duke of Wellington for the
formation of a ministry was entirely at an end.

Nothing then was now left for the king but to yield to
the almost unanimous wishes of his people, and recall Earl
Grey. It was evident that not only were the lower classes
almost to a man in favour of the bill, but that even in the
upper and middle classes the desire that it should be passed
speedily and without any considerable change was rapidly
spreading. Of this fact the character of the daily papers of
the period affords a sufficient proof. These papers circulated
almost exclusively among the classes we have just mentioned,
and it appeared that out of thirteen, which was the whole
number of them at the time, ten were on the side of Reform,
and that while, during the last ten days, more than 400,000
stamps had been issued to the papers favourable to Reform,
those issued to the anti-reform journals were under 40,000.
The violence of language in which the former class of papers
indulged at this period, also furnishes an index to the feelings
of their readers. A writer in the *Morning Chronicle*,
denominated the Bishop of Exeter " that obscene renegade

CHAP. IV. Philpotts." Royalty itself was not spared. The queen was
1832. stigmatized as "a nasty German frow." Another writer uses
the following language in reference to the king's natural
children :—" The bye blows of a king ought not to be his
body guard. Can anything be more indecent than the
entry of a sovereign into his capital with one bastard riding
before him and another by the side of his carriage? The
impudence and rapacity of the Fitz-Jordans is unexampled
even in the annals of Versailles and Madrid. The demands
made on the person of their poor drivelling begetter are
incessant," &c., &c. In fact, the king's popularity was now
completely gone. He was no longer "the patriot king,"
or "the sailor king." Dirt was thrown into his carriage as
he came up to London, and he was received in the metropolis with hisses, groans, execrations, and obscene outcries,
and was only protected from personal violence by the
exertions of the guards who surrounded his carriage.

May 17.   Earl Grey at once obeyed his sovereign's summons,
Earl Grey accompanied as usual by Lord Brougham. The king received
and Lord
Brougham them with evident ill-humour, and, contrary to his usual
have an
interview practice, kept them standing during the interview. But
with the he at once gave his consent to the creation of as many
king.
peers as the ministry might think necessary to enable them
to carry the Reform Bill through the House of Lords, with
the understanding that this power was not to be exercised
until every means of avoiding the necessity for it had been
tried—a condition which the two lords readily agreed to, as
they and all their colleagues were extremely averse to the
proposed step, and many of them would even have abandoned
a great part of their bill, if they dared, rather than have
recourse to it. This having been arranged, and it being understood that the ministers retained their offices, the king asked—
"Is there anything more?" "Sire," said Lord Brougham, "I
have one further request to make." "What." replied the king,

"have I not yet conceded enough?" "Yes," replied the Chap. IV.
Chancellor, "I do not wish to ask any fresh concessions of   1832.
your Majesty, but simply to request you to put in writing   May 17.
the promise you have made us."

The king was evidently irritated at a demand which
seemed to imply a want of confidence in his promise, but he
also felt that he could not resist. After a moment's hesitation, he took a small piece of paper, on which he wrote the
following words, which he then handed to Lord Brougham:—
"The king grants permission to Earl Grey and to his Chancellor, Lord Brougham, to create such a number of peers as
will be sufficient to ensure the passing of the Reform Bill—
first calling peers' eldest sons.   Signed,
   "Windsor, May 17, 1832.   WILLIAM R."

The same evening, Sir Herbert Taylor, who had been
present at this interview, wrote the following circular note to
the most active of the opposition lords :—

   "My dear Lord,

   "I am honoured with His Majesty's commands to acquaint
your lordship that all difficulties to the arrangements in
progress will be obviated by a declaration in the house of
peers to-night, from a sufficient number of peers, that in
consequence of the present state of affairs they have come to
the resolution of dropping their opposition to the Reform
Bill, so that it may pass without delay, and as nearly as
possible in its present shape."

   "I have the honour to be, yours sincerely,

                    "HERBERT TAYLOR."

On the evening on which this letter was written the Explana-
Duke of Wellington, in his place in the House of Lords, gave   tions.
a full explanation of the share he had taken in the transactions
which had followed Earl Grey's resignation. He then withdrew from the house, and did not make his appearance in it
again until the day following the passing of the Reform Bill.

Lords Grey and Brougham, on the other hand, did not even yet choose to declare positively that they would retain their offices. "All I can state," said the former, "is that my continuance in office will depend on my conviction of my ability to carry into full effect the bill on your lordships' table, unimpaired in principle and in all its essential details." "We shall not return to office," said the Chancellor, "except upon the condition not only of our possessing the ability to carry the bill efficiently through the house, but also of being able to carry it through with every reasonable dispatch consistent with the due discussion of its various provisions."

The fact is that ministers were not, at this moment, aware of the proceeding of Sir Herbert Taylor, and they were most unwilling to use the power that the king had given them to the extent that would be required to carry the bill unimpaired, if the anti-reform peers persisted in their opposition to it. Therefore, notwithstanding their triumph, they were still in the greatest perplexity. They hesitated to use the power they had obtained. There were the people behind them, instant with loud voices, demanding the bill. They had conjured up a spirit they could not lay and could not resist. They have been gravely censured for this, but most unjustly. The situation was most difficult, but the difficulty arose from the fault of those who had delayed Reform so long, that it was necessary to do in one bill and at one time what ought to have been done long before in twenty bills, spread over more than a century. That which—done in time—might have been effected quietly and without danger, was now attended with imminent peril. The longer the delay the greater the danger, and the more violent the required change. The chief merit of the Grey ministry was that they dared to face the difficulties of the situation before it was too late, and by proposing a strong measure of Reform to prevent a revolution.

The success of Sir Herbert Taylor's communication to the CHAP. IV.
peers removed every difficulty, and Earl Grey being asked, 1832.
on the following evening, by the Earl of Harewood, whether it May 18.
was settled that ministers should continue in office, replied—
" In consequence of my having received the king's request to
that effect, and in consequence of my now finding myself in
a situation which will enable me to carry through the bill
unimpaired in its efficiency, I and my colleagues continue in
office." He accordingly moved that the bill should be proceeded with on Monday.

Lord Harewood, after bitterly complaining that the inde- The bill in committee.
pendence of the house was destroyed, announced his intention
of withdrawing from further opposition, and a large number
of peers followed the same course. A small minority disregarded the king's request, and still offered a pertinacious and
often violent opposition to its progress, and, if they did not
succeed in their endeavours, at least had the satisfaction of
venting their indignation, which they did in no measured
terms. Here is a specimen scene. In the course of a discussion on the enfranchisement of Oldham, Lord Kenyon
exclaimed—

" The bill will be the destruction of the monarchy; by May 22.
forcing this measure on his reluctant sovereign, the noble
earl has placed the king in a situation in which he could
make no choice of a minister; and his advice to exercise his
prerogative in so unconstitutional a manner as to destroy the
independence of this house is abandoned and atrocious."

Earl Grey (interrupting, with great warmth and amidst
vehement cheering): "Atrocious! my lords. I put it to your
lordships, is it consistent with the usages of this house, or
with ordinary propriety, that the noble lord should apply
such words to me ? For my part I can only reject the words
with contempt and scorn."

Lord Kenyon : "I repeat that I think such conduct most

CHAP. IV. abandoned and atrocious. Whether the noble lord be pleased
1832. or not with my using the word *atrocious*, the privileges of
May 22. the house have not been abrogated to such an extent that
the noble earl can prevent me from saying that I shall always
feel that it was a most atrocious act of the minister to give
such advice to the king."

Earl Grey : "Anything more unparliamentary, disorderly,
and atrocious, than the applying of such words to me I never
heard in this house. It is for the house to act as may seem
befitting its own dignity; but for me, all that remains to me
is to throw back those words with the utmost scorn, contempt,
and indignation.   ."

After some further bickerings, the Duke of Cumberland
interposed as a peacemaker, and the business of the committee
proceeded.

These efforts only served to delay the period of the final
adoption of the bill, and to introduce some very trifling modifications of its details. In six days it went through the
committee, and on the 4th of June it was read a third time
and passed, 106 peers voting for it and only 22 against it.
Lords Wharncliffe and Harrowby, by whose assistance the
second reading was carried, evidently thought that they had
been duped by the ministry, and took the opportunity afforded
them by the debate on the third reading to give utterance to
their disappointment and indignation.

June 5.   On the 5th of June, the amendments introduced into the
The amend- bill by the House of Lords were submitted to the lower house
ments of
the Lords and assented to. No objection was made to them from any
accepted by
the Com- quarter, nevertheless a long discussion took place, which had
mons.
very little reference to the question before the house, but
which presented one or two remarkable features. In the course
of this debate Lord Milton avowed and justified his intention to resist the payment of taxes in case the Wellington
administration had been formed. Sir R. Peel also made the

following remarks, to which subsequent events gave peculiar Chap. IV.
interest and significance :—" Whenever government come to 1832.
deal with the Corn Laws, the precedent formed by the present
occasion will be appealed to, and if they should be placed in
similar circumstances of difficulty and excitement, the danger
to the public tranquillity will be made a plea for overturning
the independence of the House of Lords." Little did he then
dream that when the dire commotion, which he thus
lugubriously predicted, arrived, he himself would be the man
who, by the aid of a reformed House of Commons, would con-
strain a reluctant House of Lords to sanction the entire
abolition of the Corn Laws, and the subversion of the policy
with which they were identified. It was also in the course
of this debate that Lord J. Russell made the celebrated
"finality" declaration, which has so often been referred to as a
proof that he and his colleagues were pledged to resist any
attempt to carry further than they had done by their bill the
Reform of the House of Commons. His words were these : "I
think that so far as ministers are concerned this is a final
measure. I declared on the second reading of the bill that
if only a part of the measure were carried it would lead to
new agitations, that is now avoided by the state in which the
bill has come from the other house." To every candid mind
it must be evident that these words were intended to convey
nothing more than that so far as the Grey administration
was concerned the Reform Bill was intended to settle the
question with which it dealt, but that they did not pledge
Lord J. Russell or the other members of the Grey cabinet to
abstain from assisting in the further extension of the franchise,
or the remedy of other evils and injustices which their bill
left untouched.

The bill, thus at length adopted by the legislature, swept Results of
away fifty-six nomination boroughs, returning 112 members, the bill.
semi-disfranchised thirty more, making a sum total of

disfranchisement of 142 seats in the lower house of parliament. It gave the counties sixty-five additional representatives, and conferred the right of sending members to the House of Commons on Manchester, Leeds, Birmingham, and thirty-nine other large and flourishing towns previously unrepresented. On the other hand it greatly impaired the direct influence of the working classes in the elections, by diminishing the number of the franchises in Preston and other towns, where, before the Reform Bill was carried, the suffrage was nearly universal. It must also be confessed that the mechanism of the measure was in many respects faulty. This was admitted by the late Lord Spencer—the Lord Althorp of our history—and has been pointed out by the late Sir J. Stephen, Mr. Chadwick, and other authorities. For this, however, the opponents of the bill were much more to blame than its framers and supporters. Their efforts were exerted not to amend the bill but to delay and defeat it. Not only did they bring forward themselves a multitude of motions with this view, but they also availed themselves of all the amendments proposed by the friends of Reform to forward their obstructive designs. But the defects thus occasioned, though much to be regretted, are as dust in the balance when weighed against the solid gain which was obtained by the abolition of the crying abuses and mischievous working of the system which the bill swept away, as well as by the positive benefits of the system which it introduced. It conferred on some of the most powerful interests in the nation not perhaps all the influence in the framing of our laws to which their growing importance entitled them, but an influence sufficient to secure attention to their needs and requirements. The vast expansion of our trade, commerce, and manufactures, which has since taken place could not have been effected if the landed interest had continued to possess that virtual monopoly of legislation which was taken from it by the Reform Bill.

Nothing now remained in order to give the bill the force CHAP. IV.
of law but the formal assent of the king. It was earnestly 1832.
hoped that he would have given it in person, and had he done The Royal
so he would probably have recovered a considerable portion of assent.
the popularity he had lost by his refusal to create peers. His
ministers implored him to go down to the House of Lords; the
Reform journals urged him to attend, and promised a most
enthusiastic reception, which most unquestionably would have
been given to him, for the people, now that their wishes were
gratified, were quite prepared to forgive his past conduct.
But the treatment he had received after Lord Grey's resignation, and the abuse with which he had been loaded by the
Reform journals at that period, had made a deep impression
on his mind, and he peremptorily refused to give his assent
to the bill in person. It was consequently given by commission; the commissioners being the Lord Chancellor, Earl
Grey, the Marquis of Lansdowne, the Marquis of Wellesley,
Lord Durham, and Lord Holland. The ministerial benches
were crowded, those usually occupied by the opposition were
empty. One single prelate, Dr. Maltby, the new Bishop of
Chichester, represented the episcopal bench on the occasion.
The Speaker, followed by all the members present in the
house, with the single exception of Sir R. H. Inglis, went up
to the House of Lords, and announced on his return that the
royal assent had been given to the bill. The announcement
was received in silence, and the absence of the king gave rise
to gloomy presentiments. The bill had now become law, but
its results yet remained to be seen. The agitation which the
struggle had caused and the passions it had roused had by no
means subsided, and the state of the public mind was such as
to give rise to anxious forebodings even in the hearts of the
most sanguine supporters of the measure as to the use which
the nation would make of its victory. These fears we all know
were proved by the event to be unfounded. The dangers which

CHAP. IV. menaced the state have passed away. The constitution has
1832.   acquired new vigour—tranquillity, contentment, security, and
wealth of the nation have increased enormously, and many
excellent measures have passed, to the great advantage of all
classes, which an unreformed parliament never would have
entertained. It is no part of the historian's province to speak
of any future extension which the principles of the bill may
receive, but he may at least be permitted, in concluding, to
draw this lesson from the experience of the past, that if so
great and organic a change, carried by strong popular feeling,
could be effected without injury to our institutions, but even
with a great increase of their stability and of the national
prosperity, we may be quite sure that no danger can attend
the comparatively trifling changes which the lapse of time,
or the unavoidable imperfections of this first measure of
Reform, may have rendered necessary.

THE END.

APPENDIX.

Authentic Copy of a Petition praying for a Reform in Parliament, presented to the House of Commons by CHARLES GREY, Esq., on Monday, 6th May, 1793 ; and signed only by the Members of the Society of the Friends of the People, associated for the Purpose of obtaining a Parliamentary Reform.

" To the Honourable the Commons of Great Britain in Parliament assembled.

"Sheweth,—That by the form and spirit of the British constitution, the king is vested with the sole executive power.

"That the House of Lords consists of lords spiritual and temporal, deriving their titles and consequence either from the crown, or from hereditary privileges.

" That these two powers, if they acted without control, would form either a despotic monarchy, or a dangerous oligarchy.

" That the wisdom of our ancestors hath contrived, that these authorities may be rendered not only harmless, but beneficial, and be exercised for the security and happiness of the people.

" That this security and happiness are to be looked for in the introduction of a third estate, distinct from, and a check upon the other two branches of the legislature; created by, representing, and responsible to the people themselves.

" That so much depending upon the preservation of this third estate, in such its constitutional purity and strength, your petitioners are reasonably jealous of whatever may appear to vitiate the one, or to impair the other.

" That at the present day the House of Commons does not fully and fairly represent the people of England, which, consistently with what your petitioners conceive to be the principles of the constitution, they consider as a grievance, and therefore, with all becoming respect, lay their complaints before your honourable house.

" That though the terms in which your petitioners state their grievance may be looked upon as strong, yet your honourable house is entreated to believe that no expression is made use of for the purpose of offence.

" Your petitioners in affirming that your honourable house is not an adequate representation of the people of England, do but state a fact, which

APPENDIX. if the word 'representation' be accepted in its fair and obvious sense, they
are ready to prove, and which they think detrimental to their interests, and
contrary to the spirit of the constitution.

"How far this inadequate representation is prejudical to their interests,
your petitioners apprehend they may be allowed to decide for themselves;
but how far it is contrary to the spirit of the constitution, they refer to the
consideration of your honourable house.

"If your honourable house shall be pleased to determine that the people
of England ought not to be fully represented, your petitioners pray that such
your determination may be made known, to the end that the people may be
apprised of their real situation; but if your honourable house shall conceive
that the people are already fully represented, then your petitioners beg leave
to call your attention to the following facts:—

"Your petitioners complain, that the number of representatives assigned
to the different counties is grossly disproportioned to their comparative extent,
population, and trade.

"Your petitioners complain, that the elective franchise is so partially and
unequally distributed, and is in so many instances committed to bodies of
men of such very limited numbers, that the majority of your honourable
house is elected by less than fifteen thousand electors, which, even if the
male adults in the kingdom be estimated at so low a number as three millions,
is not more than the two-hundredth part of the people to be represented.

"Your petitioners complain, that the right of voting is regulated by no
uniform or rational principle.

"Your petitioners complain, that the exercise of the elective franchise is
only renewed once in seven years.

"Your petitioners thus distinctly state the subject matter of their complaints, that your honourable house may be convinced that they are acting
from no spirit of general discontent, and that you may with the more ease be
enabled to enquire into the facts, and to apply the remedy.

"For the evidence in support of the first complaint, your petitioners refer
to the return book of your honourable house. Is it fitting that Rutland and
Yorkshire should bear an equal rank in the scale of county representation;
or can it be right, that Cornwall alone should, by its extravagant proportion
of borough members, outnumber not only the representatives of Yorkshire
and Rutland together, but of Middlesex added to them? Or, if a distinction
be taken between the landed and the trading interests, must it not appear
monstrous that Cornwall and Wiltshire should send more borough members
to parliament than Yorkshire, Lancashire, Warwickshire, Middlesex, Worces-
tershire, and Somersetshire united? and that the total representation of all
Scotland should but exceed by one member the number returned for a single
county in England?

"The second complaint of your petitioners is founded on the unequal
proportions in which the elective franchise is distributed, and in support
of it,

"They affirm that seventy of your honourable members are returned by
thirty-five places, where the right of voting is vested in burgage and other

tenures of a similar description, and in which it would be to trifle with the patience of your honourable house to mention any number of voters whatever, the elections at the places alluded to being notoriously a mere matter of form. And this your petitioners are ready to prove.

"They affirm that, in addition to the seventy honourable members so chosen, ninety more of your honourable members are elected by forty-six places, in none of which the number of voters exceeds fifty. And this your petitioners are ready to prove.

"They affirm that, in addition to the hundred and sixty so elected, thirty-seven more of your honourable members are elected by nineteen places, in none of which the number of voters exceeds one hundred. And this your petitioners are ready to prove.

"They affirm that in addition to the hundred and ninety-seven honourable members so chosen, fifty-two more are returned to serve in parliament, by twenty-six places, in none of which the number of voters exceeds two hundred. And this your petitioners are ready to prove.

"They affirm that, in addition to the two hundred and forty-nine so elected, twenty more are returned to serve in parliament for counties in Scotland, by less than by one hundred electors each, and ten for counties in Scotland by less than two hundred and fifty each. And this your petitioners are ready to prove, even admitting the validity of fictitious votes.

"They affirm that, in addition to the two hundred and seventy-nine so elected, thirteen districts of burghs in Scotland, not containing one hundred voters each, and two districts of burghs not containing one hundred and twenty-five each, return fifteen more honourable members. And this your petitioners are ready to prove.

"And in this manner, according to the present state of the representation, two hundred and ninety-four of your honourable members are chosen, and, being a majority of the entire House of Commons, are enabled to decide all questions in the name of the whole people of England and Scotland.

"The third complaint of your petitioners is founded on the present complicated rights of voting. From the caprice with which they have been varied, and the obscurity in which they have become invólved by time and contradictory decisions, they are become a source of infinite confusion, litigation, and expense.

"Your petitioners need not tender any evidence of the inconveniences which arise from this defect in the representation, because the proof is to be found in your journals, and the minutes of the different committees who have been appointed under the 10th and 11th of the king. Your honourable house is but too well acquainted with the tedious, intricate, and expensive scenes of litigation which have been brought before you, in attempting to settle the legal import of those numerous distinctions which perplex and confound the present rights of voting. How many months of your valuable time have been wasted in listening to the wrangling of lawyers upon the various species of burgagehold, leasehold, and freehold ! How many committees have been occupied in investigating the nature of scot and lot, pot wallers, commonalty, populacy, resiant inhabitants, and inhabitants at large !

APPENDIX. What labour and research have been employed in endeavouring to ascertain
the legal claims of borough-men, aldermen, port-men, select-men, burgesses,
and council-men ! And what confusion has arisen from the complicated
operation of clashing charters, from freemen resident and non-resident, and
from the different modes of obtaining the freedom of corporations by birth,
by servitude, by marriage, by redemption, by election, and by purchase !
On all these points it is however needless for your petitioners to enlarge,
when your honourable house recollects the following facts, namely—that
since the 22nd of December, 1790, no less than twenty-one committees have
been employed in deciding upon litigated rights of voting. Of these, eight
were occupied with the disputes of three boroughs, and there are petitions
from four places yet remaining before your honourable house, waiting for a
final decision to inform the electors what their rights really are.

"But the complaint of your petitioners on the subject of the want of an
uniform and equitable principle in regulating the right of voting, extends as
well to the arbitrary manner in which some are excluded as to the intricate
qualifications by which others are admitted to the exercise of that privilege.

"Religious opinions create an incapacity to vote. All Papists are
excluded generally, and, by the operation of the Test Laws, Protestant
Dissenters are deprived of a voice in the election of representatives in about
thirty boroughs, where the right of voting is confined to corporate officers
alone ; a deprivation the more unjustifiable because, though considered ɩs
unworthy to vote, they are deemed capable of being elected, and may be the
representatives of the very places for which they are disqualified from being
the electors.

" A man possessed of one thousand pounds per annum, or any other sum,
arising from copyhold, leasehold for ninety-nine years, trade, property in the
public funds, or even freehold in the city of London, and many other cities
and towns having peculiar jurisdictions, is not thereby intitled to vote.
Here again a strange distinction is taken between electing and representing,
as a copyhold is a sufficient qualification to sit in your honourable house.

" A man paying taxes to any amount, how great soever, for his domestic
establishment, does not thereby obtain a right to vote unless his residence
be in some borough where that right is vested in the inhabitants. This
exception operates in sixty places, of which twenty-eight do not contain
three hundred voters each, and the number of householders in England and
Wales (exclusive of Scotland), who pay all taxes, is 714,911, and of householders who pay all taxes but the house and window taxes is 284,459, as
appears by a return made to your honourable house in 1785; so that, even
supposing the sixty places above-mentioned to contain, one with another,
one thousand voters in each, there will remain 939,370 householders who
have no voice in the representation unless they have obtained it by accident
or by purchase. Neither their contributions to the public burdens, their
peaceable demeanour as good subjects, nor their general respectability and
merits as useful citizens, afford them, as the law now stands, the smallest
pretensions to participate in the choice of those who, under the name of their
representatives, may dispose of their fortunes and liberties.

"In Scotland the grievance arising from the nature of the rights of voting has a different and still more intolerable operation. In that great and populous division of the kingdom not only the great mass of the householders, but of the landholders also, are excluded from all participation in the choice of representatives. By the remains of the feudal system in the counties, the vote is severed from the land and attached to what is called the superiority. In other words, it is taken from the substance and transferred to the shadow, because, though each of these superiorities must, with very few exceptions, arise from the present annual value of four hundred pounds sterling, yet it is not necessary that the lands should do no more than give a name to the superiority, the possessor of which may retain the right of voting notwithstanding he be divested of the property. And on the other hand, great landholders have the means afforded them, by the same system, of adding to their influence, without expense to themselves, by communicating to their confidential friends the privilege of electing members to serve in parliament. The process by which this operation is performed is simple. He who wishes to increase the number of his dependent votes surrenders his charter to the crown, and, parcelling out his estate into as many lots of four hundred pounds per annum as may be convenient, conveys them to such as he can confide in. To these new charters are, upon application, granted by the crown, so as to erect each of them into a superiority, which privilege once obtained the land itself is re-conveyed to the original granter; and thus the representatives of the landed interest in Scotland may be chosen by those who have no real or beneficial interest in the land.

"Such is the situation in which the counties of Scotland are placed. With respect to the burghs, everything that bears even the semblance of popular choice has long been done away. The election of members to serve in parliament is vested in the magistrates and town councils, who having by various innovations constituted themselves into self-elected bodies, instead of officers freely chosen by the inhabitants at large, have deprived the people of all participation in that privilege, the free exercise of which affords the only security they can possess for the protection of their liberties and property.

"The fourth and last complaint of your petitioners is the length of the duration of parliament. Your honourable house knows that, by the ancient laws and statutes of this kingdom, frequent parliaments ought to be held; and that the 6th of William and Mary, c. 2 (since repealed), speaking while the spirit of the revolution was yet warm, declared that 'frequent and new parliaments tend very much to the happy union and good agreement between king and people;' and enacted that no parliament should last longer than three years. Your petitioners, without presuming to add to such an authority by any observations of their own, humbly pray that parliament may not be continued for seven years.

"Your petitioners have thus laid before you the specific grounds of complaint from which they conceive every evil in the representation to spring, and on which they think every abuse and inconvenience is founded.

"What those abuses are, and how great that inconvenience is, it becomes

your petitioners to state, as the best means of justifying their present
application to your honourable house.

" Your petitioners then affirm that, from the combined operation of the
defects they have pointed out arise those scenes of confusion, litigation, and
expense, which so disgrace the name, and that extensive system of private
patronage which is so repugnant to the spirit of free representation.

" Your petitioners entreat of your honourable house to consider the
manner in which elections are conducted, and to reflect upon the extreme
inconvenience to which electors are exposed, and the intolerable expense to
which candidates are subjected.

" Your honourable house knows that tumults, disorders, outrages, and
perjury, are too often the dreadful attendants on contested elections as at this
time carried on.

" Your honourable house knows that polls are only taken in one fixed
place for each county, city, and borough, whether the number of voters be
ten or ten thousand, and whether they be resident or dispersed over England.

" Your honourable house knows that polls, however few the electors, may
by law be continued for fifteen days, and even then be subjected to a scrutiny.

" Your honourable house knows that the management and conduct of
polls is committed to returning officers, who, from the very nature of the
proceedings, must be invested with extensive and discretionary powers, and
who, it appears by every volume of your journals, have but too often
exercised those powers with the most gross partiality and the most scandalous
corruption.

" Of elections arranged with such little regard to the accommodation of
the parties, acknowledged to require such a length of time to complete, and
trusted to the superintendence of such suspicious agents, your petitioners
might easily draw out a detail of the expense. But it is unnecessary. The
fact is too notorious to require proof, that scarce an instance can be
produced where a member has obtained a disputed seat in parliament at a
less cost than from two to five thousand pounds ; particular cases are not
wanting where ten times these sums have been paid, but it is sufficient for
your petitioners to affirm, and to be able to prove it if denied, that such is the
expense of a contested return that he who should become a candidate, with
even greater funds than the laws require him to swear to as his qualification
to sit in your honourable house, must either relinquish his pretensions on the
appearance of opposition, or so reduce his fortune in the contest, that he could
not take his seat without perjury.

" The revision of the original polls before the committees of your honourable house, upon appeals from the decisions of the returning officers, affords
a fresh source of vexation and expense to all parties. Your honourable house
knows that the complicated rights of voting, and the shameful practices
which disgrace election proceedings, have so loaded your table with petitions
for judgment and redress, that one-half of the usual duration of a parliament
has scarcely been sufficient to settle who is entitled to sit for the other half;
and it was not till within the last two months that your honourable house had
an opportunity of discovering that the two gentlemen, who sat and voted

near three years as the representatives of the borough of Stockbridge, had APPENDIX.
procured themselves to be elected by the most scandalous bribery ; and that
the two gentlemen who sat and voted during as long a period for the borough
of Great Grimsby had not been elected at all.

"In truth all the mischief of the present system of representation are ascertained by the difficulties which even the zeal and wisdom of your honourable
house experiences in attending to the variety of complaints brought before
you. Though your committee sit five hours every day from the time of
their appointment, they generally are unable to come to a decision in less
than a fortnight, and very frequently are detained from thirty to forty days.
The Westminster case in 1789 will even furnish your honourable house with
an instance, where, after deliberating forty-five days, a committee gravely
resolved that ' From an attentive consideration of the circumstances relating
to the cause, a final decision of the business before them could not take place
in the course of the session, and that not improbably the whole of the parliament'—having at that time near two years longer to sit—' might be consumed in a tedious and expensive litigation;' and they recommended it to
the petitioners to withdraw their petition, which, after a fruitless perseverance of above three months they were actually obliged to submit to.

"Your petitioners will only upon this subject farther add that the expense
to each of the parties who have been either plaintiff or defendant in petitions
tried before your honourable house in the present session, has, upon an
average, amounted to above one hundred pounds per day; and that the
attorneys' bills in one cause, the trial of which in point of form only lasted
two days, and in point of fact only six hours, amounted to very near twelve
hundred pounds. And this your petitioners are ready to prove.

" Your petitioners must now beg leave to call the attention of your
honourable house to the greatest evil produced by these defects in the
representation of which they complain, namely, the extent of private parliamentary patronage ; an abuse which obviously tends to exclude the great
mass of the people from any substantial influence in the election of the
House of Commons, and which, in its progress, threatens to usurp the
sovereignty of the country, to the equal danger of the king, of the lords, and
of the commons.

" The patronage of which your petitioners complain is of two kinds : that
which arises from the unequal distribution of the elective franchise, and the
peculiar rights of voting by which certain places return members to serve in
parliaments ; and that which arises from the expense attending contested
elections, and the consequent degree of power acquired by wealth.

" By these two means, a weight of parliamentary influence has been
obtained by certain individuals, forbidden by the spirit of the laws, and in its
consequences most dangerous to the liberties of the people of Great Britain.

" The operation of the first species of patronage is direct, and subject to
positive proof. Eighty-four individuals do by their own immediate authority
send one hundred and fifty-seven of your honourable members to parliament.
And this your petitioners are ready, if the fact be disputed, to prove, and to
name the members and the patrons.

"The second species of patronage cannot be shewn with equal accuracy, though it is felt with equal force.

"Your petitioners are convinced, that in addition to the one hundred and fifty-seven honourable members above mentioned, one hundred and fifty more, making in the whole three hundred and seven, are returned to your honourable house, not by the collective voice of those whom they appear to represent, but by the recommendation of seventy powerful individuals, added to the eighty-four before-mentioned, and making the total number of patrons altogether only one hundred and fifty-four, who return a decided majority of your honourable house.

"If your honourable house will accept as evidence the common report and general belief of the counties, cities, and boroughs, which return the members alluded to, your petitioners are ready to name them, and to prove the fact; or if the members in question can be made parties to the inquiry, your petitioners will name them, and be governed by the testimony which they themselves shall publicly give. But if neither of these proofs be thought consistent with the proceedings of your honourable house, then your petitioners can only assert their belief of the fact, which they hereby do in the most solemn manner, and on the most deliberate conviction.

"Your petitioners entreat your honourable house to believe that, in complaining of this species of influence, it is not their intention or desire to decry or to condemn that just and natural attachment which they, who are enabled by their fortune, and inclined by their disposition, to apply great means to honourable and benevolent ends, will always insure to themselves. What your petitioners complain of is, that property, whether well or ill employed, has equal power; that the present system of representation gives to it a degree of weight which renders it independent of character; which enables it to excite fear as well as to procure respect, and which confines the choice of electors within the ranks of opulence, because, though it cannot make riches the sole object of their affection and confidence, it can and does throw obstacles, almost insurmountable, in the way of every man who is not rich, and thereby secures to a select few the capability of becoming candidates themselves, or supporting the pretensions of others. Of this your petitioners complain loudly, because they conceive it to be highly unjust, that while the language of the law requires from a candidate no greater estate, as a qualification, than a few hundred pounds per annum, the operation of the law should disqualify every man whose rental is not extended to thousands; and that, at the same time that the legislature appears to give the electors a choice from amongst those who possess a moderate and independent competence, it should virtually compel them to choose from amongst those who themselves abound in wealth, or are supported by the wealth of others.

"Your petitioners are the more alarmed at the progress of private patronage, because it is rapidly leading to consequences which menace the very existence of the constitution.

"At the commencement of every session of parliament, your honourable house, acting up to the laudable jealousy of your predecessors, and speaking

APPENDIX.

the pure, constitutional language of a British House of Commons, resolve, as APPENDIX. appears by your journals, 'That no peer of this realm hath any right to give his vote in the election of any member to serve in parliament;' and also, 'That it is a high infringement upon the liberties and privileges of the Commons of Great Britain, for any lord of parliament, or any lord-lieutenant of any county to concern themselves in the elections of members to serve for the Commons in parliament.'

" Your petitioners inform your honourable house, and are ready to prove it at your bar, that they have the most reasonable grounds to suspect that no less than one hundred and fifty of your honourable members owe their elections entirely to the interference of peers ; and your petitioners are prepared to show, by legal evidence, that forty peers, in defiance of your resolutions, have possessed themselves of so many burgage tenures, and obtained such an absolute and uncontrolled command in very many small boroughs in the kingdom, as to be enabled by their own positive authority to return eighty-one of your honourable members.

" Your petitioners will, however, urge this grievance of the interference of peers in elections no farther, because they are satisfied that it is unnecessary. Numbers of your honourable members must individually have known the fact, but collectively your honourable house has undoubtedly been a stranger to it. It is now brought before you by those who tender evidence of the truth of what they assert, and they conceive it would be improper in them to ask that by petition, which must be looked for as the certain result of your own honourable attachment to your own liberties and privileges.

" Your petitioners have thus laid before your honourable house, what the michiefs are which arise from the present state of the representation, and what they conceive to be the grounds of those mischiefs, and therefore pray to have removed.

" They now humbly beg leave to offer their reasons, why they are anxious that some remedy should be immediately applied.

" Your petitioners trust they may be allowed to state, because they are ready to prove, that seats in your honourable house are sought for at a most extravagant and increasing rate of expense.

"What can have so much augmented the ambition to sit in your honourable house, your petitioners do not presume accurately to have discovered, but the means taken by candidates to obtain, and by electors to bestow that honour, evidently appear to have been increasing in a progressive degree of fraud and corruption. Your petitioners are induced to make this assertion by the legislature having found it necessary, during the last and present reigns, so much to swell the statute book with laws for the prevention of those offences.

" As far as conjecture can lead your petitioners, they must suppose that the increasing national debt, and the consequent increase of influence, are the causes of the increased eagerness of individuals to become members of the House of Commons, and of their indifference as to the means used to gratify their speculations. To prove that they do not state this wantonly, or without substantial grounds, they humbly beg to call your attention to the

APPENDIX. following table, all the vouchers for which are to be found in the journals of
your honourable house, or in different Acts of Parliament.

"It is upon this evidence of the increase of taxes, establishments, and
influence, and the increase of laws found necessary to repel the increasing
attacks upon the purity and freedom of elections, that your petitioners
conceive it high time to inquire into the premises.

"Your petitioners are confident that in what they have stated, they are
supported by the evidence of facts, and they trust that, in conveying those
facts to your honourable house, they have not been betrayed into the language of reproach or disrespect. Anxious to preserve in its purity a constitution they love and admire, they have thought it their duty to lay before
you, not general speculations deduced from theoretical opinions, but positive
truths susceptible of direct proof, and if in the performance of this task they
have been obliged to call your attention to assertions which you have not
been accustomed to hear, and which they lament that they are compelled to
make, they intreat the indulgence of your honourable house.

"Your petitioners will only further trespass upon your time, while they
recapitulate the objects of their prayer, which are—

"That your honourable house will be pleased to take such measures, as
to your wisdom may seem meet, to remove the evils arising from the unequal manner in which the different parts of the kingdom are admitted to
participate in the representation.

"To correct the partial distribution of the elective franchise, which com-
mits the choice of representatives to select bodies of men of such limited
numbers as renders them an easy prey to the artful, or a ready purchase to
the wealthy.

"To regulate the right of voting upon an uniform and equitable principle.

"And, finally to shorten the duration of parliaments, and by removing
the causes of that confusion, litigation, and expense, with which they are at
this day conducted, to render frequent and new elections, what our ancestors
at the revolution asserted them to be, the means of a happy union and good
agreement between the king and people.

"And your petitioners shall ever pray."

	Public revenue	Peace establishment	Number of statutes
At the Revolution ...	The public revenue did not exceed £2,100,000	The peace establishment had not exceeded £1,900,000	The number of statutes found necessary to preserve the freedom and independence of parliament, and to regulate elections, and to prevent frauds, bribery, &c., amounted only to 14
At the death of William III.	The public revenue had increased to about ... £3,950,000	The peace establishment had increased to about £1,950,000	The number of statutes found necessary to preserve the freedom of parliament, to prevent bribery, &c., increased to 23
At the death of Queen Anne	The public revenue had increased to about ... £6,000,000	The peace establishment had increased to about £2,000,000	The number of statutes found necessary to preserve the freedom of parliament, &c., increased to 35
At the death of George I.	The public revenue had increased to about ... £6,800,000	The peace establishment had increased to about £2,600,000	The number of statutes found necessary to preserve the freedom of parliament, &c., increased to 37
At the death of George II.	The public revenue had increased to about ... £8,600,000	The peace establishment had increased to about £2,800,000	The number of statutes found necessary to preserve the freedom of parliament, &c., to prevent bribery, &c., increased to 49
In the 31st year of the reign of his present majesty ...	The public revenue had increased to above ... £16,000,000	The peace establishment had increased to about £5,000,000	The number of statutes found necessary to preserve the freedom of parliament, &c., to prevent bribery, &c., increased to 65

INDEX.